The Golden Era of
Amateur Wrestling:
1980s

The Golden Era of Amateur Wrestling: 1980s

REGINALD E. ROWE

ARCHWAY PUBLISHING

Archway Publishing books may be ordered through booksellers or by contacting:

Archway Publishing
1663 Liberty Drive
Bloomington, IN 47403
www.archwaypublishing.com
1 (888) 242-5904

Cover image: Reginald E. Rowe

ISBN: 978-1-4808-2962-6 (sc)
ISBN: 978-1-4808-2963-3 (e)

Library of Congress Control Number: 2016905312

Print information available on the last page.

Archway Publishing rev. date: 5/9/2016

DEDICATION

This book is dedicated to the millions of grade school, middle school, high school, club, collegiate and international wrestlers who have endured more physical pain, anguish, elation, deprivation, agony and exhaustion in one month of wrestling than most people face in a lifetime – all because they love their sport. There are no million-dollar contracts awaiting them upon graduation from college, just a chance to win a World or Olympic medal if they can work even harder to become the best of the best.

ACKNOWLEDGMENTS

So many people contributed their time, effort and insight in the development of this book which began with a conversation with close friend Roger Frizzell, four-time all-American wrestler at the University of Oklahoma from 1980-83. Roger postulated that collegiate wrestling in the 1980s produced the best amateur wrestlers in U.S. history and took the sport to new heights.

Having covered high school and college wrestling in Oklahoma in the 1970s as a sportswriter, I was well aware of the many Oklahoma-based wrestlers who excelled in college: Frizzell, John and Lee Roy Smith, Rick Stewart, Kenny Monday, Dave and Mark Schultz, Steve Williams, Mike Sheets, Andre Metzger, Melvin Douglas, Dan Chaid and Clar Anderson, among others. Intrigued by Frizzell's comments, I began researching the decade and reaching out for help. My first call went to Lee Roy Smith, executive director of the National Wrestling Hall of Fame and Museum in Stillwater, OK. When I told him that I believed the 1980s were the golden era of collegiate wrestling, he said it wasn't just the greatest decade for college wrestling but for all amateur wrestling: college, freestyle and Greco-Roman. At that moment, the title of the book became *The Golden Era of Amateur Wrestling: 1980s.*

Lee Roy couldn't have been more gracious in his assistance. He immediately set up an interview with his brother, John, the most successful amateur wrestler in U.S. history and head wrestling coach at Oklahoma State University. John was as gracious as his older brother, giving my wife and me a tour of the OSU athletic offices and historical displays. Lee Roy opened up the archives at the museum for my research and involved his staff in assisting me; especially helpful was Maghan Cawlfield, office manager, who assisted with archives and providing numerous photographs.

Many wrestlers from the 1980s responded to my emails and calls to talk about the Golden Era, provide their personal perspective and vote on the top 10 collegiate wrestlers from the 1980s. Their names are peppered throughout this book for their wrestling prowess in college and beyond.

A number of wrestlers who went on to become NCAA head coaches also contributed their time, effort and insight to this project including the incomparable Dan Gable, Stan Abel, Barry Davis, Jim Gibbons, Joe McFarland, Jim Heffernan, Rob Eiter, Steve Martin, Lennie Zalesky, and Terry and Tom Brands. The Brands brothers, Jim and Joe Gibbons,

John and Lee Roy Smith, and Ed and Lou Banach took time from their busy schedules to talk with me about their wrestling careers and share childhood memories.

Photographs in this book were provided by individual wrestlers and universities and their sports information departments. Heartfelt thanks to Tim Vanni for providing an incredible pictorial history of his stellar international career and Nancy Schultz for providing a remarkable photo of the late Dave Schultz. Andy Rein, Gene Mills, Barry Davis and Joe Gonzales also shared their personal photos. Head Coach Tom Brand and Christopher Brewer at the University of Iowa; Head Coach John Smith and Taylor Miller at Oklahoma State University; Head Coach Mark Cody and Micah Thompson at the University of Oklahoma; Head Coach Kevin Jackson, Mike Green and Zachary Gourley at Iowa State University; Head Coach Joe McFarland and Leah Howard at the University of Michigan; Head Coach Tom Ryan and Michael Basford of Ohio State University; Head Coach Rob Koll and Jeremy Hartigan of Cornell University; and Head Coach Mark Manning and Connor Stange at the University of Nebraska generously provided pictures from university archives. In addition, Bloomsburg University Sports Information Director Tom McGuire and Administrative Assistant Donna Gillaspy provided photos, as did University of Pittsburgh SID for Wrestling Julie Jurich and Administrative Assistant Kim Robertson, and Ace Hunt, Director of Athletic Media Relations at Indiana State University.

Special thanks to my beautiful wife of 44 years, Sally Cameron Disney Rowe. She not only encouraged me to write this book, but was my chief researcher and accompanied me to the National Wrestling Hall of Fame on numerous occasions for that purpose. I have the sneaking suspicion it was the seasoned French fries at Eskimo Joe's in Stillwater that got her excited about a four-hour drive from our home in McKinney, TX.

This book would never have been attempted had it not been for close friend and the nicest man I've ever known, Roger Frizzell. *The Golden Era of Amateur Wrestling* was his idea. He provided ongoing encouragement, laser-focused insight and took time to reach out to the wrestling community to engage numerous wrestlers in the project. I am honored to be one of his many, many friends.

FOREWORD

Early in 2015, I received a telephone call from a former sportswriter requesting access to the archives at the National Wrestling Hall of Fame to do research for a book he was just beginning. I didn't know him, but he was a close friend of Roger Frizzell, a four-time all-American at the University of Oklahoma, a member of the Oklahoma Chapter of the National Wrestling Hall of Fame and a great ambassador for the sport of wrestling. That was good enough for me. Reg Rowe and his wife, Sally, visited the Hall several times. In our first meeting, he offered that 1980-89 was the best decade in the history of collegiate wrestling. I told him I thought it might be the best decade for U.S. amateur wrestling period and challenged him to prove it. He certainly proves it beyond a shadow of doubt in these pages.

Not only did he uncover numerous statistics to back up my memories of the decade – 33 four-time all-Americans, seven of the top nine winningest wrestlers in NCAA history, the top five most prolific amateur wrestlers in history who accounted for seven NCAA titles, three Olympic gold medals, six World gold medals and 41 U.S. National championships – but also he uncovered great stories of some of the best individual wrestlers, storied rivalries and exciting moments in our incredible sport. A virtually unknown collegiate wrestler (Tim Vanni), relegated to providing wrestling room workouts for national champions at Cal State-Bakersfield, never quit and became an international star. Rick Stewart's defeat of the late Dave Schultz in the 1981 NCAA finals, long considered a tremendous upset, was more about motivation, desire and strategy. Six sets of brothers who wrestled in the '80s, including my brother John and me, are profiled as well. Gene Mills, who owns the NCAA record for most career pins, took his patented half-nelson overseas in 1980 and pinned virtually every opponent in a display of dominance. His memory of an all-out war against an Iranian wrestler will have you laughing out loud. A chapter on Andre Metzger, the winningest amateur wrestler of all time, provides insight into his technical superiority and what it takes to compete at the highest level – even beyond the age of 50. And the book closes with poignant remembrances of Dave Schultz by men who wrestled with and against him.

The 1980's was indeed an era of innovation with wrestlers demonstrating a plethora of upper and lower body takedown skills and a variety of turning combinations from the top position on the mat. It was an era when "mercy rules" were adopted because winning wrestlers often produced a scoring margin over opponents in the upper teens, twenties and even thirties.

As Reg Rowe reflects on this era, we should recall the structure from which the Golden Era emerged. Thanks should go to people like International Wrestling Federation President Milan Ercegan who ushered in a concept referred to as Total Wrestling. Just as it implies, total wrestling demanded action and skill execution at all times and from all positions. Another key element to the maturation of the Golden Era in the United States was the national governing body for the sport, USA Wrestling, was provided with vital support from its elite club programs like the New York Athletic Club and the Sunkist Kids. Their influence gave birth to the national team program in the USA, providing critical financial and coaching support to the top wrestlers in each weight class so they could train and compete year round.

Thus, the era of specialization in wrestling took firm root in this era and produced some of the greatest champions at the collegiate and international levels of our sport in the United States. I am proud to have been a part of it and truly enjoyed remembering it through this book.

Lee Roy Smith
Executive Director
National Wrestling Hall of Fame and Museum

CONTENTS

CHAPTER 1

Golden Anniversary

Wrestling is the original human sport and the first event contested in the ancient Olympic Games in Greece. It also is a nondiscriminatory sport: size doesn't matter; gender doesn't matter. You can be a lightweight, a heavyweight, or anywhere in between—male or female—and still wrestle competitively. It is, without a doubt, the hardest sport in which to compete. Think about it. It is the only sport where the action is nonstop between opponents. There is no place to hide. It is the only sport in which opponents of similar size and strength are in constant contact throughout the event. Except for injury or a ruling challenge, there are no timeouts—not even between periods in the collegiate ranks. Wrestlers are the best-conditioned athletes in the world. And because wrestlers have to be smart, strong, quick, and more dedicated in their training and diet, a very strong case could be made that wrestlers are the best athletes, period.

Let me state up front that I did not wrestle competitively. A few matches in high school gym class don't count. I played baseball (high school, collegiate, and professional) but always admired the dedication and toughness of wrestlers I knew at Tulsa Memorial High School (**Phil Carmen, John** and **Jim Buchan**) and in college. It wasn't until 1974 in Oklahoma, after I became the sports editor of *The Duncan Banner* daily newspaper, that I fell in love with the sport at the age of twenty-five, sitting on the edge of the mat while snapping photographs of Demon wrestlers up close and personal. To better understand the intricacies of wrestling so I could write about it with some authority, I asked Duncan High School wrestling Coach **Mike Reding** (a three-time all-American at OSU who was the top seed at 147 pounds in the 1964 NCAA Championships but lost an overtime decision in the finals) if I could work out with the team. Reding asked me how much running I did. I said about four miles a day. He said, "Okay, come to practice tomorrow. I'll get you a singlet and some shoes."

I showed up the next afternoon, got dressed, and was ready to learn some slick moves from stars **Rick Stewart**, **Jeff Howe**, the **Russell** brothers (**Brent** and **Brad**), and the **Schlittler** brothers (**Billy** and **Ronnie**). Ronnie's patented double chicken wing was high on my list. "Hit the stairs," Reding called to his team. I followed them into the gym where we ran up, down, and across the bleachers in those crazy heelless shoes until I thought I'd pass out. Then we went into the super-heated wrestling room to loosen up. Fifteen minutes later, I was asking Reding when we were going to wrestle.

"Are you loose?" he asked, his thick eyebrows arching.

"Yeah," I gasped.

After going through some drills and getting further fatigued, Mike paired me with his outstanding heavyweight **Gary Morgan**, who also starred on the Duncan football team at defensive tackle. I locked up with Morgan, and the next thing I knew, I was on my back on the mat. Morgan was holding my left leg in his right arm and laughing as I tried to squirm away. He let me up. Then he took me down again and ground me into the mat, put in a deep half nelson, and easily put me on my back for a fall.

That's how it went for what seemed like six hours. It was maybe six minutes. I crawled across the mat and into the restroom, pulled myself up on the porcelain pew, and discharged my lunch, breakfast, previous night's dinner, and an unidentifiable internal organ. (Can you live without a pancreas?) It was the closest to death I have ever been. My gums were blue. I was in oxygen deprivation.

Reding's wrestlers were still hard at it when I sheepishly returned to the mat. The laughter still rings in my ears.

Rick Stewart
(Courtesy Oklahoma
State University)

I covered the Duncan Demons throughout the '70s and learned lessons in Reding's wrestling room, such as how to pop my dislocated fingers back in place and just how intense a competitor Reding was. When Stewart was getting ready to take the mat in the Oklahoma's class 3A championship as a sophomore, Reding was so amped about Stewart potentially being his first state champ that he slapped Rick on the rear with extreme force. After Stewart won his first title, mounted the winner's podium, showered, dressed, and returned to the arena, he told me he still carried Reding's handprint on his gluteus maximus.

I learned the intricacies of the sport thanks to Reding and saw many outstanding high school wrestlers around the state in the process: **Rick Stewart** and **Harold Young** of Duncan; **Roger Frizzell, Paul Ameen**, and **Richard Evans** from Midwest City; **Lee Roy Smith** of Del City; **Rod Hooks, Thomas Landrum, Kenny Monday, Paul "Booger" Parker**, and **Edcar Thomas** of Tulsa Washington; **Robert Ritchie** of Oklahoma City Southeast; **Isreal Sheppard** of Tulsa Kelley; **Mike Sheets** of Tahlequah; **Pat Pace** of Pawhuska; **Mike Pollock** of Ardmore; **Chazz Richards** and **Shelby Stone** of Putnam City; and **Woody Beisel** of Perry. All except Hooks, Landrum, Monday, Ritchie, Sheppard, and Thomas made the *Wrestling USA Magazine* High School All-America Team in their careers. Stewart (1977) and Frizzell (1978) were named to the magazine's dream team of all-Americans for those years.

As a sophomore, Stewart walked up to Reding at the first practice and tapped him on the shoulder. "He said, 'Come out on the mat,'" Reding recalled. "I was still in halfway decent shape so I stepped on the mat. Ricky grabbed me by the wrist, and the next thing I knew, he had taken me down. I never had a wrestler who was so naturally strong. His grip was just incredible."

Joining Stewart (two-time NCAA champion and four-time all-American) on the 1977 dream team were **Bobby Weaver**, **Randy Lewis**, and **Dave Schultz**. Weaver became an

NCAA all-American at Lehigh and went on to qualify for the 1980 Olympic Games (boycotted by the United States), won an Olympic gold medal in 1984, was a silver medalist in the 1979 World Games, and took fifth in the 1983 World Games. Lewis was a two-time NCAA champion and four-time all-American at Iowa, qualified for the 1980 Olympic team, and won an Olympic gold in 1984. He placed fourth in the Worlds in 1982. Schultz was an NCAA champion and three-time all-American at Oklahoma and Oklahoma State, an Olympic gold medalist (1984), and a five-time medal winner (one gold, two silver, and two bronze) in the World Games.

Also on that 1977 high school all-America team, at 158 pounds, was the aforementioned Evans, class 4A state champion from Midwest City. He was set to be Stewart's opponent at the Oklahoma Grand State Wrestling Tournament (champions from all four classifications competing following the state tournament). "I advised Ricky not to wrestle. There was just too much to lose," said Reding. "Generally, the guy who wins goes on to stardom, while the runner-up seems to fade away. I knew Ricky would get a scholarship from OSU or OU, but I still didn't want him to wrestle."

Stewart wasn't going to wrestle. "But an article appeared in the *Daily Oklahoman* that had an interview with Evans," said Stewart. "He basically bragged that class 4A was so much tougher than class 3A. I cut out that article and taped it to my headboard. It became my motivation."

Stewart was so motivated that he scored more than twenty points on Evans. "I put him on his back with my first takedown and that was pretty much the end. I let him up and took him down a lot."

The 1978 dream team included two future teammates of four-time all-American Frizzell at Oklahoma: four-time all-American and two-time 142-pound national champion **Andre Metzger** and four-time all-American heavyweight **Steve Williams**. It also included future NCAA champion and three-time all-American **Jim Gibbons** (Iowa State), NCAA champion **Adam Cuestas** (Cal State-Bakersfield), four-time NCAA all-American **Mike Mann** (Iowa State), and two-time NCAA all-American **Jerry Kelly** (Oklahoma State).

Wrestling was huge in Oklahoma in that era. It still is, thanks to some traditional high school programs that crank out outstanding wrestlers year after year, such as Broken Arrow, Collinsville, Choctaw, Lawton MacArthur, Sand Springs, Stillwater, Tulsa Union, Tulsa Washington, and Tuttle. And when it comes to team success, no one stands taller than Perry High School. The Maroon grapplers, through 2015, have won a national record of forty state championships in sixty-three seasons, including an Oklahoma state record of eleven in a row (1971–1981). To clarify: no other high school in America has won more state championships or crowned more individual champions *in any sport,* according to the National Federation of High School Sports. In the 1950s, Perry produced perhaps the greatest collegiate wrestler in history: three-time national champion **Dan Hodge**. Unbeaten in high school, Hodge was a beast at the University of Oklahoma, going 46–0 with thirty-six pins, including a record twenty-four in a row. He won two outstanding wrestler awards at the NCAA tournament and was *never taken down his entire college career.*

Dan Hodge going for the pin. (Courtesy National Wrestling Hall of Fame)

In 1955, Hodge registered three falls and a 7–3 decision on his way to his first title at 177. In 1956, he pinned all four opponents and was named outstanding wrestler. That year, he went on to pin his way through the national freestyle and Greco-Roman tournaments as well. In his senior year, he led Oklahoma to a national team championship by registering four falls (5:50, 0:50, 0:28, and 7:31) and an 8–2 decision on his way to the championship and a second outstanding wrestler award. Of note, five of OU's ten wrestlers on the 1957 team were from Perry High School. In three NCAA tournaments, Hodge pinned eleven of thirteen opponents, including falls in all three finals matches. On April 1, 1957—no joke—*Sports Illustrated* featured Hodge on the cover. The joke is that SI has never featured another collegiate wrestler on its cover—not the first four-time national champion **Pat Smith** of Oklahoma State or four-time national champions **Cael Sanderson** of Iowa State, **Kyle Dake** of Cornell, and **Logan Steiber** of Ohio State. Sanderson (2000-2002) is the only three-time winner of The Dan Hodge Trophy, begun in 1995, which is wrestling's equivalent to football's Heisman Trophy. Dake (2013) and Steiber (2015) each won the award.

My wife, Sally, remembers "Danny" Hodge as a very nice elementary school student assistant teacher at University School on the campus of OU in 1956 who took time to help her with woodshop projects. Hodge has entertained many audiences over the years by crushing an apple in one hand, which he still can do today in his eighties. He also can break a pair of pliers in his powerful right hand. He attributes his freakish hand strength to being born with double tendons.

Many of those Oklahoma high school wrestlers I had the privilege of watching in the 70's went on to wrestling greatness in the 1980s, a decade unequaled in U.S. amateur wrestling history.

In 1980, the seminal year of The Golden Era of Amateur Wrestling, there were 374 schools in all NCAA divisions with wrestling programs or approximately 10,000 collegiate wrestlers. In 2014, there were just 227 programs with some 6,000 competitors. Since 1972, 670 college wrestling programs (including 95 Division I schools) have been dropped. Forty-eight U.S. states and the District of Columbia had schools drop wrestling.

Was it coincidence or karma that 1980 marked the Golden Anniversary of the NCAA Division I Wrestling Tournament and simultaneously launched The Golden Era of Amateur Wrestling? The decade produced a group of U.S. wrestlers unmatched in collegiate and international history. 1980 was the first time the U.S. ever defeated the Soviet Union in the World Cup's 21-year history at that time. That feat would be repeated by the U.S. squad in 1982. And the U.S. defeated Russia, 19-18, head-to-head in the 1989 World Cup, but lost the title on total points scored in the event.

In the field of the 50th NCAA event in 1980, held at Oregon State University in Corvallis, were 11 wrestlers who would become four-time NCAA all-Americans. Of note, two other four-time all-Americans, **Gene Mills** of Syracuse and **Mike DeAnna** of Iowa, missed the tournament to train for the 1980 Olympic Games, but completed their four-year sweeps in 1981.

The names of the 11 four-time all-Americans who wrestled in the 1980 national tournament are etched in the pantheon of collegiate wrestling excellence: national champions

Howard Harris (Heavyweight) of Oregon State University, who earned the Outstanding Wrestler Award; **Randy Lewis** (134) and **Ed Banach** (177) of the University of Iowa; and **Rick Stewart** (158) representing Oklahoma State University. National runners-up **Andre Metzger** (142) of the University of Oklahoma and **Darryl Burley** (134) of Lehigh University were joined by fourth-place finishers **Roger Frizzell** (150) of the University of Oklahoma and **Mike Mann** (190) of Iowa State University; and fifth-place finishers **Geno Savegnago** (190) of Eastern Illinois University and **Steve Williams** (Heavyweight) of the University of Oklahoma. Rounding out the four-timer list was seventh-place finisher **Mike Brown** (190) of Lehigh University. What a lineup!

While the number of future four-time all-Americans wrestling in the 1980 tournament is incredibly impressive, the list of other legendary wrestlers in the field is equally incredible: 118-pound national champion **Joe Gonzales** and 126-pound winner **John Azevedo**, both of California State-Bakersfield; 142-pound kingpin **Lee Roy Smith** of Oklahoma State; 150-pound champion **Andy Rein** of Wisconsin; and future undefeated national champion (44-0) in 1982, **Bruce Baumgartner** of Indiana State University.

Baumgartner went on to become the most decorated international freestyle wrestler in U.S. history by winning four Olympic medals (two gold); 10 World Games medals (three gold); and four Pan American Games medals (three gold).

Gonzales set an NCAA record with a 55-0 ledger his senior year (1980) at Cal State-Bakersfield including two national championships (Div. I and Div. II). He was a five-time national freestyle champion, an Olympian in 1984 and placed third, fourth and fifth in three World Games appearances. He also holds the record for most takedowns in an NCAA season, 448 in 1980.

Azevedo went 122-2 in his collegiate career, made the 1980 Olympic team (boycotted by the U.S.) and placed fourth in the World Games in 1982. Without Azevedo and Gonzales in the CSUB wrestling room, future two-time 126-pound national champion **Dan Cuestas** (1981-82) might have been a four-time champion and future international star **Tim Vanni** may have captured a title or two. I would have loved to watch the battles that took place in the Roadrunners' one-mat wrestling room between those outstanding athletes.

Rein had a magical 1980 season, winning 40 straight matches. He went on to win four national freestyle titles and qualified for two Olympic teams, winning a silver medal in 1984. Smith, the oldest of the Smith family wrestling dynasty, won a silver medal in the 1983 World Games. He is currently the executive director of the National Wrestling Hall of Fame in Stillwater, OK.

Also competing in the 1980 NCAA Wrestling Championship at 150 pounds was a future three-time NCAA national champion, the incomparable **Nate Carr** of Iowa State, and a future three-time all-American, **Colin Kilrain** of Lehigh.

The head coach of the Iowa Hawkeyes in 1980 was a pretty fair wrestler in his own right. He led the Hawkeyes to a record nine straight NCAA titles (15 in 21 years, including seven in the decade). His name: **Dan Gable**. The legendary Iowa State wrestler took a 118-0 record into the 1970 NCAA finals but lost a somewhat controversial 13-11 decision to second-seeded University of Washington sophomore **Larry Owings**.

In addition, five wrestlers in the 1980 tournament have been inducted into the National Wrestling Hall of Fame as Distinguished Members: **Ed Banach** (1993), **Bruce Baumgartner** (2002), **Nate Carr** (2003), **Joe Gonzales** (2015) and **Randy Lewis** (1998).

Focusing on 1980-84, that five-year period produced 15 four-time all-Americans when you add Iowa's **Jim Zalesky** and Oklahoma State's **Mike Sheets** who completed their careers in 1984, along with **Gene Mills** and **Mike Deanna**. Those 15 wrestlers accounted for 19 national individual championships.

To further state the case that the 1980s was the Golden Era of Amateur Wrestling, there were a number of firsts, bests and milestones in the decade:

1980

- Marked only the second time that the NCAA Championships were held on the West Coast (Oregon State).
- First time two freshmen met in the NCAA finals when unseeded **Matt Reiss** of North Carolina State upset second-seeded **Perry Hummel** of Iowa State, 4-2, at 167 pounds.
- First time three freshmen made it to the NCAA semifinals in the same weight class: Reiss, Hummel and Navy's **John Reich.**
- Eighth-seeded **Noel Loban** (190) became the first individual national champion in Clemson history.
- **Joe Gonzales**, Cal State-Bakersfield, set an NCAA record for most wins without a loss or tie (55) en route to two national championships (Div. I and Div. II) at 118. His 428 takedowns is also an NCAA record.
- **Howard Harris**, Oregon State heavyweight, becomes only the sixth man to pin all opponents in the NCAA Championships and establishes the record for most victories in a career at 169.

1981

- **Gene Mills**, Syracuse, ends his career with a 144-5-1 record and an NCAA record 107 pins.
- **A record twelve future National Wrestling Hall of Fame Distinguished Members** wrestled in the NCAA event: **Ed Banach** (1993), **Lou Banach** (1994), **Bruce Baumgartner** (2002), **Nate Carr** (2003), **Barry Davis** (2007), **Gene Mills** (2000), **Randy Lewis** (1998), **Kenny Monday** (2001), **Dave Schultz** (1997), **Mark Schultz** (1995), **Bobby Weaver** (2008) and **Jim Zalesky** (2004).

1982

- In what many consider the greatest NCAA finals match in history, **Mark Schultz** of Oklahoma scored back points late in his 177-pound match with Iowa's defending national champion **Ed Banach** to win, 16-8.
- **Twelve future National Wrestling Hall of Fame Distinguished Members** wrestled in the NCAA event, tying the record set in 1981: **Ed Banach** (1993), **Lou**

Banach (1994), **Bruce Baumgartner** (2002), **Nate Carr** (2003), **Barry Davis** (2007), **Kenny Monday** (2001), **Bill Scherr** (1998), **Jim Scherr** (2002), **Dave Schultz** (1997), **Mark Schultz** (1995), **Bobby Weaver** (2008) and **Jim Zalesky** (2004).

- Iowa scores an NCAA record 131.75 points (since broken) to win the team title.

1983

- **Eleven future National Wrestling Hall of Fame Distinguished Members** wrestled in the NCAA event: **Ed Banach** (1993), **Lou Banach** (1994), **Nate Carr** (2003), **Barry Davis** (2007), **Kevin Jackson** (2003), **Kenny Monday** (2001), **Bill Scherr** (1998), **Jim Scherr** (2002), **Mark Schultz** (1995), **Bobby Weaver** (2008) and **Jim Zalesky** (2004).

- First time two 400-plus pound wrestlers met in the NCAA Championships as fifth-seeded **Mitch Shelton** of Oklahoma State decisioned North Carolina State's fourth-seeded **Tab Thacker**, 5-0, in the quarterfinals.

- **Ed** (190) and **Lou Banach** (UNL) of Iowa become the first twins to win national championships in the same year.

- The fastest pin (collegiate rules) in the NCAA tournament was registered by **Clarence Richardson** of LSU over **Scott Mansur** of Portland State (nine seconds).

1984

- The **Schultz** (**Dave** and **Mark**) and **Banach** (**Ed** and **Lou**) brothers win gold medals in the Los Angeles Olympic Games, the only time that has occurred.

- The U.S. wins the team gold in the Olympics for the first time in 52 years (1932).

- **Seven future National Wrestling Hall of Fame Distinguished Members** wrestled in the NCAA event: **Melvin Douglas** (2013), **Kevin Jackson** (2003), **Kenny Monday** (2001), **Bill Scherr** (1998), **Jim Scherr** (2002), **John Smith** (1997) and **Jim Zalesky** (2004).

- The first and only time a wrestler scored 35 points in an NCAA Championship came when Oklahoma's **Melvin Douglas** defeated **John Hanlon** of Boston College, 35-5, in the first round at 167. It also is the largest margin of victory.

- Unseeded **Rudy Isom** of Wisconsin was the first wrestler to become an all-American without winning a match, winning by forfeit twice in the consolations. He finally scored a 1-0 win in the consolations (his only win) and finished sixth.

1985

- Tennessee's **Chris Edmond** (167) becomes the Volunteers' first and only wrestling national champion with a 14-10 decision over Hofstra's **Pete Capone**.

- **Wade Hughes** (126 pounds) of George Washington surpasses **Howard Harris** on the list for most career victories with 174.

- **Barry Davis** sets an Iowa record for career wins (162) to rank fourth on the NCAA all-time list.

- **Five future National Wrestling Hall of Fame Distinguished Members** wrestled in the event: **Ricky Bonomo** (2008), **Barry Davis** (2007), **Melvin Douglas** (2013), **Kevin Jackson** (2003) and **John Smith** (1997).

1986

- The Iowa Hawkeyes under Coach **Dan Gable** win their ninth consecutive NCAA championship, a record that still stands. The team set a tournament record with 158 points (since broken by Iowa in 1997 with 170 points). The five individual titles is a record that was tied by Iowa's 1997 squad and Oklahoma State's 2005 team.
- **Two future National Wrestling Hall of Fame Distinguished Members** wrestled in the NCAA event: **Ricky Bonomo** (2008) and **Melvin Douglas** (2013).

THE LEGEND, Dan Gable, celebrates another Hawkeye dual victory. Gable led Iowa to nine consecutive NCAA titles, a record. (Courtesy University of Iowa)

1987

- **Tim Wright**, SIU-Edwardsville (Div. II) becomes the first-ever four-time national collegiate champion. In the NCAA Div. I tournament that year, Wright places third at 118.
- **Four future National Wrestling Hall of Fame Distinguished Members** wrestled in the event: **Ricky Bonomo** (2008), **Kevin Jackson** (2003), **John Smith** (1997) and **Carlton Haselrig** (2016).

1988

- Arizona State becomes only the third national champion outside of the states of Iowa and Oklahoma and the first to win the title without a national champion. Other teams to win a title without an individual champ were Minnesota (2001) and Oklahoma State (2005).
- The NCAA tournament produced the closest finish in history among the top four teams: ASU 93, Iowa 85.5, Iowa State 83.75, and Oklahoma State 80.5.
- **John Smith** of Oklahoma State becomes the first World Champion to wrestle in the NCAA Championships and wins his second national title at 134.
- **Four future National Wrestling Hall of Fame Distinguished Members** wrestled in the NCAA event: **Kendall Cross** (2002), **Zeke Jones** (2005), **John Smith** (1997) and **Carlton Haselrig** (2016).

1989

- **John Fisher** of Michigan (134 pounds) sets the NCAA record for most wins in a career with 183, while **Jack Cuvo** of East Stroudsburg (118 pounds) moves into fourth place on the NCAA career wins list with 164, passing **Barry Davis** of Iowa.
- For the first time, U.S. women enter the World Wrestling Championships in Martigny, Switzerland. **Asia DeWeese** (50 kg) and **Leia Kawaii** (70 kg) capture silver medals and **Afsoon Roshanzamir** (47 kg) takes home a bronze.
- **Four future National Wrestling Hall of Fame Distinguished Members** wrestled in the NCAA event: **Tom Brands** (2001), **Kendall Cross** (2002), **Zeke Jones** (2005) and **Carlton Haselrig** (2016).

CHAPTER 2

1980 NCAA Wrestling Championship

Held at Oregon State University with a NCAA record 128 schools represented, and with the previously mentioned 11 four-time all-Americans in the field and future NCAA and international wrestling superstars competing, the 1980 NCAA Wrestling Championship featured the usual team battle between Iowa, Oklahoma State, Iowa State and Oklahoma, collectively known as The Big Four. Through 2015, 86 team titles have been earned (there were no events in 1943-45). Oklahoma State owns 34 titles (three unofficial), followed by Iowa (23), Iowa State (8) and Oklahoma (7). That's 72 titles or 83.7% of the total. Other team champions are Penn State University (5), University of Minnesota (3), Arizona State (1), Michigan State (1), University of Northern Iowa (1), Cornell (1), Indiana (1) and Ohio State University, 2015 national champ.

1980 NCAA Champions: Back, L-R: Rick Stewart, Oklahoma State; Matt Reiss, North Carolina State; Ed Banach, Iowa; Noel Loban, Clemson; Howard Harris, Oregon State. Front, L-R: Joe Gonzales, Cal State-Bakersfield; John Azevedo, Cal State-Bakersfield; Randy Lewis, Iowa; Lee Roy Smith, Oklahoma State; Andy Rein, Wisconsin. (Courtesy Joe Gonzales)

The domination of the Big Four is underscored by the number of individual champions those schools produced in the decade. Of the 100 titles (10 weight classes in 10 NCAA Championships) won, the Big Four captured 55. University of Iowa wrestlers won 22, followed by Iowa State (13), Oklahoma State (11) and Oklahoma (9). The Big 8 led all conferences with 35 national champions, followed closely by the Big 10 with 30.

Iowa and Oklahoma State each produced two national champions in 1980: **Randy Lewis** at 134 and **Ed Banach** at 177 for the Hawkeyes; **Lee Roy Smith** (142) and **Rick Stewart** (158) for the Cowboys. In the end, Iowa won its third of nine consecutive national championships (1978-86) with 110.75 points, followed by OSU (87), Iowa State (81.75) and Oklahoma (67.5).

Fittingly, hometown favorite **Howard Harris** of Oregon State captured his only national title at heavyweight, was named Outstanding Wrestler and won the Gorriaran Award by becoming the eighth wrestler to pin every opponent in the tournament. Previous champions who pinned their way through the tournament were **Earl McCready**, Oklahoma State, 1930 (Heavyweight); **Wayne Martin**, Oklahoma, 1936 (134); **Bill Koll**, Northern Iowa, 1948 (147); **Dan Hodge**, Oklahoma, 1956 (177); **Dan Gable**, Iowa State, 1969 (142); **Chris Taylor**, Iowa State, 1973 (Heavyweight); and **Bruce Kinseth**, Iowa, 1979 (150). The Gorriaran Award is named in honor of **Manuel "Manny" Gorriaran**, who is credited with developing the sport in his native country, Cuba, and for helping to launch what has become the Pan American Games for athletes in the Western Hemisphere.

In the 1980 tournament were three wrestlers who were nominated for the 75th Anniversary NCAA Wrestling Team in 2005: **Darryl Burley**, **Nate Carr** and **Ed Banach**. Carr reeled off a pair of lopsided wins in his first two matches, then faced fellow Big 8 freshman **Roger Frizzell** of Oklahoma in the quarterfinals, losing 13-6.

1980 Weight-By-Weight Highlights

118 – **Joe Gonzales**, CSU-Bakersfield, completed an undefeated season (55-0) with a tough 6-3 victory over second-seeded, three-time all-American **Dan Glenn** of Iowa. Gonzales racked up an astonishing 94 points in 5 matches (pigtail victory by disqualification not included), winning by an average margin of 19-7.

126 – **John Azevedo**, CSU-Bakersfield, won his only national title after a pair of runner-up finishes in 1978 and 1979. Azevedo defeated Oklahoma State's **Jerry Kelly**, 17-9. Kelly, a seventh-seed, had an incredible run to the finals, knocking off second-seeded **Byron McGlathery** of Tennessee-Chattanooga and third-seeded **Ricky Dellagatta** of Kentucky.

134 – **Randy Lewis** and **Darryl Burley** met in the finals, but had to weather a pair of close matches to get there. Lewis survived an 8-7 battle with unseeded **Derek Glenn** of Colorado. Glenn had the tournament of his life, pinning his way into the semifinals including knocking off the #9 and #5 seeds. In the pigtails, he beat #4 **Frank DeAngelis** of Oklahoma (who had injured his ribs in the Big 8 tourney), #11 **Thomas Landrum** of Oklahoma State and Old Dominion's unseeded **Buddy Lee** to claim third place. Burley had a wild quarterfinal match with **Joe Romero** of Arizona State University, winning 10-7. In the finals, Lewis dominated Burley, 11-3.

A familiar sight: Randy Lewis wins again.
(Courtesy University of Iowa)

142 – Top-seeded **Lee Roy Smith** of Oklahoma State survived one of the toughest weight classes in the event, defeating Oklahoma's second-seeded **Andre Metzger** in the finals, 10-7, in what many believe was one of the best finals matches in NCAA history. Smith was steady throughout the tournament, while Metzger roared into the semifinals with two lopsided wins and a fall before decisioning third-seeded **Bill Cripps** of Arizona State, 11-7. Also in the field was Iowa's **Lennie Zalesky**, who finished fourth and fourth-seeded **Dave Brown** of Iowa State, who finished sixth.

Lee Roy Smith attempts a fireman's carry. (Courtesy Oklahoma State University)

150 – Wisconsin's top-seeded **Andy Rein** registered a rugged 4-2 win over Oregon's #2 **Scott Bliss** to finish 40-0 and win his only national title in three all-American seasons. This weight was perhaps the toughest in the tourney, with Rein, Bliss, Iowa's **King Mueller** (third), Oklahoma's **Roger Frizzell** (4th), and future three-time national champion **Nate Carr** of Iowa State. Frizzell turned a headlock into back points early and defeated Carr, 13-6, earning the right to meet Rein in the semifinals. That defeat forced Carr into the consolations, where he lost and, for the only time in his career, didn't earn all-American honors. Rein barely prevailed over Frizzell in the semis, 9-6. In addition, future all-Americans **Matt Skove** of Georgia and **Wes Roper** of Missouri were in the field. When Georgia dropped its program after the 1980 season, Skove transferred to Oklahoma State and wrestled for the Cowboys for three years, earning all-American honors with a fourth-place finish at 158 in 1983.

158 – Upsets were the norm in this division, with fourth-seeded **Donny Owen** of Brigham Young University falling in the first round and second-seeded **Dave Musselman** of Arizona getting knocked off in the second round. Top-seeded **Dave Zilverberg** of the University of Minnesota made it to the semifinals, but dropped a heartbreaking 9-9, 2-1 overtime decision to fifth-seeded **William Smith** of Morgan State in the semifinals. In the other half of the bracket, third-seeded **Rick Stewart** of Oklahoma State powered into the semifinals where he met the tournament's hottest wrestler, seventh-seeded **Isreal Sheppard** of Oklahoma who had beaten Stewart at 150 pounds (a tough pull for Stewart from 158) in the 1977 Oklahoma High School All-State Tournament. Sheppard had scored three straight falls and took Stewart to the limit before Stewart notched a razor-thin 8-6 win to reach the finals against Smith, a Division II national champion with an impressive 44-1 record entering the event. Stewart took control early and scored an 11-6 decision to win his first of two national championships. Of note, **Tom Pickard** of Iowa State scored three straight falls in the consolation bracket, then beat Zilverberg 9-6 before losing 9-4 to Sheppard in the third-place match.

167 – **Matt Reiss** of North Carolina State was the biggest feel-good story in the tournament. Unseeded, Reiss proceeded to defeat the fifth seed, fourth-seeded **Dave Evans** of Wisconsin, and eighth-seeded **John Reich** of Navy. Reiss had been beaten by Reich in the Pennsylvania state prep tournament semifinals the previous year. In the finals against second-seeded **Perry Hummel** of Iowa State, Reiss registered a major upset with a defensive 4-2 win over the future two-time all-American Hummel. It marked the only time in NCAA history that two freshmen made the finals. In addition, Reich made the penultimate round – the only time three freshmen have reached the semifinals.

177 – Perhaps the biggest upset in the tournament occurred in the first round when un-seeded **Gary Chadwick** of the Air Force Academy defeated top-seeded **Rick Worel** of Cal Poly-San Luis Obispo, 7-3. Because Chadwick was defeated in the second round and didn't "pull" Worel through, Worel did not get a chance to wrestle in the consolation rounds and missed out on all-American honors. Second-seeded redshirt freshman **Ed Banach** of Iowa (missed 1979 with an injury) breezed through his first three matches with two falls and a superior decision before facing third-seeded **Colin Kilrain** of Lehigh. Trailing 8-0, Banach roared back and squeaked out a 12-11 thriller to reach the finals. He defeated fourth-seeded **Dave Allen** of Iowa State 16-5 to claim his first of three national titles. Of note, Banach had lost three previous bouts to the Cyclone star.

190 – Defending national champion and three-time all-American **Eric Wais** of Oklahoma State would have been heavily favored to win a second consecutive crown, but suffered a career-ending knee injury following his Big 8 tournament title and missed the big event. With top seed **Mike Brown** of Lehigh defeated in the quarterfinals, No. 2 **Dan Severn** of Arizona had a national title in sight. He scored three falls and a major decision to reach the finals against eighth-seeded **Noel Loban** of Clemson. Finishing regulation time at 4-4, Loban took an improbable 5-2 decision and the 190-pound crown over Severn – the first individual national championship in Clemson history.

UNL – As mentioned earlier, **Howard Harris** of Oregon State (who had moved up from 190 the previous year) pinned every opponent on his way to his only national title, deck-ing **Bruce Baumgartner** in 4:35 in the finals. He remains the only heavyweight to win the Outstanding Wrestler Award. Baumgartner had reached the finals with a 4-2 decision over Oklahoma's **Steve Williams**, a four-time all-American who went on to a professional wrestling career as "Dr. Death."

CHAPTER 3

1981 NCAA Wrestling Championship

While the 1980 Golden Anniversary tournament launched The Golden Era of Amateur Wrestling, the 1981 national tourney had the most talent ever assembled under one roof. Contested on the campus of Princeton University, the event showcased seven future nominees for the NCAA's 75th Anniversary Wrestling Team (2005): **Ed Banach**, **Darryl Burley**, **Nate Carr**, **Randy Lewis**, **Gene Mills**, **Mark Schultz** and **Jim Zalesky**. No other NCAA tournament has ever had more than five NCAA 75th Anniversary Team nominees. Banach was one of just five wrestlers named to the NCAA 75th Anniversary Wrestling Team in the heavyweight classification (177 and over).

In addition, 12 wrestlers in the tournament would be inducted into the National Wrestling Hall of Fame as Distinguished Members: **Ed Banach** (1993), **Lou Banach** (1993), **Mark Schultz** (1995), **Dave Schultz** (1996), **Randy Lewis** (1998), **Gene Mills** (2000), **Kenny Monday** (2001), **Bruce Baumgartner** (2002), **Nate Carr** (2003), **Jim Zalesky** (2004), **Barry Davis** (2007) and **Bobby Weaver** (2008).

This tournament featured – in my opinion – the toughest weight class in history (134), with three other weight classes nearly as tough (118, 158 and 167), underscoring the amazing amount of talent gathered in Princeton.

Gene Mills of Syracuse is seconds away from pinning Michigan's John Hartupee in the finals at 118 pounds. (Courtesy Gene Mills)

The Big Four again dominated, with the team title again going to the Iowa Hawkeyes with 129.75 points, followed by Oklahoma (100.25), Iowa State (87.75) and Oklahoma State (68.5). Mills (118) was named Outstanding Wrestler, while **Jerry Kelly** of Oklahoma State received the Gorriaran Award.

1981 Weight-By-Weight Highlights

118 – It was the **Gene Mills** coronation as the future Hall of Famer won four matches by fall – including a pin of Central Michigan's **John Hartupee** in the finals – and had a 28-4 superior decision in the semifinals. He came within a whisker of becoming the seventh wrestler to pin

all tournament opponents. Unseeded **Tom Reed** of SIU-Edwardsville upset second-seeded **Randy Willingham** of Oklahoma State in the opening round, and kept winning into the semifinals where he was edged by Hartupee, 2-2, 5-2 in overtime. In the consolation bracket, Willingham gained some payback by pinning Reed in the third-place match. Also competing in one of the toughest weights in history were future Hall of Fame members **Barry Davis** of Iowa (7th) and **Bobby Weaver** of Lehigh (DNP) and future four-time all-American **Joe McFarland** of Michigan.

126 – Out from under the shadow of **John Azevedo**, second-seeded Cal State-Bakersfield's **Dan Cuestas** pinned his way into the finals and then registered a tougher-than-expected 7-5 win over eight-seeded **Dave Cooke** of North Carolina. Oklahoma's national championship aspirations took a major hit when top-seeded Big 8 champion **Derek Glenn** was edged 6-6, 3-2 in overtime by unseeded **Ed Pidgeon** of Hofstra. Pidgeon's loss in the next round ended Glenn's tournament and OU's chances.

134 – Arguably the toughest weight in NCAA history included two-time national champion **Randy Lewis** of Iowa and future champs **Darryl Burley** of Lehigh (1983) and **Clar Anderson** of Auburn (who would win his title as an OSU Cowboy in 1983). Also in the group was two-time Big 8 champion and two-time all-American **Johnnie Selmon** of Nebraska and three-time all-American **Ricky Dellagatta** of Kentucky. And yet, it was Iowa State's sixth-seeded **Jim Gibbons** (eventual three-time all-American) who went on a tear, upsetting third-seeded arch rival Lewis, 13-6, in the quarterfinals. In the finals, he outscored Lehigh's top-seeded **Darryl Burley**, 16-8, for his only NCAA title. Also in the weight was Oklahoma State all-American **Thomas Landrum**. This unmatched group of wrestlers accounted for six national titles and 20 all-American designations in their careers.

142 – Another very tough weight with #1 **Lennie Zalesky** of Iowa; #2 **Andre Metzger** of Oklahoma; #3 **Dave Brown** of Iowa State; #4 **Kenny Monday** of Oklahoma State; and #5 **Gene Nighman** of Cornell. Metzger breezed into the semifinals where he pinned tenth-seeded **Shawn White** of Michigan State at 1:29. White had registered a 10-9 upset of Brown in the second round. Brown battled back through the consolation bracket and defeated White 10-5 to grab third place. Monday, a freshman who would win an NCAA title in 1984 after two runner-up finishes in '82 and '83, stormed into the quarterfinals with a superior decision and a fall, but dropped a wild 13-9 decision to **Bernie Fitz** of Penn State. In the consolations, Monday was eliminated by Nighman, 15-6. Metzger scored a solid 10-6 decision over Zalesky for his first of back-to-back wins over the Iowa wrestler in the finals.

150 – Sophomore **Nate Carr** of Iowa State powered his way through the weight class by an average score of 17-6, downing second-seeded **Scott Trizzino** of Iowa, 10-5, in the finals. It was the first of Carr's three straight NCAA titles. Trizzino reached the finals with a tough 10-6 victory over Oklahoma's **Roger Frizzell**, who beat **Fred Boss** of Central Michigan, 10-3, for third.

158 – Top-seeded **Dave Schultz** of Oklahoma breezed into the semifinals, but then ran into **Perry Shea** of Cal State-Bakersfield, the fifth seed. Shea pushed Schultz to the max, but the OU star held on for a 6-5 win. In the finals, Schultz faced defending 158-pound national champion **Rick Stewart** of Oklahoma State. Stewart had roared into the finals, scoring 66 points in his first four matches including a solid 8-4 decision over third-seeded **Jim Zalesky** in the semis. Schultz had beaten Stewart two straight times, including the Big 8 Tournament finals, and was a heavy favorite. In one of the top-ranked finals matches in NCAA history, Stewart (trailing 3-1 after being hit with two penalty points) took down Schultz with a near arm-far leg late in the second period, put the Sooner star on his back, stuck in the half and registered the fall at 4:58 for his second consecutive national championship.

167 – Among the toughest weight divisions in any NCAA tournament, this featured #1 **Mike DeAnna** of Iowa; #2 **Perry Hummel** of Iowa State; #3 **Mark Schultz** of Oklahoma; #5 **Matt Reiss** of North Carolina State (defending NCAA champion at 167); and unseeded Oklahoma State freshman **Mike Sheets,** who placed seventh and would become a four-time all-American and two-time NCAA champ in his storied career. Schultz went unchallenged in his first three matches, but had to face Hummel in the semifinals. The two superstars battled to a 4-4 tie in regulation, with Schultz prevailing 4-0 in overtime. DeAnna pinned ninth-seeded **John Hanrahan** of Penn State in 43 seconds to reach the finals. Schultz then claimed a 10-4 victory over DeAnna to win his first of three straight NCAA crowns.

177 – **Ed Banach** of Iowa shredded the field by scoring two superior decisions and two falls to reach the finals against fourth-seeded **Charlie Heller** of Clarion. Banach flattened Heller in 4:15 to win his second-straight NCAA title.

Iowa's Ed Banach rides in-state rival John Forshee of Iowa State. (Courtesy University of Iowa)

190 – This weight provided the most upsets in the tourney, with eighth-seeded **Tom Martucci** of the College of New Jersey edging unseeded **Tony Mantella** of Temple, 4-3, in the finals. Three other unseeded wrestlers – **Craig Blackman** of Franklin & Marshall (5th), **Henry Milligan** of Princeton (7th) and **Pat McKay** of Michigan (8th) – earned all-American status. Top-seeded **John Forshee** of Iowa State dropped a heart-breaking 2-1 decision to Martucci in the semi-finals and finished sixth.

UL – Another tough weight. Third-seeded **Lou Banach** of Iowa pinned top-seeded **Bruce Baumgartner** of Indiana State at 5:45 to join his brother on the winner's podium. Oklahoma's fifth-seeded **Steve Williams** pinned second-seeded **Dan Severn** of Arizona State at 3:40 to capture third. Severn placed second in 1980 at 190 pounds.

CHAPTER 4

1982 NCAA Wrestling Championship

Held at Iowa State University in Ames, IA, this tournament was in doubt until the last consolation match. The theme of this tournament for Iowa, Iowa State and Oklahoma (top three finishers) was "what might have been." Oklahoma had two seeded wrestlers – **Mark Zimmer** #7 at 126 and **Derek Glenn** #11 at 134 and unseeded **Dave Rynda** at 118 – who all went one-and-done. "The first 30 minutes of the first round were a complete disaster," Sooner Coach Stan Abel said.

The gut-punch of the three losses came in the final 30 seconds at 126 when Zimmer was reversed and put on his back to lose to unseeded **Cliff Berger** of Oregon State, 10-9. Glenn was disqualified for stalling, while trailing, in his match with Wisconsin freshman **John Giura**. Incredibly, it was the second NCAA stalling disqualification for Glenn at the Hilton Coliseum. He was eliminated there while wrestling for Colorado in 1979.

Oklahoma still managed to make it a race by winning three national titles – **Andre Metzger**, 142; **Dave Schultz**, 167; and **Mark Schultz**, 177 – to finish in third, two points behind runner-up Iowa State (111). Iowa, with champions **Barry Davis** (118), **Jim Zalesky** (158) and **Pete Bush** (190) took home its fifth straight team championship with 131.75 points.

The first "what might have been" for Iowa State came at 134 pounds where top-seeded Cyclone **Jim Gibbons** squeaked out three straight wins (7-4 over unseeded **Mike Enzien**, Boston University; 7-6 over 12-seed **Mike Barfuss**, Cal Poly-SLO; and 5-4 over #8 **Clar Anderson** of Oklahoma State) to make the semifinals, but dropped a 10-5 decision to fifth-seeded **Don Reese** of Bloomsburg.

The second "what might have been" came at 190 where second-seeded **Mike Mann** of ISU took on the fourth-seeded **Pete Bush** of Iowa in the finals. In an exciting overtime match, Bush registered a 3-3, 2-2 criteria victory for his only NCAA title.

Iowa's "what if" came at 126 where second-seeded **Mark Trizzino** lost a second-round match, 3-2, to #11 **Derek Porter** of Eastern Illinois. Because Porter didn't advance to the semifinals, Trizzino's tournament was over.

The Big 8 conference set a record for the decade with 25 wrestlers earning all-American status including four champions, five runners-up, four third-place finishers and four wrestlers who placed fourth. The power of the conference was most evident at 150 pounds where Iowa State's **Nate Carr** (1st), Oklahoma State's **Kenny Monday** (2nd), Oklahoma's **Roger Frizzell** (3rd) and Missouri's **Wes Roper** (4th) swept the top four placings.

Twelve wrestlers in the tournament (tying the record set the previous year) would be inducted into the National Wrestling Hall of Fame as Distinguished Members: **Ed Banach** (1993), **Lou Banach** (1993), **Mark Schultz** (1995), **Dave Schultz** (1996), **Bill Scherr** (1998), **Kenny Monday** (2001), **Bruce Baumgartner** (2002), **Jim Scherr** (2002), **Nate Carr** (2003), **Jim Zalesky** (2004), **Barry Davis** (2007) and **Bobby Weaver** (2008).

1982 Weight-By-Weight Highlights

118 – Top-seeded **Barry Davis** of Iowa won his first of two national titles with a tough 7-5 decision over third-seeded **Kevin Darkus** of Iowa State, who had knocked off #2 **Joe McFarland** of Michigan, 5-3, in the semifinals. Ninth-seeded and under-sized **Bobby Weaver** of Lehigh, who would go on to international freestyle stardom at 105.5 pounds, lost a 13-13, 7-3 overtime battle with fourth-seeded **Randy Willingham** of Oklahoma State in the semifinals. Weaver narrowly missed a fall in regulation.

The best wrestler on the best team, Iowa's Barry Davis works for another pin. (Courtesy University of Iowa)

126 – No. 1 and defending champion **Dan Cuestas** of Cal State-Bakersfield scored 68 points in five matches to win his second straight national title. He defeated un-seeded **Scott Barrett** of Boise State, 10-4 in the finals, but had to survive a nail-biter in the second round. Twelfth-seeded **Frank Famiano** of SUNY-Brockport pushed Cuestas to the limit before falling, 7-6. Barrett's incredible run to the finals included a tense 2-1 victory over third-seeded **Joe Gibbons** of Iowa State in the semis.

134 – Second-seeded **C.D. Mock** of North Carolina, one of six #2 seeds to win a national title in this event, survived an overtime win over Old Dominion's **Buddy Lee**, 2-2, 4-0, in the quarterfinals, before defeating fifth-seeded **Don Reese** of Bloomsburg, 9-2, in the finals.

142 – Top-seeded **Lennie Zalesky** of Iowa and second-seeded **Andre Metzger** of Oklahoma powered their way through their respective brackets, although Metzger had a tough defensive semifinal win, 3-1, over third-seeded Big 8 rival **Johnnie Selmon** of Nebraska. In the finals, Metzger won a hotly-contested match, 9-6, over Zalesky for his second straight NCAA title. Metzger benefitted from four penalty points against Zalesky including a two-point penalty assessed when Zalesky illegally grabbed Metzger's uniform.

150 – Second-seeded **Nate Carr** of Iowa State gained a measure of revenge for a Big 8 tourney loss by fall to **Kenny Monday** of Oklahoma State, prevailing in one of the best finals matches, 3-3, 2-0 in overtime on an escape and a penalty point for locked hands against Monday. Carr also gained revenge in the semi-finals, surviving a wild match with Oklahoma's **Roger Frizzell**, 13-10, regarded by many as the second-best match of the tournament. Frizzell had beaten Carr in the 1980 NCAA tourney. Frizzell defeated Missouri's **Wes Roper**, 9-2, to claim third place after having narrowly beaten the Tiger star, 5-4, in the quarterfinals.

Iowa State's incomparable Nate Carr, future three-time NCAA champion. (Courtesy Iowa State University)

158 – Top-seeded and two-time defending champion **Rick Stewart** of Oklahoma State was on his way to a third title when fourth-seeded **Perry Shea** of Cal State-Bakersfield handed him an 8-3 semifinal loss. Shea then fell to Iowa's **Jim Zalesky** 10-3 in the finals. It was Zalesky's first of three straight NCAA titles at 158. Stewart placed third with a 3-2 decision over Oklahoma's **Isreal Sheppard** and earned all-American laurels for the fourth straight year.

167 – Oklahoma State's **Mike Sheets** (29-4) stormed into the tourney fresh off a Big 8 tourney finals win over second-seeded **Dave Schultz** (32-3) of Oklahoma. Two of Schultz's losses were at the hands of Sheets. In a Bedlam Battle encore in the finals, the pair didn't disappoint. After a 4-4 tie, the two titans went 1-1 in overtime with Schultz earning the title on criteria.

177 – In what many people believe was the greatest finals match of all-time, **Mark Schultz** of Oklahoma became the sixth #2 seed to win a championship in the event with a thrilling, closer-than-it-sounds 16-8 win over Iowa's stellar two-time defending champion **Ed Banach**. It marked the only time Banach lost in four appearances in the finals. Banach had three falls and a superior decision en route to the finals, while Schultz had to survive a grueling 2-1 semifinals victory over Iowa State's exceptional **Perry Hummel**. The finals match was more Greco Roman than collegiate style as the two superstars continually locked up in the familiar over-and-under of Greco. Both wrestlers had big throws and counters and both went to their backs. Leading 10-8 late in the match, Schultz countered a Banach throw attempt and put the Hawkeye on his back for a five-point move and the win, 16-8.

190 – A very tough weight with **Colin Kilrain** of Lehigh (#1), **Mike Mann** of Iowa State (#2), **Bill Scherr** of Nebraska (#3) and **Geno Savegnago** of Eastern Illinois (#6). Those four accounted for 14 all-American finishes in their careers and Scherr would win a national title in 1984. The big surprise was fourth-seeded **Pete Bush** of Iowa who took a rugged 3-3, 2-2 criteria decision over Mann in the finals for his only NCAA championship. Bush had reached the finals with a narrow 8-7 win over fifth-seeded **Kirk Myers** of Northern Iowa in the quarterfinals and then put Kilrain on his back with a throw and registered a fall in just 44 seconds to advance to the finals. Mann made the finals by edging Scherr, 8-7, in the semifinals.

UL – **Bruce Baumgartner** of Indiana State, two-time runner-up and top seed, stepped on the NCAA winner's podium for the only time in his career with a hard-earned 4-2 win over Oklahoma's third-seeded **Steve Williams**, who had reached the finals with a 7-4 victory over defending champion and second-seeded **Lou Banach** of Iowa.

* * *

When wrestling aficionados put together lists of the all-time best U.S. wrestlers based on international and NCAA success, they are weighted heavily toward Olympic and World freestyle gold and silver medals. Using that criterion, there were a dozen wrestlers in the 1982 event who rank among the very best ever. In fact, five of the top 10 best U.S. wrestlers in history (based on Olympic, World Games and NCAA placements) were in the field: **Bruce Baumgartner**, **Dave Schultz**, **Bill Scherr**, **Kenny Monday** and **Mark Schultz**.

With more total Olympic, World and NCAA medals (15) than any U.S. wrestler in history, heavyweight Baumgartner ranks as everyone's top pick. He amassed four Olympic medals (two gold), eight World medals (two gold), one NCAA title and two runner-up finishes. **Dave Schultz** earned an Olympic gold medal and five World medals (one gold, two silver and two bronze) on top of his three NCAA all-American placements (one title). **Bill Scherr** won an Olympic bronze medal and four World medals (gold, two silvers and a bronze) to go with three NCAA top-four finishes (one first). **Kenny Monday** won gold and silver medals in the Olympics and World championships to add to his three top-two NCAA placements (one title). And **Mark Schultz** won an Olympic gold medal and two World gold medals, as well as three consecutive NCAA championships.

Is there any question that the 1980s were The Golden Age of Amateur Wrestling? If there is, we can add to the case with the list of the top 15 wrestlers registering the most wins in their collegiate careers. The winningest collegiate wrestler is **John Fisher** of Michigan. From 1984 through 1989, Fisher compiled an incredible **183 wins** against 21 losses, a record likely to stand forever. Of the top 26 wrestlers based on wins, 17 wrestled in the 1980s:

Rank	Wins	Wrestler	Weight	School	Years
1.	183	**John Fisher**	134	Michigan	1984-1989
2.	175	Otto Olson	174	Michigan	1996-2002
3.	174	**Wade Hughes**	126	George Washington	1982-85
4.	169	**Howard Harris**	190-HWT	Oregon State	1977-80
5.	168	Larry Bielenberg	HWT	Oregon State	1974-77
6.	167	**Pat Santoro**	142	Pittsburgh	1986-89
7.	166	**Joe McFarland**	118-126	Michigan	1980-85
8.	164	**Jack Cuvo**	118	E. Stroudsburg	1986-89
9.	162	**Barry Davis**	118-126	Iowa	1981-83, 1985
T10.	160	Jeff Catrabone	158-167	Michigan	1995-98
T10.	160	Michael Swift	142-150	California (PA)	1990-93
T12.	159	Cael Sanderson	184	Iowa State	1999-2002
T12.	159	**Ed Giese**	118	Minnesota	1982-86
14.	158	**Tom Brands**	126-134	Iowa	1989-92
15.	156	**Jim Jordan**	134	Wisconsin	1984-86
T16.	155	**Jim Baumgardner**	177-190	Oregon State	1981-84
T16.	155	**Jim Martin**	118-126	Penn State	1986-89
T16.	155	Cole Konrad	HWT	Minnesota	2003-2007
19.	154	**John Smith**	126-134	Oklahoma State	1984-85, 87-88
T20.	153	Wade Schalles	150-158	Clarion	1970-73
T20.	153	Ben Askren	174	Missouri	2004-2007
22.	151	**Ed Potokar**	177	Ohio State	1980-83
T23.	150	**Dan Chaid**	177-190	Oklahoma	1982-86
T23.	150	**Matt Demaray**	150	Wisconsin	1989-92
T23.	150	Kerry McCoy	190-HWT	Penn State	1993-95, 97
T23.	150	**Rob Koll**	150-158	North Carolina	1985-88

CHAPTER 5

1983 NCAA Wrestling Championship

Conducted at The Myriad in Oklahoma City, OK, with Oklahoma and Oklahoma State hosting, Iowa ran away with the team title by 53 points over the Cowboys by crowning four champions, the most for the Hawkeyes in their nine-year streak until the 1986 team crowned five. Seven No. 1 seeds and one No. 2 earned titles to provide the seeding committee with a measure of satisfaction for a job well done. However, two wrestlers disregarded the seedings, winning titles from the fifth and seventh slots. The event also produced four national champions from two high schools: **Barry Davis** and **Jim Zalesky** from Cedar Rapids (IA) Prairie High School, and **Ed** and **Lou Banach** from Port Jervis (NY) High School.

There were eleven wrestlers in the tournament who would be inducted into the National Wrestling Hall of Fame as Distinguished Members: **Ed Banach** (1993), **Lou Banach** (1993), **Mark Schultz** (1995), **Bill Scherr** (1998), **Kenny Monday** (2001), **Jim Scherr** (2002), **Nate Carr** (2003), **Kevin Jackson** (2003), **Jim Zalesky** (2004), **Barry Davis** (2007) and **Bobby Weaver** (2008).

1983 Weight-By-Weight Highlights

118 – The craziest weight class in the tourney saw the top three seeds fail to place. Top-seeded **Randy Willingham** of Oklahoma State lost 8-7 to unseeded **John Thorn** of Iowa State in the quarterfinals and lost in the consolations; No. 2 **Carl DeStefanis** of Penn State (future national champion in 1984) was pinned in the first period of the first round by **Robin Morris** of Wisconsin and didn't get pulled through the consolations; and No. 3 **Bobby Weaver** of Lehigh lost 7-5 in his first match to **Brad Anderson** of BYU and was out of the tourney when Anderson didn't reach the semifinals. **Adam Cuestas**, a seventh seed from Cal State-Bakersfield, powered his way into the finals and registered a 14-4 major decision over fourth-seeded **Charlie Heard** of Tennessee-Chattanooga.

126 – The seedings held here as No. 1 and 1982 champ at 118 **Barry Davis** of Iowa plowed through the field until meeting Arizona State's second-seeded **Gary Bohay** in the finals. Davis controlled the action and registered a solid 5-2 victory. The big story was Northern Iowa's No. 12 **Randy Majors'** comeback from a 22-11 drubbing by Davis in the quarterfinals

to win five straight matches (including wins over the 3rd, 5th and 8th seeds) to capture a hard-earned and well-deserved third.

134 – The second biggest surprise of the event was Oklahoma State's **Clar Anderson** clawing his way to the top from the fifth seed. Anderson finished third in the Big 8 tournament, but rode the rollercoaster at nationals winning 6-4, 11-1, 2-1 and 11-3 to reach the finals against Oklahoma's second-seeded **Clint Burke** whom had beaten Anderson three times. Anderson scored a takedown with 16 seconds left for a thrilling 5-3 victory and the title.

142 – It was a coronation for the incomparable **Darryl Burley** of Lehigh who steamrolled four straight opponents by a score of 47-11 before getting an injury default win at 2:37 of the finals over second-seeded **Al Freeman** of Nebraska. Burley would have been the outstanding wrestler had Oklahoma State's **Mike Sheets** (167) not been in the tournament.

150 – The top four seeds all came from the Big Four and finished exactly where they were seeded. In a battle for the ages, Big 8 rivals **Nate Carr** (#1) of Iowa State and **Kenny Monday** (#2) of Oklahoma State struggled to a 3-3 stalemate after regulation as both got two penalty points and an escape. Carr led 3-2 when he took down Monday at the buzzer for the 5-2 overtime win and his second of three NCAA crowns. Monday had to survive a very tough semifinals war with Oklahoma's **Roger Frizzell**, narrowly prevailing, 7-5. Frizzell's third-place default win over fourth-seeded **Jim Heffernan** of Iowa, was his 115th career victory, an OU record at that time.

158 – In another superb finals match, Iowa's top-seeded **Jim Zalesky** downed second-seeded **Lou Montano** of Cal Poly-SLU, 7-4, for his second consecutive title. Eighth-seeded **Kevin Jackson** of Louisiana State University had the tournament of his life, narrowly falling to Zalesky in the quarterfinals, 9-7, then reeling off four straight wins to place third.

167 – The Outstanding Wrestler Award went to Oklahoma State's top-seeded **Mike Sheets** who decimated the field in a way rarely seen at any weight. Sheets registered three shutouts, gave up just three points, was never taken down and scored an incredible 68 points in five matches. He shut out Navy's second-seeded **John Reich** 14-0 in the finals. Can you say DOMINANT?

177 – After three relatively easy wins, top-seeded **Mark Schultz** of Oklahoma ran into a determined **Ed Potokar**

Oklahoma State's Mike Sheets decimated the field at 167, including a shutout of Navy's John Reich in the finals to register his first of two national championships. (Courtesy Oklahoma State University)

(#5) of Ohio State in the semifinals, squeaking out a 4-4, 6-0 win to reach the finals against third-seeded **Duane Goldman** of Iowa. In a close match, Schultz edged out Goldman, 4-2, using a first-period takedown, riding time and an escape for his third and final national championship for the Sooners. Potokar won two matches in the consolations to claim third place. Of special note, this weight produced the two fastest falls in NCAA history. **Clarence Richardson** of LSU pinned **Scott Mansur** of Portland State in just nine seconds in the opening round, while **Wayne Catan** of Tennessee decked Arizona State's **Tom Kolopus** in 13 seconds in the consolations.

Swarmed by teammate Andre Metzger and Coach Stan Abel, Mark Schultz celebrates his third consecutive national championship. (Courtesy University of Oklahoma)

190 – Moving up a weight after a runner-up finish at 167 in 1982, second-seeded **Ed Banach** of Iowa powered his way into the finals with two falls, a 13-7 decision and a 15-4 major decision. On the opposite side, top-seeded **Mike Mann** of Iowa State had an easy path into the finals as well, setting up the match everyone wanted to see. The two all-Americans (Banach four times, Mann three) didn't disappoint the crowd as Banach came away with a hard-earned 4-3 win and his third NCAA championship. It was Banach's only win over Mann in four bouts.

UL – For the first time in NCAA history, two 400-pound wrestlers met. Oklahoma State's fifth-seeded **Mitch Shelton** blanked fourth-seeded **Tab Thacker** of North Carolina State, 5-0. Shelton pushed prohibitive favorite **Lou Banach** of Iowa in their semifinal match, but fell 3-1. Banach pinned second-seeded **Wayne Cole** of Iowa State at 2:57 in the finals to earn his second national championship.

CHAPTER 6

1984 NCAA Wrestling Championship

Seven top seeds and two second seeds won titles at The Meadowlands, NJ (Princeton hosting). Outstanding depth again proved to be the difference for Iowa in the team race, winning just one individual title but placing second in four weights and adding a fourth, fifth and sixth. Oklahoma State's championship hopes were damaged by sub-par performances from five Cowboy wrestlers including a top seed finishing fifth. Six of Iowa's eight seeded wrestlers exceeded or equaled their placements. Based on seeds, OSU should have claimed the national trophy, but that's why they wrestle the matches.

1984 Weight-By-Weight Highlights

118 – The big story here was eighth-seeded Northern Iowa's **Bob Hallman** defeating top-seeded **Charlie Heard** of Tennessee-Chattanooga, 7-6, in the quarterfinals. Hallman battled Penn State's second-seeded **Carl DeStefanis** on even terms in the finals before falling, 6-4. Heard registered two incredibly lopsided victories, 30-8 and 32-12, which may be a record two-match total for the NCAA Championships.

126 – Two-time all-American **Kevin Darkus** of Iowa State lived up to his No. 1 seed by sweeping into the semifinals. Fourth-seeded **Mark Trizzino** of Iowa gave Darkus all he could handle in the semis, but the Cyclone held on for a 5-3 victory. In the finals, Darkus met second-seeded **Joe McFarland** of Michigan and came away with a wild 9-6 win and his only national championship. Of note, third-seeded freshman **John Smith** of Oklahoma State (future two-time NCAA champion and the most successful U.S. international wrestler in history) lost a second-round match to Cleveland State's **Dan Foldesy**, 6-2, and did not get pulled through the consolations.

134 – Top-seeded **Clar Anderson** of Oklahoma State and second-seeded **Clint Burke** of Oklahoma fell in the semifinal round to fifth-seeded **Scott Lynch** of Penn State and third-seeded **Greg Randall** of Iowa. Lynch completed his run to the title with a convincing 13-6 win over Randall and was the only wrestler not seeded one or two to grab a championship.

142 – In the highest-scoring match of the finals, top-seeded **Jesse Reyes** of Cal State-Bakersfield defeated sixth-seeded **John Orr** of Princeton, 19-11. Reyes' 19 points were the most scored in the finals during the decade. That record total was tied by **Cael Sanderson** in 2000. Orr's improbable run to the finals included a narrow 6-5 victory over third-seeded **Jeff Kerber** of Iowa and a wild 16-13 decision over second-seeded **Luke Skove** of Oklahoma State.

After placing second the two previous years, Oklahoma State's Kenny Monday captured his only NCAA title for the Cowboys by avenging a Big 8 Tournament loss to Missouri's John Sonderegger (above) with a second-period fall. (Courtesy Oklahoma State University)

Iowa's Jim Zalesky won his third straight NCAA crown at 158 and was named Outstanding Wrestler. (Courtesy University of Iowa)

150 – Oklahoma State's **Kenny Monday** earned his only national title after placing second to **Nate Carr** the two previous years. Monday opened with a 12-3 victory and a fall before meeting Missouri's **John Sonderegger** in the quarterfinals. Sonderegger had upset Monday 6-6, 2-2 criteria in the Big 8 finals two weeks earlier. Monday avenged that loss with a second-period fall (3:47) and then scored an 11-5 semifinal victory over Arizona State's fifth-seeded **Eddie Urbano**. He won the crown with a solid 7-2 win over **Marty Kistler** (#3) of Iowa. Oklahoma's unseeded **Darren Abel**, son of OU Coach **Stan Abel,** had an exceptional tournament, reaching the semifinals with wins over the #11 and #2 seeds. Kistler scored a 5-1 win in the semis to send Abel to the consolation bracket and an eventual fifth-place finish.

158 – Iowa's remarkable **Jim Zalesky** won his third straight title at 158 and registered his 90th straight victory, knocking off unseeded **Greg Evans** of Minnesota; #12 **Chris Aragona** of William & Mary; #4 **Johnny Johnson** of Oklahoma; and #6 **Mark Schmitz** of Wisconsin, 9-5, in the finals.

167 – Top-seeded and defending national champion **Mike Sheets** of Oklahoma State cruised into the finals and for the second straight year pitched a shutout, 9-0 over #2 **Lindley Kistler** of Iowa. As an aside, Sheets was the only blemish (a tie) on **Kenny Monday's** undefeated high school career (140-0-1). Also of note, Oklahoma's **Melvin Douglas** scored

the most points and largest margin of victory in the 1980s, a 35-5 superior decision in the first round – a score that cannot be surpassed. The next year, the NCAA implemented the Technical Fall Rule, ending matches when one wrestler was ahead by 15 points, keeping Douglas's record safe. Speaking of Douglas, he failed to make weight in the consolations and didn't gain all-American status. That allowed unseeded **Rudy Isom** of Wisconsin to become an all-American without winning a match. Isom did score a 1-0 win in the consolations and eventually finished sixth.

177 – Iowa's top-seeded **Duane Goldman**, 1983 runner-up to **Mark Schultz** at 177 (4-2), again blistered the field (17-3, 17-5, 17-7) before rallying past fourth-seeded **Dan Chaid** of Oklahoma, 6-5 in the semis. Solid second-seeded **Jim Scherr** of Nebraska edged Goldman, 3-2, to win his only NCAA title for the Cornhuskers.

190 – Top-seeded **Bill Scherr** of Nebraska joined his brother atop the medal podium with lopsided wins on his way to the finals: 26-8 over unseeded **Doug Morse** of SUNY-Oswego; a fall in 4:59 over #12 **Ernie Badger** of SIU-Edwardsville; a fall in 2:42 over #8 **Paul Diekel** of Lehigh; and 20-6 over #5 **Jim Beichner** of Clarion. In the finals, Scherr dispatched second-seeded **Jim Baumgardner** of Oregon State, 13-4, for his lone NCAA title.

UL – With no **Lou Banach** or **Bruce Baumgartner** to contend with, two-time all-American behemoth (447 pounds) **Tab Thacker** (#1) notched his lone NCAA championship by edging fourth-seeded **Mike Holcomb** of Miami of Ohio, 4-4, 1-0, in overtime in the semifinals and sixth-seeded **Gary Albright** of Nebraska, 3-1, in the finals.

CHAPTER 7

1985 NCAA Wrestling Championship

Interest in the sport of wrestling was raised in February when the movie *Vision Quest* was released starring Matthew Modine as Louden Swain, a high school wrestler dropping down two weights to wrestle the defending state champion in a dual match. A month later, the second half of The Golden Era of Amateur Wrestling began with the Iowa Hawkeyes cruising to their eighth straight national team title (a record at that time), followed by Oklahoma, Iowa State and Oklahoma State. Eleven four-time all-Americans were in the Oklahoma City field. Highlighting the event at The Myriad in Oklahoma City were two finals between four-time all-Americans at 126 (**Barry Davis** vs. **Joe McFarland**) and 190 (**Dan Chaid** vs. **Duane Goldman**).

1985 Weight-By-Weight Highlights

Ricky Bonomo, Bloomsburg University, controls an opponent from the top. Bonomo roared to the 118-pound title with a 17-3 win in the finals. (Courtesy Bloomsburg University)

118: Second-seeded **Ricky Bonomo** of Bloomsburg made his case to become Outstanding Wrestler of the tournament (awarded to **Barry Davis** of Iowa) by decimating the field. No opponent got closer than 14 points, including Iowa's #8 **Matt Egeland** who fell 17-3 in the finals. Egeland had upset top-seeded **Mark Perry** of Oklahoma State by a razor-thin 9-8 margin. Perry dropped into the consolations, where he fought back to a fifth-place finish. Ninth-seeded freshman **Joe Melchiore** of Oklahoma battled his way to a fourth-place finish, his first of four all-American designations.

126: Top-seeded and defending 126-pound champion **Barry Davis** of Iowa plowed through the field until encountering #5 **Wade Hughes** of George Washington in the semifinals. Davis won a wild and wooly 16-11 decision over Hughes, who ended his career as the winningest collegiate wrestler in history (174) at that time. Davis advanced to the finals against second-seeded Big 10 rival **Joe McFarland** of Michigan and came away with his third national championship, 8-4.

134: Wisconsin junior all-American **Jim Jordan** lived up to his top seed with a workmanlike trip into the finals with solid wins over #8 **John Fisher** of Michigan, 6-1, in the quarterfinals, and 6-3 over fourth-seeded **Alan Grammer** of Southern Illinois University-Edwardsville, who finished third in the event. In the title match, he faced second-seeded freshman **John Smith** of Oklahoma State. Despite wrestling with an injured shoulder, Smith gave Jordan all he could handle before falling, 7-4. Both Jordan and Smith would win two NCAA titles in their storied careers.

142: Second-seeded **Kevin Dresser** of Iowa and No. 3 **John Orr** of Princeton pounded their way into the semifinals with lopsided wins, with Orr prevailing 10-6 in the semifinals. Top-seeded **Joe Gibbons** of Iowa had a tougher time, nipping unseeded **John Effner** of Indiana State, 7-4, in the quarterfinals before surviving a 3-3, 1-1 criteria win in the semis against fifth-seeded **Lew Sondgeroth** of Northern Iowa. In the finals, Gibbons and Orr engaged in an epic defensive struggle, with Gibbons hanging on for a 4-3 win.

Iowa's Barry Davis, wrestling in a dual (above) in Iowa City, was named the tournament's Outstanding Wrestler after beating Michigan's talented Joe McFarland in the finals. (Courtesy University of Iowa)

150: Third-place finisher in 1984 at 150, **Eddie Urbano** of Arizona State defended his No. 1 seed but not without difficulty. Fifth-seeded **Chris Bevilacqua** of Penn State pushed Urbano to the max before falling to the Sun Devil star, 3-3, 3-1 in overtime. On the other side of the bracket, Iowa's #2 **Jim Heffernan** had to survive overtime matches in the first two rounds and a 7-5 decision over No. 7 **Luke Skove** of Oklahoma State in the quarterfinals. Urbano took a solid 4-1 decision over Heffernan in the finals for his lone national title.

158: Two unseeded wrestlers – **Dave Ewing** of Iowa State (third place) and **Dave Lilovich** of Purdue (fourth place) – had the tournaments of their careers, but the day belonged to Iowa's top-seeded **Marty Kistler**. Kistler survived early one-point and two-point wins, then moved into the finals with a fall over #8 **Tony Tracey** of Louisiana State and a 6-1 decision over #5 **Ernie Blazeff** of Michigan State. In the finals, Kistler scored a 4-3 victory over third-seeded **Greg Elinsky** of Penn State for his first of two NCAA titles.

167: This topsy-turvy weight class saw three unseeded wrestlers place eighth (**Tad Wilson**, North Carolina), sixth (**Mike Van Arsdale**, Iowa State) and fourth (**John Monaco**, Montclair State), and a #9 seed (**John Laviolette**, Oklahoma) place third. Top-seeded **Kevin Jackson** of Louisiana State was edged 6-5 in the first round by the unseeded Monaco, who had the tournament of his career as he advanced to the semifinals against fifth-seeded **Chris Edmond** of Tennessee. Edmond narrowly prevailed, 8-5, to reach the finals. On the other side of the bracket, second-seeded **Lindley Kistler** of Iowa was upset in the semifinals by third-seeded **Pete Capone** of Hofstra, 5-1. Capone and Edmond had the most entertaining finals match of the tourney with Edmond outlasting Capone, 14-10.

Oklahoma's Dan Chaid (top, earlier dual match) captured his only NCAA title with a thrilling come-from-behind win over Iowa's outstanding Duane Goldman, 5-3, in the finals. (Courtesy University of Oklahoma)

177: This weight held to form, but not without some close calls. Top-seeded **Melvin Douglas** of Oklahoma edged eighth-seeded **Doug Dake** (father of future four-time national champion Kyle) of Kent State, 4-3, and fourth-seeded **Tom Kolopus** of Arizona State, 7-3, to reach the finals. Third-seeded **Wayne Catan** of Syracuse survived a 1-1, 3-1 overtime scare against sixth-seeded **Roger Sayles** of Cal Poly-San Luis Obispo in the quarterfinals and nipped second-seeded **Booker Benford** of SIU-Edwardsville, 8-7. In a defensive struggle in the finals, Douglas outlasted Catan, 3-2, for his first of two NCAA crowns.

190: Two future four-time all-Americans, Oklahoma's second-seeded **Dan Chaid** and top-seeded **Duane Goldman** of Iowa, clashed in the 190-pound final. To get there, Chaid had to survive a 3-2 decision over #11 **John Heropoulos** of Iowa State in the second round and a 1-0 decision over sixth-seeded **Mark Cody** of Missouri in the semifinals. Goldman easily rolled into the semifinals with wins of 15-6, 21-4 and 16-5, before registering an 8-4 decision over fifth-seeded **Koln Knight** of tiny Augustana College (South Dakota). In a tense, physical battle between four-time all-Americans in the finals, Chaid piled up riding time but trailed 3-2 when he was hit with a stalling call with just 32 seconds left. With 26 seconds left, Chaid got in on a single leg, ran the pipe and took Goldman down at the edge of the mat with 10 seconds remaining to pull out a tough 5-3 decision to win his lone NCAA title for the Sooners.

UNL: Three unseeded wrestlers (**Rick Brunot**, Youngstown State, third; **Darryl Peterson**, Iowa State, fifth; and **Rod Severn**, Arizona State, seventh) gained all-American honors while the #1 and #3 seeds didn't. Top-seeded **Rick Petersen** of Lock Haven breezed into the quarterfinals but fell, 10-8, to eighth-seeded **Kirk Trost** of Michigan in the quarterfinals. Third-seeded **Gary Albright** of Nebraska lost a titanic struggle to tenth-seeded **Steve Sefter** of Penn State, 1-1, 1-1 criteria in the second round. Trost scored a 7-3 decision over fourth-seeded **Kahlan O'Hara** of Oklahoma State to reach the finals. Second-seeded **Bill Hyman** of Temple had a technical fall (15-0) and two pins (4:27 and 4:23) before a narrow 5-4 decision over Sefter in the semis. Hyman then dominated future national champion Trost, 12-2, for the title.

CHAPTER 8

1986 NCAA Wrestling Championship

The 1986 tournament in Iowa City saw Iowa cruise to a record ninth-straight team championship with a record 158 points and five national champions: third-seeded **Brad Penrith** at 126; top-seeded **Kevin Dresser** at 142; second-seeded **Jim Heffernan** at 150; #1 **Marty Kistler** at 167; and top-seeded **Duane Goldman** at 190. Oklahoma finished second for the second consecutive year, followed by Oklahoma State and Iowa State. The Big 10 conference dominated the event with eight individual championships. Bloomsburg's **Ricky Bonomo** (118) and Oklahoma's **Melvin Douglas** (177) were the only non-Big 10 wrestlers to capture titles.

Ten four-time all-Americans were in the field: Heffernan; Goldman; **Jim Martin** of Penn State (fourth at 118); **Joe Melchiore** of Oklahoma (seventh at 118); third-seeded **Joe Gibbons** of Iowa State (third at 142); unseeded **Pat Santoro** of Pittsburgh (sixth at 142); top-seeded **Tim Krieger** of Iowa State (fifth at 150); top-seeded **Greg Elinsky** (second at 158); fifth-seeded **Rob Koll** of North Carolina (third at 158); and third-seeded **Dan Chaid** (second at 190). Kistler was a three-time all-American.

1986 Weight-By-Weight Highlights

118: It was the **Ricky Bonomo** show as the top-seeded defending national champion from Bloomsburg powered his way 20-5, 15-2, 5-0 and 14-5 into the finals against sixth-seeded **Al Palacio** of North Carolina. Palacio had knocked off third-seeded **Joe Melchiore** of Oklahoma, 9-6, and second-seeded **Ed Giese** of Minnesota, 9-4, before falling to Bonomo, 9-4, in the finals. It was Bonomo's second of three straight NCAA championships at 118.

126: When top-seeded **Alan Grammer** of SIU-Edwardsville and second-seeded **Bill Kelly** of Iowa State lost in the championship round, it opened the door for third-seeded **Brad Penrith** of Iowa. Penrith registered workmanlike 10-5, 11-7, 8-6 and 7-4 decisions to reach the finals against the hottest wrestler in the weight class, ninth-seeded **Dennis Semmel** of Army. Semmel defeated eight-seeded **Rocky Bonomo** of Bloomsburg, 5-2, then engaged in a wild quarterfinals match with the top-seeded Grammer. Following an 11-11 tie in regulation, Semmel came alive to notch an 11-2 overtime victory, then upset fourth-seeded

31

Cordel Anderson of Utah State, 9-7, to reach the finals. Penrith then powered his way to a solid 9-4 win over Semmel and his lone NCAA title.

134: While the top two seeds met in the final, the highlight of this weight was the placement of three unseeded wrestlers, as well as a 10th seed and a 12th seed. After dropping their second-round matches, unseeded **David Ray** of Edinboro and 12th-seeded **Leo Bailey** of Oklahoma State battled through the consolations with five straight wins apiece to reach the third-place match. Ray prevailed in a tight bout, 7-6. Top-seeded and defending NCAA champion at 134 **Jim Jordan** of Wisconsin had a steady trip into the finals where he met second-seeded two-time all-American **Greg Randall** of Iowa. Jordan picked up his second title with a solid 6-2 win.

142: One of the toughest weights ever, it featured defending champion **Joe Gibbons** of Iowa State and two eventual champions: **Peter Yozzo** of Lehigh (1987) and **Pat Santoro** of Pittsburgh (1988 and 1989). The seeding committee was perfect with its top four as #1 **Kevin Dresser** of Iowa defeated #2 Yozzo, 11-6, for his only NCAA title. Dresser missed an inside trip early in the match and was taken down to trail Yozzo, 2-0. But it was Dresser's four-point fireman's carry in the second period that spelled the difference. Dresser had three pins en route to his title and should have been the Outstanding Wrestler given the difficult weight. Gibbons edged fourth-seeded **Luke Skove** of Oklahoma State for third place. Three unseeded wrestlers earned all-American status including Santoro, an eventual four-time all-American.

150: Two future four-time all-Americans headlined this weight: top-seeded **Tim Krieger** of Iowa State and second-seeded **Jim Heffernan** of Iowa. Krieger suffered a very tough 5-5, 1-0 overtime loss to ninth-seeded **Scott Turner** of North Carolina State in the quarterfinals, while Heffernan dominated three foes 16-2, 10-2, 16-4 and then scored a fall in 4:55 over sixth-seeded **Joey McKenna** of Clemson in the semifinals. Heffernan cruised to a 10-3 win over fourth-seeded **Adam Cohen** of Arizona State in the finale.

158: Sixth-seeded **Jude Skove** of Ohio State survived a 3-2 thriller with third-seeded **Royce Alger** of Iowa on his way to the finals where he met top-seeded **Greg Elinsky** of Penn State. Elinsky barely reached the finals, surviving a 3-3, 5-1 overtime win over future national champion and four-time all-American **Rob Koll** of North Carolina. Skove won the championship with a solid 5-2 decision. Oklahoma's fourth-seeded **Johnny Johnson** suffered a loss by fall to Koll in the quarterfinals, then battled back to meet Koll for third place, losing a 7-0 decision.

167: Defending national champ at 158, Iowa's **Marty Kistler** earned the top seed at 167 and didn't disappoint. He was untested as he steamrolled into the finals with wins of 14-6, 21-8, TF 20-4 and a 9-3 semifinals win over in-state rival and sixth-seeded **Mike Van Arsdale** of Iowa State. Oklahoma State's third-seeded **Mark Van Tine** had an equally easy road until the semifinals where he eked out a 2-1 win over tenth-seeded **Dave Lee** of Stanford. Kistler prevailed over Van Tine in the finals, 15-3 and took home the O.W. award.

177: Oklahoma's top-seeded and defending NCAA champion **Melvin Douglas** raced into the finals with 18-6, 18-6, 14-4 and 10-2 decisions to set up a match against second-seeded **Wayne Catan** of Syracuse. In a rematch of the 1985 finals, Douglas again prevailed with a 9-5 win and his second straight 177-pound crown. Catan had to weather a 5-4 decision over seventh-seeded **Mark Tracey** of Cal Poly-SLO in the quarters and a 4-3 decision over #3 **Rico Chiapparelli** of Iowa in the semis.

Oklahoma's Melvin Douglas celebrates his second straight NCAA championship at 177. (Courtesy University of Oklahoma)

190: In a finals rematch between four-time all-Americans, **Duane Goldman** of Iowa scored the only takedown of the match and held on for a 5-4 victory over third-seeded and defending NCAA champion **Dan Chaid** of Oklahoma to avenge his finals loss to the Sooner in 1985. Leading 5-2 in the third period, Goldman was hit with two stalling calls but held on for the win, 5-4.

UNL: All four top seeds finished in the top four, but it was third-seeded **Kirk Trost** of Michigan taking on fourth-seeded **John Heropoulos** of Iowa State in the finals. Trost had edged second-seeded **Gary Albright** of Nebraska, 4-2, in the semifinals. In the finals, Trost scored a 6-3 decision over Heropoulos to claim the title.

Duane Goldman (right) looks for an opening in an earlier dual meet. Goldman edged Oklahoma's Dan Chaid to win his lone NCAA title.

CHAPTER 9

1987 NCAA Wrestling Championship

The University of Maryland was the site of the 1987 tournament and marked the end of Iowa's record nine-year run atop the team standings as archrival Iowa State crowned four champions and outdistanced the Hawkeyes, 133-108, under the guidance of second-year coach **Jim Gibbons**. Penn State finished third, followed by Oklahoma State. Taking down titles for Iowa State were second-seeded **Bill Kelly** (126), top-seeded **Tim Krieger** (150), fourth-seeded **Stewart Carter** (158) and second-seeded **Eric Voelker** (190).

Four-time all-Americans in the field were Krieger; **Jim Martin** of Penn State (second at 118); **John Fisher** of Michigan (fourth at 134); **Pat Santoro** of Pittsburgh (second at 142); **Jim Heffernan** of Iowa (second at 150); **Rob Koll** of North Carolina (third at 158); **Kevin Jackson** of Iowa State (second at 167); **Greg Elinsky** of Penn State (third at 167); and **Mike Funk** of Northwestern (fourth at 177).

1987 NCAA National Champion Iowa State Cyclones. L-R: Bill Kelly, 1st at 126; Kevin Jackson, 2nd at 167; Stewart Carter, 1st at 158; Coach Jim Gibbons; Eric Voelker, 1st at 190; Tim Krieger, 1st at 150; Jeff Gibbons, 3rd at 134. (Courtesy Iowa State University)

1987 Weight-By-Weight Highlights

118: It was same song, third verse as **Ricky Bonomo** of Bloomsburg made his case for the Outstanding Wrestler Award by plowing through the field to capture his third NCAA championship for the Huskies. Bonomo's toughest match came in the semifinals against fourth-seeded and future two-time NCAA champ **Jack Cuvo** of East Stroudsburg, a wild 9-6 decision. In the finals, Bonomo bested third-seeded **Jim Martin** of Penn State, 8-4. Martin would win his lone NCAA title in '88 and become a four-time all-American in 1989.

Of note, Martin beat the first-ever NCAA four-time national champion (Division II) **Tim Wright** of Southern Illinois-Edwardsville in the quarterfinals, 8-2. Wright placed third.

126: It was a battle of the top two seeds as No. 1 defending champion **Brad Penrith** of Iowa met second-seeded **Bill Kelly** of cross-state rival Iowa State in the finals. In the first round, Penrith avoided a huge upset with a narrow 10-9 decision over Oklahoma State's unseeded **Kendall Cross**. Cross would go on to win an NCAA title in '89 at 126 and become a three-time all-American. Kelly had a monumental battle against seventh-seeded **Ken Chertow** of Penn State, 4-4, 2-1 in overtime to make it to the semifinals, where he

Second-seeded Bill Kelly of Iowa State (top, earlier match) registered a fall over top-seeded Brad Penrith to win the NCAA title at 126 pounds. (Courtesy Iowa State University)

squeezed past third-seeded **Marc Sodano** of North Carolina State, 4-3. Kelly scored a mild upset by pinning Penrith at 6:31 for his lone NCAA title.

134: Oklahoma State's **John Smith** returned to the NCAA tournament after a year's absence and earned the top seed. In a display worthy of the Outstanding Wrestler Award he won, Smith used his patented low single leg to devastating effect as he rolled up wins by fall (6:30), technical falls of 23-8 and 22-7, and a 20-9 major decision over fourth-seeded **Rob Johnson** of Ohio University in the semifinals. Second-seeded **Gil Sanchez** of Nebraska was equally dominant with wins of 16-2, 16-1 and 11-4. In the semis, he dispatched sixth-seeded **Paul Clark** of Clarion, 7-4. In the finals, it was all Smith as he continued the scoring clinic with an 18-4 victory, the biggest victory margin in any finals match of the decade. The win avenged an earlier dual meet loss to Sanchez, who was the last collegiate wrestler to defeat Smith. Also in the field was future four-time all-American **John Fisher** of Michigan who finished third.

142: No. 1 **Peter Yozzo** of Lehigh had smooth sailing into the semifinals where he met unseeded **Mike Cole** of Clarion. Cole, the biggest surprise of the weight, had

OSU's John Smith, right, (earlier match) avenged a Big 8 Tournament finals loss to Nebraska's Gil Sanchez with an 18-4 romp in the NCAA finals at 134. (Courtesy Oklahoma State University)

upset fourth-seeded **Greg Randall** of Iowa, 9-2, and fifth-seeded **Karl Monaco** of Montclair State by fall (4:31) to earn the slot versus Yozzo. He gave Yozzo everything he could handle before succumbing, 9-8. In the bottom bracket, second-seeded **Nick Neville** of Oklahoma battled third-seeded all-American **Pat Santoro** of Pittsburgh in the semis, with Santoro edging the Sooner, 8-6. In the finals, Yozzo caught Santoro in the second period and registered a fall at 3:52 for his lone title.

150: Two four-time all-Americans met in the match of the tournament in the finals at 150. Top-seeded **Tim Krieger** of Iowa State and second-seeded **Jim Heffernan** of Iowa battled in the closest finals match of the event, ending regulation tied at 1-1. Heffernan barely missed a takedown at the edge of the mat with seconds left in regulation. In the overtime session, Krieger escaped to lead 1-0, but Heffernan was awarded a point when Krieger backed off the mat and was tagged for the one-point stalling penalty. Krieger narrowly missed a takedown at the edge of the mat with 30 seconds left in the second overtime period. He then won the title on criteria 5 (more escapes). **Darrin Higgins** of Oklahoma finished third with a 7-3 decision over **Jeff Jordan** of Wisconsin.

158: Top-seeded **Rob Koll** of North Carolina was pinned (6:47) by unseeded **John Heffernan** of Iowa in the second round and had to battle back through the consolations to a third-place finish and his second all-American designation. Heffernan then fell 8-0 to fourth-seeded **Stewart Carter** of Iowa State in the semifinals. Third-seeded **Ken Haselrig** of Clarion advanced to the finals with a grueling 1-1, 1-1 criteria overtime win over second-seeded **Glen Lanham** of Oklahoma State, who finished fifth. In the finals, Carter scored a solid 6-3 decision over Haselrig to win his only NCAA championship.

167: **Royce Alger** of Iowa (#1) was virtually untested when the eighth and fourth seeds were beaten early in the tournament and he had to only face one seeded wrestler before the finals, #9 **Craig Martin** of Missouri, whom he beat 16-5. Four-time all-American and second-seeded **Kevin Jackson** of Iowa State had a smooth run into the semis, but ran into two-time NCAA runner-up at 158 and four-time all-American **Greg Elinsky**. In a tense defensive struggle, Jackson survived with a 2-2, 1-1 criteria victory. Alger controlled Jackson in the finals, winning 10-4 for his first of two titles.

177: Top-seeded **Darryl Pope** of Cal State-Bakersfield and second-seeded **Rico Chiapparelli** of Iowa were set on a collision course to the finals. Pope ran roughshod over his bracket, registering a fall in 0:36, superior decision (17-5), TF 15-0, and another fall in the semifinals over fifth-seeded **Reggie Wilson** of Chicago State in 5:22 to reach the finals. Chiapparelli's road to the title bout was a bit tougher including a narrow 3-2 win over third-seeded **Dan Mayo** of Penn State in the semis. In the finals, Chiapparelli held the high-scoring Pope to just two points and took home his only NCAA title, 5-2.

190: Quarterfinal losses by top-seeded **Eric Mittlestead** of Cal State-Bakersfield and third-seeded **Scott Kelly** of Navy opened the door for the rest of the field. Second-seeded **Eric Voelker** of Iowa State and eighth-seeded **Dave Dean** of Minnesota stepped through the door and into the finals. Voelker edged Dean, 4-3, for his first of two NCAA championships.

275: The legend of top-seeded **Carlton Haselrig** of Pittsburgh-Johnstown, one of the greatest heavyweights in NCAA (Division I & II) history, began in 1987 as he survived a second-round 5-4 decision over unseeded **Andy Cope** of Iowa State and a 6-5 decision over sixth-seeded **Rod Severn** of Arizona State to reach his first of three finals. Fifth-seeded **Dean Hall** of Edinboro, a three-time all-American, had the tourney of his life by knocking off fourth-seeded **Joel Greenlee** of Northern Iowa, 10-9, and top-seeded **Tom Erikson** of Oklahoma State, 11-6, to make the finals. Haselrig scored a 4-2 decision for his first Division I championship.

CHAPTER 10

1988 NCAA Wrestling Championship

Conducted at Iowa State, the 1988 tournament marked the end of a 20-year run atop the standings by the Big Four – Iowa, Iowa State, Oklahoma and Oklahoma State – as Arizona State edged Iowa 93-85.5 without crowning a single champion. Five points separated the second, third and fourth placers, Iowa, Iowa State (83.75) and Oklahoma State (80.5). Seven Sun Devils earned all-American honors including runner-up at 190 **Mike Davies** and third-place finishers **Chip Park** (126), **Dan St. John** (158) and **Jim Gressley** (167).

Six four-time all-Americans were in the field: 126-pound champion **Jim Martin** of Penn State; 134-pound runner-up **Joe Melchiore** of Iowa and 134-pound third-place finisher **John Fisher** of Michigan; 142-pound champ **Pat Santoro** of Pittsburgh; 150 runner-up **Tim Krieger** of Iowa State; and 158-pound titlist **Rob Koll** of North Carolina. The top-seeded Koll registered the fastest finals fall of the decade, pinning sixth-seeded **Joe Pantaleo** of Michigan in 1:14.

1988 Weight-By-Weight Highlights

118: The fifth-place finisher in 1987, **Jack Cuvo** of East Stroudsburg entered the 1988 tournament with the top seed and high expectations as the only returning placer. He more than lived up to those expectations by averaging nearly 21 points in his first three matches. Fourth-seeded **Cory Baze** of Oklahoma State stayed within six points, falling 14-8. Seventh-seeded **Keith Nix** of Minnesota made a career run, knocking off second-seeded **Ken Chertow** of Penn State, 10-8, in the quarterfinals and sixth-seeded **Craig Corbin** of Lock Haven, 11-7, in the semis. In the finals, Cuvo dominated, 11-4, to claim his first of back-to-back NCAA titles.

126: Iowa's top-seeded **Brad Penrith** was dominant in his first four matches, including a technical fall (18-2) over fourth-seeded **Steve Knight** of Iowa State in the semifinals. Second-seeded **Jim Martin** of Penn State had a tougher road to the finals, slipping past tenth-seeded **Peter Gonzalez** of Montclair State, 3-2, in the quarters, and sixth-seeded **Kendall Cross** of

Oklahoma State, 8-7, in the semis. In the finals, Martin held on for a 5-4 win over Penrith and his lone NCAA title in four trips to all-American status.

134: This weight was loaded with talent. Four-time all-Americans **Joe Melchiore** of Iowa (Oklahoma transfer) and **John Fisher** of Michigan faced the unenviable task of trying to unseat defending NCAA champion and reigning World Games champion senior **John Smith** of Oklahoma State. Smith was the first world champion to compete in an NCAA tournament. He scored a fall in 6:26, a superior decision 21-8, and a fall in 6:29 to reach the semifinals where he flattened fifth-seeded **Jeff Gibbons** of Iowa State in 6:07. Reaching the finals from the other bracket was seventh-seeded Melchiore of Iowa who, next to Smith, was the hottest wrestler at 134. Melchiore scored a fall in 5:43, beat No. 10 **Thierry Chaney** of William & Mary, 13-5, major decisioned the second-seeded Fisher, 14-4, in a huge upset, and topped sixth-seeded **Joei Bales** of Northwestern, 10-2. Smith proved too much for Melchiore in the finals, prevailing 9-2 for his second consecutive NCAA championship and 90th straight win.

142: Top-seeded **Pat Santoro** of Pittsburgh zipped into the semifinals, but ran into a determined fourth-seeded **Karl Monaco** of Montclair State. Santoro managed a tense 3-2 victory to set up a finals bout with third-seeded **Sean O'Day** of Edinboro. O'Day had notched a narrow 8-8, 10-2 overtime win over unseeded **Larry Gotcher** of Michigan who had upset second-seeded **Kurt Shendenhelm** of Northern Iowa, 8-5. Santoro and O'Day hooked up in the most entertaining final of the tournament, with Santoro pulling out an exciting 16-11 win for his first title.

150: In the only weight where the top eight seeds all earned all-American honors, top-seeded and defending national champion **Tim Krieger** of Iowa State faced second-seeded **Scott Turner** of North Carolina State in the finals. To get there, Krieger barely nipped Oklahoma's eighth-seeded **Junior Taylor**, 4-3, in the quarterfinals and fought off fifth-seeded **Dave Morgan**

Oklahoma State's John Smith (top, earlier match), the reigning World Champion, won his second consecutive NCAA title with a 9-2 decision over Iowa's Joe Melchiore. (Courtesy Oklahoma State University)

Grinding for back points, Pittsburgh's Pat Santoro (top) defeated Edinboro's Sean O'Day in a wild finals bout, 16-11, for his first of back-to-back national championships at 142. (Courtesy University of Pittsburgh)

of Bloomsburg, 8-2 in the semis. Turner blanked three straight opponents (12-0, 8-0 and 13-0) before edging third-seeded **Jeff Jordan** of Wisconsin, 1-0, to enter the finals unscored upon. In the closest finals match of the event, Turner gave up his first point – but just one – and took a rugged 1-1, 1-0 overtime win over Krieger for his only NCAA title. He was named Outstanding Wrestler.

158: Entering the tournament as a three-time all-American, (8th, 3rd and 3rd), North Carolina's top-seeded **Rob Koll** was a man on a mission in his final NCAA appearance. Unseeded **Kenny Fischer** of Oklahoma almost derailed Koll's quest for gold, pushing the senior to the limit before falling, 3-1. Wins over eighth-seeded **Mike Carr** of West Virginia (6-2) and fifth-seeded **Chris Limbeck** of Northern Iowa (8-1) put him in the finals against surprising sixth-seeded **Joe Pantaleo** of Michigan. Pantaleo had upset third-seeded **Dan St. John** of Arizona State, 4-3, en route to the finals. Koll fittingly capped his exceptional career with a first period fall (1:14) over Pantaleo for his only NCAA title.

167: The big story was Michigan's unseeded **Mike Amine** who upset fourth-seeded **John Kohls** of Brigham Young University, 4-4, 4-2 in overtime in the second round and twelfth-seeded **Joe Decamillis** of Wyoming in the quarterfinals. In the semis, Amine again was up to the task, shocking eighth-seeded **Jim Gressley** of Arizona State, with a fall in just 35 seconds. Gressley had pinned top-seeded **Dave Lee** of Wisconsin at 3:36. Second-seeded **Mike Van Arsdale** of Iowa State edged seventh-seeded **Jerry Umin** of Eastern Michigan, 4-2, in the quarterfinals and topped third-seeded **Eric Osborne** of Cal Poly-SLO, 10-4, to reach the finals. Van Arsdale then rolled to an 8-2 victory over Amine to win his lone NCAA championship.

177: The seeding committee was spot on with the top four. **Royce Alger** of Iowa, the 167-pound champ in 1987, earned the top seed and won his second NCAA title with a 6-4 win over determined **Dan Mayo** of Penn State. Alger's toughest match along the way was an 8-2 decision over fourth-seeded **Chris Barnes** of Oklahoma State in the semifinals, while Mayo won a gritty 3-1 decision over third-seeded **Brad Lloyd** of Lock Haven in the semis.

190: Defending champion **Eric Voelker** of Iowa State was seeded second to Ohio State's **Mark Coleman**. When Voelker was upset in the second round, 5-4, by **Bill Freeman** of Lock Haven it opened the door for third-seeded **Mike Davies** of Arizona State, and he took full advantage. Davies bulled his way into the finals with wins of 19-4, WBF 2:45, 11-4, and 11-2 over tenth-seeded **Andy Voit** of Penn. Coleman controlled Davies and scored the only shutout in the finals, 5-0, to earn his only NCAA title. Voelker registered three falls and won the Gorriaran Award.

275: Defending champion and top-seeded **Carlton Haselrig** of Pittsburgh-Johnstown powered his way into the finals with two falls (6:13 and 4:32), a 9-1 decision over eighth-seeded **Mark Tatum** of Oklahoma (who would place third), and a 6-3 semifinals decision over fifth-seeded **Rod Severn** of Arizona State. Unseeded **Dave Orndorff** of Oregon State had a career tourney, upsetting sixth-seeded **Mike Lombardo** of North Carolina State, 7-4, eleventh-seeded **Jon Cogdill** of Wyoming, WBF 4:19, third-seeded **Dean Hall** of Edinboro, 9-5, and seventh-seeded **Mark Sindlinger** of Iowa, 6-5, to reach the finals. Orndorff's magical run ended with a 12-2 loss to Haselrig.

CHAPTER 11

1989 NCAA Wrestling Championship

The 1989 tournament in Oklahoma City, the last year of collegiate wrestling's most dynamic decade, featured two wrestlers (**Carlton Haselrig** and **Tom Brands**) who would be named to the NCAA 75th Anniversary Wrestling Team and become Distinguished Members of the National Wrestling Hall of Fame. It also featured the return to the top of the team race by a Big Four school after a one-year absence. The Oklahoma State Cowboys crowned two champions: third-seeded **Kendall Cross** at 126 and second-seeded **Chris Barnes** at 177 en route to a 20.75-point victory over defending national champion Arizona State.

There were nine four-time all-Americans in the field: top-seeded **Jim Martin** of Penn State and second-seeded freshman **Tom Brands** of Iowa at 126; #2 **Joe Melchiore** of Iowa and #1 **John Fisher** of Michigan at 134; top-seeded **Pat Santoro** of Pittsburgh at 142; top-seeded **Tim Krieger** of Iowa State at 150; third-seeded **Steve Hamilton** of Iowa State at 158; seventh-seeded **Mike Funk** of Northwestern at 177; and unseeded heavyweight **Kirk Mammen** of Oklahoma State. Santoro and Krieger claimed NCAA titles. There were three of the lowest-scoring finals matches in NCAA history.

1989 Weight-By-Weight Highlights

118: Defending champion **Jack Cuvo** of East Stroudsburg had anything but an easy time reaching the finals again, narrowly besting fourth-seeded **Ken Chertow** of Penn State, 6-6, 2-1in overtime in the semifinals. Third-seeded **Doug Wyland** of North Carolina survived a 5-5, 5-1 overtime decision over sixth-seeded **Chris Bollin** of Oklahoma in the quarter-finals, and registered a 9-5 win over second-seeded **Jack Griffin** of Northwestern to reach the finals. In a back-and-forth finale, Cuvo emerged victorious over Wyland, 10-8, for his second straight title.

126: Defending national champion **Jim Martin** of Penn State notched a 4-3 quarterfinals win over eighth-seeded **Gary McCall** of Iowa State, but suffered an excruciatingly close semifinal match loss (2-2, 2-2 criteria) to fifth-seeded **Michael Stokes** of North Carolina State. Third-seeded **Kendall Cross** of Oklahoma State survived three extremely close matches: 5-4 over unseeded **Curtis Wiley** of Millersville (PA) University; 8-8, 3-2 in overtime over eleventh-seeded **Jason Kelber** of Nebraska (who would win a national title at 126 in 1991); and 1-0 over future three-time national champion and second-seeded freshman **Tom Brands** of Iowa in the semifinals. In the finals, Cross ground out a tough 5-2 win over Stokes for his lone NCAA crown.

134: Edinboro's **Sean O'Day**, runner-up at 142 in 1988, pulled down to 134 and took a third seed into the tournament. He powered his way into the finals with wins of TF 21-6, 17-4, and 14-8 (over sixth-seeded **Jerry Durso** of Notre Dame) before meeting four-time all-American and second-seeded **Joe Melchiore** of Iowa in the semifinals, where he prevailed 8-3 over the Hawkeye star. In the upper bracket, Oklahoma's fourth-seeded all-American **T.J. Sewell** had the greatest tournament of his career, knocking off fifth-seeded **Anibal Nieves** of East Stroudsburg, 9-2, in the quarterfinals and stunning top-seeded **John Fisher** of Michigan, 6-6, 8-1 in overtime. In the finals, O'Day won a wild bout, 11-8, for his lone title. Fisher ended his Michigan career with a national record 183 victories, surpassing the 174 set by George Washington's Wade Hughes in 1985.

142: Defending champion **Pat Santoro** of Pittsburgh was almost unchallenged on his march to a second-straight title, handling eleventh-seed **Pat Boyd** of Notre Dame, 9-2, in the semis. Fourth-seeded **Junior Saunders** of Arizona State dispatched fifth-seeded **Larry Gotcher** of Michigan, 14-5, in the quarterfinals, and took down top-seeded **Mike Cole** of Clarion, 8-5, in the semis. Saunders gave Santoro his toughest match of the week, taking the Panther star into overtime. The match ended at 6-6, 1-1, with Santoro winning the title on criteria.

150: 1988 runner-up **Tim Krieger** of Iowa State held the top seed and reached the finals in dominating style with consecutive falls in 3:42, 3:33 and 1:27 and an 11-0 major decision in the semifinals over fifth-seeded **Todd Chesbro** of Oklahoma State. Second-seeded **Karl Monaco** of Montclair State had a much tougher time, scoring narrow decisions over unseeded **Aaron Peters** of Navy, 4-2, and seventh-seeded **Thom Ortiz** of Arizona State, 5-4. In the semis, Monaco topped sixth-seeded **Richard Bailey** of Cal State-Bakersfield, 7-3. Krieger continued his onslaught for a second title with a 5-0 blanking of Monaco in the finals and was named the tourney's Outstanding Wrestler.

Registering back points in an earlier match, Iowa State's Tim Krieger (top) scored three falls and two shutouts en route to the 150-pound title and the Outstanding Wrestler Award. (Courtesy Iowa State University)

158: No. 1 seed **Dan St. John** of Arizona State, who finished third at 158 the previous year, and second-seeded **Joe Pantaleo** of Michigan, who had placed second in '88, were set on a collision course for the finals. St. John breezed into the semifinals, but just got past a very tough fifth-seeded **Joel Smith** of Eastern Michigan, 5-2, to reach the finals. Pantaleo survived a too-close-for-comfort 4-3 win in the opening round over unseeded **Mike Flynn** of Edinboro and a 6-1 semifinal win over Navy's sixth-seeded **Scott Schleicher**, the eventual third-place winner. In the closely contested finals, St. John took a 1-1, 3-1 overtime victory over Pantaleo.

167: **Dave Lee** of Wisconsin lived up to his top seed, reaching the finals with a 9-6 quarter-finals win over ninth-seeded **Mike Amine** of Michigan and a 9-0 shutout of unseeded **Tom Marchetti** of Bucknell in the semis. Marchetti had defeated fifth-seeded **John Rippley** of Army in the second round by fall in overtime (7:37). Oklahoma's sixth-seeded **Baron Blakley** was the surprise, knocking off third-seeded **John Heffernan** of Iowa, 8-1, and second-seeded **Mike Farrell** of Oklahoma State, 5-4, in the semifinals. Lee dominated in the finals, winning 14-6 over Blakley for his only NCAA crown.

Celebrating an earlier victory, Iowa State's Eric Voelker captured his second NCAA crown with a 7-2 win over Northwestern's Mark Whitehead. (Courtesy Iowa State University)

177: Top-seeded **Brad Lloyd** of Lock Haven gave up just three points (TF 16-1, TF 15-0 and 10-2) in reaching the semifinals, then dispatched fourth-seeded **Derek Capanna** of Virginia in the semifinals, 10-2, to establish himself as the heavy favorite. However, second-seeded **Chris Barnes** of Oklahoma State was equally impressive, giving up just seven points in his four matches including a 3-1 squeaker over third-seeded **Dave Dean** of Minnesota in the semifinals. In the third finals match to go into overtime, Barnes won the NCAA title with a 1-1, 2-2 criteria decision. Also in the field was future four-time all-American **Mike Funk** of Northwestern who placed fifth.

190: Four unseeded wrestlers earned all-American status – **Chris Short**, Minnesota (third), **Todd Seiler**, Wisconsin (fourth), **Gary Horner**, Clarion (sixth) and **Nate Toedter**, St. Cloud State (eighth). But the title came down to the top two seeds, #1 **Eric Voelker** of Iowa State and #2 **Mark Whitehead** of Northwestern. Voelker, who had finished third at 190 in 1988, was taken into overtime in the quarterfinals by ninth-seeded **Matt Ruppel** of Lehigh, but prevailed 3-3, 3-2. Fourth-seeded **John Ginther** of Arizona State also pushed Voelker into overtime but dropped a 3-3, 6-1 decision. Whitehead had an easier trip to the finals with 13-5 and 12-8 decisions and a default win before scoring a hard-fought 9-7 decision over the unseeded Horner in the semis. Voelker lived up to his top billing with a solid 7-2 decision over Whitehead for his second NCAA championship.

275: Top-seeded and two-time defending national champion **Carlton Haselrig** cemented his place in NCAA wrestling history by earning his third consecutive title with a narrow 1-0 decision over second-seeded **Joel Greenlee** of Northern Iowa in the finals. The surprise of the weight class was unseeded Oklahoma State freshman **Kirk Mammen**, who placed sixth for his first of four consecutive all-American performances.

CHAPTER 12

Remembering the Golden Era

The following are recollections from those men who wrestled collegiately in the 1980s about The Golden Era of Amateur Wrestling and what made it special.

Roger Frizzell, Oklahoma (1980-83) remembers the Golden Era:

Our OU squad in those years was filled with all-Americans from top to bottom, and the crowds came out in appreciation to watch legends such as **Dave and Mark Schultz, Andre Metzger,** Dr. Death (**Steve Williams**) and future NCAA stars **Melvin Douglas, Dan Chaid, Mark Zimmer** and **Johnny Johnson** – and so many others. We regularly filled the Lloyd Nobel Arena, especially with big rivalry matches against OSU, Iowa and Iowa State. In fact, for some of those matches it was nearly impossible to get a ticket.

The style of wrestling encouraged high scoring and pinning – and that's the type of show that was put on for the fans each and every match. Every wrestler on the squad had a unique wrestling persona and it added to the hype around every event. It was the greatest show on earth and fans were coming out to watch some of the greatest wrestling in history. More importantly, they were coming out to watch college wrestling instead of basketball.

Wrestling during the decade was an odd mixture of freestyle and college style, combined with a bit of Judo (thanks to Metzger who spent time in Japan during high school) with constant high-risk throws and counters that created an exciting, high-scoring atmosphere. Dave and Andre were already among the world's best as seniors in high school and their impact on the sport was huge.

Our team was perhaps even more adept at freestyle than folkstyle as a result, with several individuals having successful international wrestling careers while in college. Our assistant coach, **Jim Humphrey**, was one of the best freestylers in the world, and he loved to hit big throws. At the start of each year, colleges from around the nation turned to freestyle – not college style – for the Great Plains Tournament (the qualifier for the U.S. team to compete in Russia) as the official kick-off to the college wrestling season. Even in the wrestling room, we wrestled freestyle in practice as much as we did college style and the two styles became embedded into one in a way that thrilled the masses and, in the process, made wrestling an absolute blast for all of us who competed.

The big four (OU, OSU, Iowa and Iowa State) were also locked in heated competition. My junior year (1982), we tied Iowa – the eventual NCAA champion that year – in the dual, but lost to Iowa State and broke even with OSU. Going into each of the matches, the outcome was far from decided and it was normally the upsets that determined the ultimate winner.

There were also great individual rivalries that added to the excitement. **Andre Metzger** versus **Lee Roy Smith**, **Dave Schultz** versus **Ricky Stewart**, **Mark Schultz** versus **Ed Banach**, along with my own matches with **Nate Carr** and **Kenny Monday**. Some of the transfers to other colleges added backstory drama to wrestling legends **Joe Gonzales** (who transferred from OU to Cal State-Bakersfield), **John Azevedo** (who transferred from OSU to Cal State-Bakersfield) and **Dave Schultz** (who transferred from OSU). The coaches themselves – **Stan Abel**, **Tom Chesbro** and **Dan Gable** – helped create an atmosphere in the sport that has never since been duplicated.

In the 1980s, the NCAA tournament also included the champions from the other NCAA divisions, so fans got to see the very best all competing under one roof to determine the true champion. Who will ever forget the NCAA finals match between **Mark Schultz** and **Ed Banach**, perhaps the greatest NCAA finals match of all. Nobody ever would have predicted that Stewart would upset Schultz, much less with a fall in his junior year. Later, Dave's matches with **Mike Sheets** were electric. Dr. Death too could thrill a crowd, coming right off the football field at OU, without a single practice, to wrestle in the Bedlam dual against OSU. **Randy Lewis**, of course, was the king of the pin and crowds adored him. He and Metzger ushered in a new era of college wrestling with exciting throws, big scoring and great counters, but always offense, offense, offense.

Almost every match I had with **Nate Carr** was in double digits with the action being non-stop. My freshman year, I hit him with a headlock in the NCAA quarterfinals and later connected with two spladles to win the match – a high-risk technique that you typically don't see any more at the NCAA tournament. It was a time of legends and legendary performances that continued throughout the decade. The run-up to the NCAA championships captured the imagination of sportswriters and the public.

My top ten NCAA wrestlers from the decade are: (1) **Mark Schultz**; (2) **Randy Lewis**; (3) **Ed Banach**; (4) **Nate Carr**; (5) **Jim Zalesky**; (6) **Andre Metzger**; (7) **Dave Schultz**; (8) **John Smith**; (9) **Kenny Monday**; and (10) **Bruce Baumgartner**. Other top wrestlers were **Melvin Douglas**, **Kendall Cross**, **Mike Sheets**, **Ricky Stewart**, **Andy Rein**, **Dan Chaid** and **Lee Roy Smith**.

John Smith, Oklahoma State (1984-88) remembers the Golden Era:

I learned more from losing to **Jim Jordan** of Wisconsin in the NCAA finals my sophomore year than anyone else I wrestled. He was as great a college wrestler as I ever wrestled. He was older and more experienced and I didn't feel like I could beat him. That was a real changing point for my career. My dream was always to be an Olympic champion, but I thought time was slipping away and I needed to be fully committed.

Randy Lewis was extremely tough. He had no fear as a competitor and a very unconventional countering style. He was as competitive as anyone and wasn't afraid to take risks. At that time, wrestling was becoming more creative. Changes were coming fast. The skills and technical innovations brought new things to the sport. The rules allowed us to create and innovate. And **Dan Gable's** influence on the sport cannot be overlooked. He created a mentality of training hard and wrestling hard, and established a culture and work ethic at Iowa that led to championships.

Rick Stewart, Oklahoma State (1979-82) remembers the Golden Era:

At that time, Gallagher Hall was full … wall-to-wall people who were loud and vocal. They stomped on the stands. When you have that atmosphere, you are the center of attention. It's powerful stuff. It's hard to explain. It was a challenge, though. You enjoy it, but you had to block it out. After you were finished, you could open up and accept the praise. But it could be crippling if you didn't perform well because 8,000 people were yelling at you. There were capacity crowds. Pure bedlam with Oklahoma. It was the same thing with Iowa. We had very knowledgeable fans. They camped out for three days in advance of a match to get tickets.

The difference in today's wrestlers is the elimination of cutting weight. They don't have to put in the hard work like we did. You had to train and do things right in my day to make it work. Today, wrestlers don't finish their moves. We had solid guys up and down our lineup. We worked very hard. Those guys were good wrestlers and good citizens. They are still good guys and good citizens. They are involved in their communities. You don't get a lot of notoriety as a wrestler.

The 1980s took the sport to a new level. There are a lot of benefits you get from wrestling. If ever there was a character builder, it's wrestling. You have to go through so much adversity. Best wrestlers: **Dave Schultz**, **Mike Sheets** (one of the best riders ever), **Kenny Monday** and **Roger Frizzell**. I told Roger when he was being recruited that he should come to OSU. Imagine what might have happened if he had gone to OSU instead of OU.

Mark Schultz (Oklahoma 1981-83) remembers the Golden Era:

It took me about 20 years after my career before I finally realized that **Stan Abel** was the greatest coach ever. He was a genius at building a team and putting wrestlers at the best weight for them and the team. When I first arrived at OU for the 80-81 season, I was wondering how I was going to beat **Isreal Sheppard** at 158 just to make the team. He was an all-American and third-place finisher in the NCAAs. He and I became mortal enemies. We had to fight every day for the spot at 158. But Stan had a vision and he redshirted Isreal that year and my brother **Dave** wrestled at that weight while I moved up to 167. The next year, Dave went up to 167, I went to 177 and Isreal wrestled at 158. That made a very strong lineup including **Roger Frizzell** at 150 and **Andre Metzger** at 142 and "Dr. Death" **Steve Williams** at heavyweight. Isreal was the only guy I could practice my most merciless techniques on because he was such a fighter and very tough.

When my OU career ended, I got on my Honda 400 motorcycle and started driving back to California. But outside of the city, I pulled off the side of the road and looked back remembering all I'd been through. All the sacrifices, the pain and the pressure I endured. I probably spent 20 minutes looking back, contemplating everything. Then I just drove away.

Barry Davis, Iowa (1981-85) remembers the Golden Era:

I really enjoyed the years I competed. Our team (Iowa) won the NCAA's every year I was in college (1981-1985). It was great knowing that as a team going into the tournament we had a great shot at winning each year. But we knew that each guy had to wrestle at or better than their seed. I think the added pressure made us perform better as a team and as individuals and I think that is what made Iowa so good. Everyone knew their role and the expectations put on them – that is why we did so well.

At that time, Iowa had an NCAA winning streak that reached nine straight. People loved us – but hated us. By being that dominant, when you went to an arena everything was sold out. Almost like an entourage to be on that team. At one time we had **Randy Lewis**, **Louis Banach**, **Eddie Banach** and myself who had won three silver and one gold medal at the Olympics; **Jimmy Zalesky** being a three-time NCAA champion and **Duane Goldman** who was an NCAA champ and four-time finalist. I think by us being that dominant, people followed us more and teams wanted to knock us off but they couldn't. Also at the time, Wide World of Sports started broadcasting the NCAA's one week after the tourney –and shortly after that they started adding more time to TV due to the popularity. It was more exciting back then. A lot of these guys are college coaches now, which has set the standard work ethic for today.

I just think the sport and the wrestlers were more active because they called stalling really fast back then .If you took a step backwards the ref would call you for stalling. There was no technical fall in the early '80s, so matches were high scoring and you had to keep wrestling aggressively because of the stalling rule. We wrestled a dual in Iowa City against Oklahoma State. After the first two matches, the score was 6-6 because the ref disqualified wrestlers for stalling.

There were so many great wrestlers in that era. Two guys that kept me motivated were **Kevin Darkus** (Iowa State) and **Joe McFarland** (Michigan). Both were elite athletes. Joe was a four-time all-American and two-time runner-up. Kevin was an NCAA champ in 1984. They were the best guys in their weight class and they kept me motivated daily. They forced me to train and focus at a high level and you need that to keep driving you daily. (Author's note: in 1981, McFarland placed fifth and Davis placed seventh at 118 in the NCAA. In 1982, Davis beat Darkus, 7-5, for the national title at 118 and McFarland placed sixth; in 1983, Davis won the title at 126 while Darkus was fifth; in 1984, Darkus edged McFarland for the title at 126; and in 1985, Davis beat McFarland 8-4 for the 126-pound title. Internationally, Davis made every U.S. team while in college: Junior World, Pan American, World and Olympics).

Sergei Beloglazov of the Soviet Union was one of the greatest Russian athletes/wrestlers of all time. From 1980 to 1988 he did not lose one match at the World level, winning two Olympic gold medals and six World Championships.

My top 10 NCAA wrestlers from the 1980s were: (1) **Randy Lewis**; (2) **Jim Zalesky**; (3) **Mark Schultz**; (4) **Ed Banach**; (5) **Nate Carr**; (6) **Ricky Bonomo**; (7) **Carlton Haselrig**; (8) **Gene Mills**; (9) **Duane Goldman**; and (10) **Tom Brands**.

Stan Abel, Oklahoma Coach (1973-1993) remembers the Golden Era:

Wrestling was better back in the 1980s. The Big Four all had great wrestlers up and down their lineups. It was an exciting time. You knew that every weight was going to be tough and you had better be ready. Of course, we had more scholarships back then, so everyone was loaded with talent. At every weight, you could have a national champion or an all-American. Every year, it seemed like the Big Four would finish 1-2-3-4 (Author's Note: the Big Four placed 1-2-3-4 in six of seven seasons from 1980-87).

Stan Abel, Oklahoma head coach. (Courtesy University of Oklahoma)

At OU, it was like coaching a bunch of gladiators. They were all so good. They were all wrestling-minded. Very smart. Dr. Death (Heavyweight **Steve Williams**) was a show unto himself. He had an aura. **Andre Metzger** was always entertaining: the good guy at home, the bad guy on the road. He had a certain presence you don't often see. **Roger Frizzell** was the nicest guy I ever coached. Other nice guys were **Rod Kilgore** and **Kenny Nelson.** They were nice guys and really good wrestlers. I was privileged to coach them.

The 1982 team was the best ever out of OU. It was a huge disappointment when we didn't win the national title. **David Rynda** (unseeded at 118), **Mark Zimmer** (No. 7 at 126) and **Derek Glenn** (No. 11 at 134) lost their first matches and were done when their opponents didn't pull them through. Totally unbelievable. The first 30 minutes of the first round were a complete disaster.

When **Dan Gable** and I were doing wrestling camps, I would say 'you kids are really lucky. Today, you have Dan Gable, national champion from Iowa State. And me, Stan Abel, national champion from OU. Or you can call us Dan and Stan. Or if you know us really well, Gabe and Abe. So remember, it's Abel, not Gable. Stan, not Dan. And Abe, not Gabe.'

Jim Heffernan, Iowa (1983, 1985-87) remembers the Golden Era:

What I remember most is all the work we did as a team and the way **Coach Gable** pushed us, more than anything I accomplished individually. We had a group that had a common goal – to win championships, not just for our team but for those who built the Iowa program into what it was at that time. Wrestling in the Big Ten and NCAA tournament was fun for that group of guys – something we really looked forward to. There was an enormous sense of pride that went along with wearing that uniform and competing for our program.

During my career, being surrounded by teammates that were some of the greats in college wrestling (**Barry Davis**, **Eddie Banach**, **Lou Banach**, **Jimmy Zalesky**, **Duane Goldman**, etc.) you usually didn't have to worry about the pressure of winning, because you were sure all the guys around you were going to do great things. It allowed you to worry about doing your best as an individual, and in turn, contributing to the team. It was a very unique team dynamic where everyone knew their role and their capabilities and how each individual could contribute, with a common goal of being the best team every single year. The longer I am in coaching, the more I understand how remarkable the chemistry was to accomplish what we did as a team. We had a lot of individuals, but everyone involved understood the team dynamic and the ultimate objective.

Looking back, I think the spectator base and excitement level for college wrestling really began to grow in the 1980s. I also think that Iowa wresting during that era, because of Coach Gable, did a lot in terms of the attention college wrestling started to receive. Internationally, as a country, we were very competitive during the 1980s, and the individuals from that era continued to have a great impact internationally during their careers. The best wrestlers I ever faced were **Kenny Monday**, **Nate Carr** and **Tim Krieger.** Kenny was very quick, had lots of length and was a really tough guy. Nate was fast, explosive, strong and physical. Tim was great defensively and very hard to score on. And he was very good from the top position.

My top ten wrestlers from the 1980s both collegiate and international would be: (1) **John Smith**; (2) **Bruce Baumgartner**; (3) **Mark Schultz**; (4) **Dave Schultz**; (5) **Eddie Banach**; (6) **Kenny Monday**; (7) **Tom Brands**; (8) **Nate Carr**; (9) **Randy Lewis**; and (10) **Barry Davis**. It's hard to leave guys like **Ricky Bonomo**, **Duane Goldman**, **Jimmy Jordan**, **Carlton Haselrig**, **Mike Sheets**, **Gene Mills**, **Marty Kistler**, **Royce Alger**, among many others, off the list.

Joe Gonzales, Cal State-Bakersfield (1977-1980) remembers the Golden Era:

The NCAA tournament in the 1980s was much tougher than it is today. You had three divisions wrestling and there were a lot more schools with wrestling programs. It's a sad fact that we don't have Division II and III going to the Division I tournament any longer.

Joe Gonzales controls East Germany's Hartmut Reich, the eventual gold medal winner, en route to a third-place finish in the 1982 World Games. (Courtesy Joe Gonzales)

The wrestling fans are getting cheated because you don't really know who the best wrestlers are at each weight. Wrestling was its own worst enemy when we voted to keep Division II and III out. The majority of Division I coaches voted them out, all except **Dan Gable**. The reason coaches wanted the other divisions out was because they were worried that it could affect a team title if some DII and DIII wrestlers knocked out a DI kid and kept them from being an all-American.

When **John Azevedo** and I won NCAA titles (1980), Cal State-Bakersfield was unofficially fourth or fifth as a team. Having Div. II and III in the tournament made it a much tougher tournament. Today, you don't see a lot of depth at each weight like you did in the 1980s. Every weight had national champs and all-Americans. In my case, I never would have been inducted into the National Wrestling Hall of Fame if I hadn't won an NCAA Division I championship.

I trained with **Yuji Takada** in Japan and he annihilated me. He was one of the greatest wrestlers in history. He wasn't exceptionally fast, but he had great mat sense and his timing was impeccable. I brought what I learned from Yuji back to the U.S. and taught **John Azevedo** and **Tim Vanni** and the other guys on our team. We added those techniques and enhanced our styles. They called it the Cal State style. We were slick, in and out, side to side. If a guy shoots, you score off his shot. A lot of guys wrestled like we did, taking guys down, letting them up, taking them down. There was a lot of scoring. Some coaches were saying that we were humiliating their wrestlers by scoring so much. Hey, I had trained my butt off and I was going to wrestle my style which was score, score, score. Then the technical fall rule came in to stop our style of wrestling.

Between my junior and season years at CS-B I worked out with Takada and got in great shape. My senior season 1979-80, I was really gunning for **Gene Mills** of Syracuse, who beat me 16-13 in the finals in 1979, but he took a redshirt to train for the Olympics. I beat the heck out of everybody that year (55-0), but I wanted Gene in the finals. Unfortunately, it didn't happen.

The best wrestlers I faced were Mills and **Randy Willingham** of Oklahoma State. Willingham was just mean. When I wrestled him, it was a street fight.

Kevin Dresser, Iowa (1983-1986) remembers the Golden Era:

In 1985, I felt I was ready to win the NCAA championship as a junior and had a superior decision, a major decision and a fall to reach the semifinals. Unfortunately, I overlooked my semifinal match against **John Orr** of Princeton and lost, 10-6. I then had a wild match with **Peter Yozzo** of Lehigh and lost, 12-9, for third.

My senior year (1986), I was determined not to let that happen again. I beat everyone in the weight during the year except **Luke Skove** of Oklahoma State. I had a 7-1 lead on him in our dual but ended up losing. The 142 weight that year proved to be one of the toughest ever. I had blinders on and didn't really take notice of how strong it was with defending champion **Jim Gibbons** of Iowa State, Skove, Yozzo and **Pat Santoro**. (Author's Note: Gibbons, Yozzo and Santoro were national champions in their careers; Santoro twice). I realize how tough it was now. I think I got ripped off for the Outstanding Wrestler Award that year. I'm a greedy son-of-a-gun, but I had three pins and won my finals match over Yozzo, 11-6. I remember I tried an inside leg trip that wasn't even close and got taken down to trail 2-0. I hit a four-point fireman's carry in the second period to pull away. He and I always had wild matches for those three years, 1984-86. I think our lowest score was 8-7. Our dual match in 1986, I won 15-12. Yozzo, Skove, Gibbons and Santoro were very tough to beat.

Lennie Zalesky, Iowa (1983-1986) remembers the Golden Era:

I have countless memories of the Iowa wrestling room and practices. The home meets at Iowa, the big crowds and going to the HAWK gatherings afterwards stand out vividly. It was motivating to have a brother who shared the same dreams and goals as you. The ability to have a brother to drill and wrestle with at that level was incredible as I look back. However, at the time, I am not sure either of us thought it was anything special. Based on the number of medalists we had in the World and Olympic competitions, it does seem that the 1980s were one of the best decades for amateur wrestling, if not the best.

Ed Banach, Iowa (1979-1983) remembers the Golden Era:

Wrestling for **Dan Gable** was a great experience. He knew exactly when you were giving it your all. I tore my ACL at The Midlands Tournament and he designed special workouts for me so I wouldn't damage the knee any further. He had me doing sprints in the armory. It was 150 yards long. I figured I would go hard the first 75 yards and then jog it the rest of the way. Then I ran back hard. He said "we'll count that as one lap, not two. You were jogging."

He also had a way of getting you to think about your matches, analyzing what you did right and what you did wrong. Why you won and why you lost. In practice, he had guys work on specific things they needed to improve on. He made everyone a better wrestler.

Iowa vs. Iowa State in 1980, we were trailing 14-7 and **Mike DeAnna** was on the way to losing his match, putting us down 17-7. **Randy Lewis** said "We're going to lose to Iowa State!" I said, 'No we won't. I'll pin **(Dave) Allen** (third-place in NCAA previous year), Lou pins **(John) Forshee** and **(Dean) Phinney** beats **(Mike) Mann**.' Lewis went over to Gable and said "Don't worry, Dan. I just talked to Eddie, we're going to win." That's exactly what happened and the Hawkeyes came away with a thrilling 22-17 victory.

Mike Mann was my toughest opponent. I wrestled him four times and only beat him once (4-3) and that was in nationals (1983). Other tough opponents were **Mark Schultz**, **Colin Kilrain**, **Charlie Heller**, **Dave Allen** and **Steve Fraser**.

Freestyle was two three-minute periods and you had to be ready to go the distance. Louie and I trained together. We went to Big Bear (CA) to train at elevation before the 1984 Olympic Games. Training at altitude boosts oxygen-carrying red blood cells that can improve performance. We were in great shape when we arrived in Los Angeles. Freestyle was in the second week, so we had a lot of time. I remember we were waiting to enter the Los Angeles Coliseum for the opening ceremonies when **Mike Adamle**, former NFL player with the Chiefs, Giants and Jets, walked up to us. He was a reporter for ABC and asked if we would do an interview. The cameraman was setting up when a female gymnast came by and they had us make an arm chair and she sat between us on our arms. After it was over, Lou asked me who the girl was. I said 'Mary Lou something.' Of course, it was soon-to-be individual all-around gold medalist **Mary Lou Retton**. Another time we ran into distance runner **Mary Decker**. It was great being around all those fantastic athletes. At the time, we didn't realize we were a part of history.

More U.S. wrestlers competing internationally in the 1980s brought a lot of new techniques into wrestling. With more throws and more scoring, matches became more exciting for the fans and helped the sport grow. In 1984, my roommate at the Tbilisi Tournament in the Soviet Union was the great **Lee Roy Smith** of Oklahoma State. I remember walking into the room and Lee Roy was reading George Orwell's 1984 in 1984 in the Soviet Union. That was surreal.

Randy Lewis and **Gene Mills** were two of the most exciting wrestlers back then, but they didn't shoot. They let you shoot, then countered and took you down. I remember before one match, Gable told us he wanted us to set the pace, to be aggressive and be the first one to shoot. No one thought Randy would do that, but he did and assistant coach J Robinson literally fell out of his chair. The official blew his whistle when he saw J fall and the ref had to take a few seconds to compose himself, he was laughing so hard at J.

Lou Banach, Iowa (1979-1983) remembers the Golden Era:

The atmosphere at Iowa was intense, but motivating. It is part of the ethos, the culture. Iowa was feared. Our group of guys making world teams and importing moves and techniques back to the Hawkeye wrestling room was elevating. There was a great sense of on-going innovation. That was as important to wrestling as it is in a business environment. Innovation and diversification are critical to success.

No one was there to win a national championship. That was clearly secondary to making World and Olympic teams. We knew we would win the Nationals. Our focus was higher than the NCAA. We were encouraged to reach for the stars; take our careers to a whole different level. **Dan Gable** almost wouldn't recruit a kid if he said he wanted to be a national champion. Gable wanted him to aim higher than that.

Lou Banach in a familiar position: on top and in control. (Courtesy University of Iowa)

Ed, Steve and I were part of the nine straight championships. We were at the start of a dynasty. We were the catalyst that won five straight while we were there under Gable, **Mark Johnson** and **J Robinson**.

Jim Gibbons, Iowa State (1979-1982) remembers the Golden Era:

It was a minefield of great wrestlers at every weight back then, making it difficult to win a national title. There were so many fantastic wrestlers such as **Dave Schultz**, **Mark Schultz**, **Andre Metzger**, **John Smith**, **Randy Lewis** and others who were innovators and teachers. They traveled around the world and brought back techniques and shared them. Andre was one of the few guys in that era who had moves named after them. I used The Metzger in the finals in 1981 and he was wrestling in that tournament and won at 142. I feel he is a Hall of Famer.

Freestyle back then was a black mark scoring system. If you pinned an opponent, you got no black marks. Anything else meant points against you, even when you won. We were incentivized to go for the fall, so matches were much more offensive and high-scoring. If you blocked with your head and backed up, you were called for stalling. The officials were much more involved back then and as a result it was not uncommon to see 20-point matches.

On his rivalry with **Randy Lewis**: What I learned from Randy Lewis was that to compete against him and win, I had to be in better shape than I was. He just countered everything you did and was great from the top position. I watched him throughout his career make great wrestlers really look their worst. He taught me that pace was more important than score.

Two things that made our matches fun was I wanted in on his leg and Randy wanted me in on his leg so there was a lot of action in our matches. He was a great counter wrestler who could throw you on your head from any position. He had the reputation of having the best scoring defense of any wrestler at any weight in the country. It was a great challenge, but I looked forward to wrestling him. I had to change angles quickly and take shallow shots at different angles to get him to react. But if you thought about the score at any point in the match he would win. I always looked forward to wrestling Randy. I admired the way he wrestled and I think he felt the same about me.

Joe Gibbons, Iowa State (1972-1986) remembers the Golden Era:

As a true freshman in 1982, I cut 17 ½ pounds before The Midlands and won. In 1983, I had a hard time making 134 so I redshirted and moved up to 142 the next year. I tore knee cartilage wrestling **Lew Sondgeroth** (Northern Iowa) in a dual and had arthroscopic surgery. In the 1984 NCAA Championships, I wrestled **Jesse Reyes** of Cal State-Bakersfield in the semifinals. I was leading 4-2 plus a couple minutes of riding time, but I wasn't confident in my conditioning after the knee injury and I got passive. He turned an inside trip into a bear hug and took me down. I rolled on my back and the referee slapped me pinned. That was a big disappointment. In my senior season, I met Sondgeroth in the semifinals and barely beat him in overtime (3-3, 1-1 criteria). In the finals, I had a tough match with Princeton's **John Orr**, but won a 4-3 decision for my only national title. In 1986 I lost to **Peter Yozzo** (Lehigh) in the semifinals, 5-4. I pinned **Pat Santoro** (Pittsburgh) in the consolations and beat **Luke Skove** (Oklahoma State) for third place.

Kevin Dresser (Iowa), **Luke Skove** and **Leo Bailey** (Oklahoma State), **Pat Santoro** (Pittsburgh), **Peter Yozzo** (Lehigh) and **Joe Reynolds** (Oklahoma) were some of the best wrestlers I faced during my career.

Terry Brands, Iowa (1989-1992) remembers the Golden Era:

In my freshman season at 118, I had beaten several nationally-ranked guys, was 26-3 and things were going well. But I lost a wrestle-off match to **Steve Martin** at the end of the year and didn't make it into the NCAA Championships in 1989. Martin was busy preparing to wrestle me, while I was busy preparing to wrestle future opponents. He got me on my heels and beat me. When I evaluated that season, I realized I just wasn't good enough yet.

Mike Moyer, West Chester (1980-83) remembers the Golden Era:

There were many really great wrestlers in the 1980s. I can attest to how great they were because I wrestled in the NCAA Championships in 1981 through 1983 at 158 pounds, the same weight class as **Jim Zalesky** (Iowa), **Dave Schultz** (Oklahoma), **Ricky Stewart** (Oklahoma State), **Isreal Sheppard** (Oklahoma), **Bill Dykeman** (LSU), **Chris Catalfo** (Syracuse), **Perry Shea** (Cal State-Bakersfield) and **Kevin Jackson** (LSU).

In 1981, I won my first match (14-8 over 10th-seeded **Robert Albert** of Clarion) but lost to Zalesky in the second round, 7-3. In '82 I pinned my first opponent (**Marty Bench**, Weber State, 3:34), but lost to Dykeman (6-4) in the second round. My senior year, it was Catalfo who got me in the first round, 16-9.

There was a lot of change going on at that time in collegiate wrestling with the influence of guys who wrestled internationally and brought back those techniques. I was a bit insulated from the international scene being at West Chester State College, a Division II school that wrestled Division I. The amount of talent was extraordinary and the coaches were exceptional. **Dan Gable** was in his prime and the other coaches were trying to catch up to him.

There were so many great rivalries back then. **Ed Banach** and **Dave Allen**. **Ed Banach** and **Mark Schultz**. **Dave Schultz** and **Ricky Stewart**. **Barry Davis** and **Kevin Darkus**. **Nate Carr**, **Kenny Monday** and **Roger Frizzell**. **Randy Lewis** and **Darryl Burley**. **Andre Metzger** and **Lennie Zalesky**. It was a great time to be a wrestling fan.

Jim Martin, Penn State (1986-89) remembers the Golden Era:

I wrestled **Brad Penrith** in the finals in 1988. He wasn't your typical Iowa wrestler. He wasn't so much of a grind, grind, grind wrestler like most of them were. He was pretty good in all phases. A little different in his style, but very good. I don't think he was as disciplined or as intense as his teammates. It was a good match since we had similar styles. I didn't wrestle all that well, but I got lucky. I was down, but at the end I got two back points with a tight waist tilt to win, 5-4. Winning a championship was awesome. Just unbelievable. You think about it when you're training and you dream about it for years. And then, there it is. It was a surreal feeling.

In 1989, it was a struggle with **Michael Stokes** of North Carolina State in the semifinals. He was strong and quick and a very talented athlete. He wrestled a smart match. He didn't want to wrestle on the mat, but he was able to ride me. We went into overtime and both scored two points to still be tied. It went to criteria and Stokes won with more riding time. I was devastated for quite a while. I was shooting to win my second championship and I knew I wouldn't be wrestling after college because of medical school. It really hurt to lose. In the consolations, I wrestled **Jason Kelber** of Nebraska. He was very tough, but I won in overtime, 6-6, 1-0. In the third place match, I wrestled **Terry Brands** of Iowa. Mentally, I don't think I was 100 percent, but I fought through it and won, 6-5.

The Penn State coaches recruited the right people who had the right mind set. Guys coming into the program expected to win and Coach **Rich Lorenzo** and Assistant Coach **John Fritz** (national champion and three-time all-American) expected them to win. We were taught not to expect Iowa to win every year. **Ken Chertow** (three-time all-American and 1988 Olympian) had a big influence on me. He expected to win every match. That kind of stuff rubs off on teammates. It becomes contagious.

What I remember most about beating Iowa in Iowa City is pretty selfish. I remember I lost to **Brad Penrith**. It was the only dual I ever lost. I had just wrestled him close in the All-Star match and was confident I could beat him, but I lost. I remember after the dual, it was eerily quiet. You could hear a pin drop. They had never lost there and the fans were stunned. It was an unusual experience for them.

CHAPTER 13

Four-time All-Americans in the 1980s

Looking back at the decade of the eighties, it is evident there has never been another quite like it. There were 11 nominees to the NCAA 75th Anniversary Wrestling Team from the decade, with four of those honored as members of the team: **Tom Brands**, Iowa (1989-92); **John Smith**, Oklahoma State (1984-88); **Ed Banach**, Iowa (1980-83) and **Carlton Haselrig**, Pittsburgh-Johnstown (1987-89). The decade also produced 33 four-time all-Americans who wrestled at least one year in the decade:

Class of 1980
Mike Brown, Lehigh: 5th (1977), 3rd (1978), 2nd (1979), 7th (1980)
Howard Harris, Oregon State: 6th (1977), 5th (1978), 5th (1979), **1st (1980)**

Class of 1981
Gene Mills, Syracuse: 3rd (1977), 4th (1978), **1st (1979)**, **1st (1981)**
Randy Lewis, Iowa: 2nd (1978), **1st (1979)**, **1st (1980)**, 7th (1981)
Mike DeAnna, Iowa: 3rd (1977), 6th (1978), 2nd (1979), 2nd (1981)

Class of 1982
Andre Metzger, Oklahoma: 5th (1979), 2nd (1980), **1st (1981)**, **1st (1982)**
Rick Stewart, Oklahoma State: 7th (1979), **1st (1980)**, **1st (1981)**, 3rd (1982)
Geno Savegnago, Eastern Illinois 8th (1979), 5th (1980), 3rd (1981), 6th (1982)
Steve Williams, Oklahoma: 6th (1979), 5th (1980), 3rd (1981), 2nd (1982)

Class of 1983
Darryl Burley, Lehigh: **1st (1980)**, 2nd (1981), 2nd (1982), **1st (1983)**
Roger Frizzell, Oklahoma: 4th (1980), 3rd (1981), 3rd (1982), 3rd (1983)
Mike Mann, Iowa State: 7th (1980), 4th (1981), 2nd (1982), 2nd (1983)
Ed Banach, Iowa: **1st (1980)**, **1st (1981)**, 2nd (1982), **1st (1983)**

Class of 1984
Jim Zalesky, Iowa: 5th (1981), **1st (1982)**, **1st (1983)**, **1st (1984)**
Mike Sheets, Oklahoma State: 7th (1981), 2nd (1982), **1st (1983)**, **1st (1984)**

Class of 1985
Barry Davis, Iowa: 7th (1981), **1st (1982)**, **1st (1983)**, **1st (1985)**
Joe McFarland, Michigan: 5th (1981), 6th (1982), 2nd (1984), 2nd (1985)

Class of 1986
Joe Gibbons, Iowa State: 4th (1982), 4th (1984), **1st (1985)**, 3rd (1986)
Duane Goldman, Iowa: 2nd (1983), 2nd (1984), 2nd (1985), **1st (1986)**
Dan Chaid, Oklahoma: 6th (1983), 4th (1984), **1st (1985)**, 2nd (1986)

Class of 1987
Jim Heffernan, Iowa: 4th (1983), 2nd (1985), **1st (1986)**, 2nd (1987)
Kevin Jackson, Iowa State/LSU: 3rd (1983), 3rd (1984), 7th (1985), 2nd (1987)
Greg Elinsky, Penn State: 7th (1984), 2nd (1985), 2nd (1986), 3rd (1987)

Class of 1988
Rob Koll, North Carolina: 8th (1985), 3rd (1986), 3rd (1987), **1st (1988)**

Class of 1989
Jim Martin, Penn State: 4th (1986), 2nd (1987), **1st (1988)**, 3rd (1989)
Joe Melchiore, Iowa/Oklahoma: 4th (1985), 7th (1986), 2nd (1988), 3rd (1989)
John Fisher, Michigan: 4th (1985), 4th (1987), 3rd (1988), 4th (1989)
Pat Santoro, Pittsburgh: 6th (1986), 2nd (1987), **1st (1988)**, **1st (1989)**
Tim Krieger, Iowa State: 5th (1986), **1st (1987)**, 2nd (1988), **1st (1989)**

Class of 1990
None

Class of 1991
Mike Funk, Northwestern: 4th (1987), 5th (1989), 4th (1990), 7th (1991)

Class of 1992
Tom Brands, Iowa: 4th (1989), **1st (1990)**, **1st (1991)**, **1st (1992)**
Steve Hamilton, Iowa State: 7th (1989), 3rd (1990), 2nd (1991), 3rd (1992)
Kirk Mammen, Oklahoma State: 6th (1989), 6th (1990), 5th (1991), 8th (1992)

There were just 10 wrestlers from the decade who placed fourth or better in all four years of eligibility. In alphabetical order: **Ed Banach, Tom Brands, Darryl Burley, John Fisher, Roger Frizzell, Joe Gibbons, Duane Goldman, Jim Heffernan, John Martin** and **Gene**

Mills. All won at least one national championship with the exception of Frizzell and Fisher who never reached the finals. **Kenny Monday** and **Nate Carr** kept Frizzell from a shot at a title in his career at Oklahoma, leaving him as the best wrestler never to reach the finals based on his placements of 4th, 3rd, 3rd and 3rd. Michigan's Fisher, the winningest wrestler in NCAA history (183), was denied by **Jim Jordan, John Smith** and **Sean O'Day**.

The Wrestlers

Ed Banach, University of Iowa (1980-1983)
All-American Placements: 1st, 1st, 2nd, 1st

Ed Banach won three national championships: 1980 and 1981 at 177 and 1983 at 190. He would have been the first four-time national champion had it not been for the sensational **Mark Schultz** of Oklahoma. Their 1982 finals match at 177 is considered by many to be the greatest finals bout in history, eventually won by Schultz in a back-and-forth match, 16-8. The big momentum changer in that bout came late with Schultz turning a Banach throw attempt into four points.

Banach's best season was 1980 when he recorded a 35-1 ledger. In the NCAA event, Banach posted a pair of falls and a 16-2 superior decision before meeting future three-time all-American **Colin Kilrain** of Lehigh in the semifinals. Banach fell behind 8-0, but roared back to come out on top, 12-11. In the finals, he dominated Iowa State's fourth-seeded **Dave Allen**, 16-5. The next year proved to be Banach's most dominant NCAA event as he won 18-6, 24-4, WBF 5:56 and 7:18 to reach the finals. However, top-seeded Kilrain was upset in the semifinals by Clarion's fourth-seeded **Charlie Heller**, 5-3. In the finals, Banach flattened Heller in 4:15 for his third national title.

He compiled an impressive 141-9-1 collegiate record and an Iowa school record of 73 career pins. In 1983, he was named Big Ten Athlete of the Year. He also ranks among the top Iowa wrestlers in season pins (22), career wins (141), season wins (41) and career winning percentage (.937).

Ed and his twin brother Lou both won NCAA titles in 1981 and 1983, and gold medals at the 1984 Summer Olympic Games in Los Angeles. Ed defeated **Akira Ota** of Japan 15-3 in the 198-pound freestyle finals despite suffering a concussion, one of many he experienced in his career.

He served as an assistant coach at Iowa State until 1987 and today works in the ISU Athletic Department in Ames, IA where he lives.

Tom Brands, Iowa (1989-1992)
All-American Placements: 4th, 1st, 1st, 1st

Tom Brands, currently the head wrestling coach for the University of Iowa, was a four-time all-American and three-time NCAA champion. After a fourth-place finish at 126 in 1989, Brands powered his way to three consecutive national championships. In 1990, he won his first title at 126, followed by consecutive championships at 134 in 1991 and 1992. His 1991 season was most memorable as he went undefeated in 45 matches and scored an incredible 93 points in four NCAA Championship matches (including a 33-19 semifinal win) leading to the finals against second-seeded **Alan Fried** of Oklahoma State. Brands earned a hard-fought 5-3 decision for title number two. In 1992, Brands and Fried again met in the finals with Brands scoring a tough 6-3 decision and earning Outstanding Wrestler honors. His career record was 158-7-2, a winning percentage of .946. He was a three-time Big Ten champion.

Brands won four U.S. National Freestyle championships (1993-1996) and earned the gold medal at 136.5 pounds in the 1996 Olympics in Atlanta. He also won a gold medal at the 1993 World Games, two World Cup gold medals (1994 and 1995) and the gold at the 1995 Pan American Games.

He was named 1993 USA Wrestling Athlete of the Year, 1993 **John Smith** Outstanding Freestyle Wrestler, and 1993 *Amateur Wrestling News* Man of the Year. He was inducted into the National Wrestling Hall of Fame in 2001.

Mike Brown, Lehigh University (1977-1980)
All-American Placements: 5th, 3rd, 2nd, 7th

Mike Brown was the first Lehigh University wrestler to become a four-time all-American. He also was a four-time EIWA Conference champion, one of just eight wrestlers to accomplish that feat. In 1977, Brown placed fifth at 177, then moved up to 190 for his final three seasons.

In the 1978 NCAA event, he won his first two matches, but was edged by third-seeded **Daryl Monasmith** of Oklahoma State, 8-7, in the quarterfinals. Brown then reeled off four straight wins including a 5-3 win over Monasmith to earn third place. His junior season was memorable as he stormed into the finals with a first-round fall, a 21-9 superior decision and a 13-3 major decision. In the semifinals, he beat future heavyweight national champion **Howard Harris** of Oregon State, 11-5. In his only finals appearance, Brown was bested by top-seeded **Eric Wais** of Oklahoma State. In his final campaign, Brown took a top seed into the NCAA event but was upset by the tournament's hottest wrestler, #8 **Noel Loban** of Clemson, 6-5. In consolations, he lost a narrow 3-1 decision to future four-time all-American **Geno Savegnago** of Syracuse to finish seventh.

He ended his storied career with school records for career wins (95) and bonus wins (67). He ranks third in Lehigh history with 36 career falls. Brown was inducted into the **Roger S. Penske**/Lehigh Athletics Hall of Fame in 2010.

Darryl Burley, Lehigh University (1980-1983)
All-American Placements: 1st, 2nd, 2nd, 1st

One of the greatest lower weight grapplers in NCAA history, the four-time all-American made the NCAA finals four times, winning two championships. As a 134-pound freshman in 1979, Burley ended the 84 match win streak of top-seeded and defending champion **Mike Land** of Iowa State, 9-7, for his first title. Following second-place finishes in 1980 (losing to the legendary **Randy Lewis**) and 1981 (losing to the superb **Jim Gibbons**), Burley took a year off, then moved up to 142 in 1983. In his finest NCAA tournament, Burley registered lopsided wins of 16-2, 9-3, 12-3 and 10-3 to reach the finals against second-seeded **Al Freeman** of Nebraska. A first-period injury forced Freeman to default and Burley had his bookend NCAA titles.

He completed his career with an exceptional 94-5-1 record and 76 bonus wins. Of note, his five losses and one tie came at the hands of Lewis and Gibbons. In 1984, Burley placed fourth at the U.S. Olympic Trials. In 2005, he was a nominee for the NCAA 75th Anniversary Wrestling Team.

He earned his law degree from Hofstra Law School and is a practicing attorney. He lives in the Pemberton, NJ area with his wife and two children.

Dan Chaid, University Oklahoma (1983-1986)
All-American Placements: 6th, 4th, 1st, 2nd

Dan Chaid, who began training with Dave and Mark Schultz at Stanford at the age of 16, was a Junior World Freestyle champion (1980) and Greco-Roman Junior National Championship gold medalist (1980). Highly recruited, Chaid followed the Schultz brothers to Oklahoma and became the sixth Sooner to earn all-American honors four times at that point in time.

Following a sixth-place finish in 1983 at 190, Chaid improved to fourth in 1984 and then nailed down his lone NCAA title with a 5-3 win over Iowa's talented **Duane Goldman** in 1985, going 39-1. Goldman, who made the finals four straight years, avenged that loss in 1986 with a 5-4 win over Chaid, who owns OU career records for wins (150) and career falls (58).

Barry Davis, University of Iowa (1981-1983, 1985)
All-American Placements: 7th, 1st, 1st, 1st

Barry Davis is the winningest wrestler in University of Iowa history with 162 victories over his incredible four-year career that included national championships in 1982, 1983 and 1985. Following a seventh-place finish in his freshman year at 118, Davis won his first title in 1982 and set the school record for wins (46) in a season. In 1983, Davis went 38-1-1 and claimed title number two, this time at 126, and defended that title in 1985 with an 8-4 decision over four-time all-American **Joe McFarland** of Michigan. That earned him the Outstanding Wrestler Award and he was named the Big Ten's Athlete of the Year. Davis redshirted in 1984 to wrestle in the Olympics and was rewarded with a silver medal at 125.5 pounds in the 1984 Los Angeles Games.

Davis was a Pan American Games gold medalist. He won a bronze medal at the 1986 World Games, and followed that with a silver medal at the 1987 World Championships after winning the Olympic Sports Festival. Also, he was a member of the 1988 U.S. Olympic Team but did not medal. He was inducted into the National Iowa Varsity Club Athletic Hall of Fame in 1998. He became a Distinguished Member of the National Wrestling Hall of Fame in 2007.

Currently the head wrestling coach at the University of Wisconsin, Davis and his wife, Nan, are the parents of two daughters, Amanda and Amy. They reside in Madison, WI.

Mike DeAnna, University of Iowa (1977-1979, 1981)
All-American Placements: 3ʳᵈ, 6ᵗʰ, 2ⁿᵈ, 2ⁿᵈ

Completing his exceptional career in 1981, DeAnna was the fifth wrestler in Big Ten history to win four consecutive conference championships. With a record of 122-18-2, he was an NCAA runner-up in his junior (1979) and senior (1981) seasons. As a junior, DeAnna upset two-time defending national champion **Mark Churella** of Michigan in the Big Ten finals, 14-14, 6-4 in what wrestling legend **Dan Gable** called "the greatest individual effort in Iowa wrestling (history)." He then powered his way into the finals as the third seed with two falls and two lopsided decisions only to lose to Churella by fall in the finals. After red-shirting in 1980, DeAnna was the top seed at 177 in '81, where he met Oklahoma's third-seeded **Mark Schultz** in the finals. Schultz pulled away to a 10-4 win, leaving DeAnna one win short of his NCAA title dream.

One of the top wrestlers from the Cleveland, OH area, DeAnna was a three-time high school champion at Bay Village going 83-0 after a 21-5-1 freshman campaign. He was named a prep all-American in 1976. In high school, he also won two U.S. Wrestling Association National Freestyle titles. DeAnna won National AAU Freestyle titles in 1983 and 1984 and was second alternate on the 1984 U.S. Olympic Wrestling Team.

Greg Elinsky, Penn State University (1984-1987)
All-American Placements: 7ᵗʰ, 2ⁿᵈ, 2ⁿᵈ, 2ⁿᵈ

Greg Elinsky was Penn State's first four-time all-American, finishing seventh, second twice and third in the NCAA tournament (18 wins), and a three-time EWL champion. He also was the first Nittany Lion to win a title at The Midlands Tournament. He was selected to wrestle in the National Wrestling Coaches Association All-Star Classic twice (1986 and 1987). He ranks among Penn State's most prolific wrestlers with 142 wins and 55 dual meet wins. Elinsky also was a National Espoir Freestyle champion (1985), a Pan American Games champion (1990), a U.S. National Open Freestyle champion (1992) and was the 1992 U.S. Olympic Freestyle Team alternate behind 1988 Olympic gold medalist **Kenny Monday**.

As a freshman, he pushed top-seeded and two-time defending national champion **Jim Zalesky** to the limit, losing a 3-2 decision in the quarterfinals to the Iowa star who would win his third straight crown. Elinsky is a member of the EWL Hall of Fame and is a vice president with Goldman Sachs in Philadelphia.

John Fisher, University of Michigan (1985, 1987-1989)
All-American Placements: 4ᵗʰ, 4ᵗʰ, 3ʳᵈ, 4ᵗʰ

Wrestling in one of the toughest weight divisions in history (134 in the 1980s), John Fisher owns the NCAA record for most career wins (183). Over four all-American seasons and three Big Ten championships, he amassed an amazing 183-21 ledger.

In 1985, Fisher placed fourth, while the future legend **John Smith** finished second (both wrestlers lost to national champion **Jim Jordan** of Wisconsin). In 1987, Smith won his first NCAA title while Fisher placed fourth, and in 1988, top-seeded Smith again won while second-seeded Fisher placed third. One of Fisher's biggest wins came in The Midlands his freshman year when he beat defending NCAA champion and Olympic silver medalist **Barry Davis** of Iowa.

Fisher was twice an alternate for the U.S. Olympic team (1992 and 1996), won a World Cup title in 1997 and was elected to the Greater Flint (MI) Area Sports Hall of Fame in 2010.

He teaches in Ann Arbor, MI where he lives with his wife, Millie, and son, John II.

Roger Frizzell, University of Oklahoma (1980-1983)
All-American Placements: 4th, 3rd, 3rd, 3rd

Roger Frizzell was a three-time state champion and *Wrestling USA Magazine* all-American Dream Team member (1977) for Midwest City (OK) High School with an incredible 86-2-2 record. He went on to become a four-time NCAA Wrestling all-American (1980-83) for the University of Oklahoma with a 115-24-2 record. His 115 wins were a record at OU at that time. He remains the most successful consolation wrestler in NCAA history who never made it to the finals (4th, 3rd, 3rd and 3rd). It took four extremely talented wrestlers – **Andy Rein**, **Scott Trizzino**, **Nate Carr** and **Kenny Monday** – to keep Frizzell from reaching the finals during his career.

In 1980, he finished fourth behind national champion Rein, who edged him, 9-6, in the NCAA semifinals at 150. Frizzell had reached the semifinals with a dominant 13-6 win over future three-time national champion Carr, hitting a headlock and two spladles in the bout. In 1981, it was Trizzino pulling out a 10-6 win, while in 1982 it was Carr holding on to register a wild 13-10 win. In his senior season, Frizzell rallied against Monday but ran out of time in a 7-5 semifinal defeat.

Frizzell was a national AAU freestyle champion and earned silver (1980) and bronze (1981) medals in the U.S. Senior Freestyle National Championships, losing to two-time NCAA champ and 1980 U.S. Olympic Team member **Chuck Yagla** (1980 finals) and the legendary **Dave Schultz** (2-1 in the 1981 semifinals). Also in 1980, Frizzell won the bronze medal in the Junior World Freestyle Championship in Mongolia.

In the 1982 Great Plains Tournament (freestyle), Frizzell beat Rein in the finals, 12-7, for the title at 150 and was named the tournament's Outstanding Wrestler. Monday placed fourth. Also competing in that weight class were OU teammate **Andre Metzger** and Trizzino, making it one of the toughest weight classes in any tournament in history with three NCAA national champions, 14 all-American designations and 13 top-four NCAA finishes including five seconds. Those wrestlers also won five World Games medals (one gold, two silver, two bronze) and three

Four-time all-American Roger Frizzell (left) and three-time national champion Mark Schultz served as co-captains of Oklahoma's 1982-83 team. (Courtesy University of Oklahoma)

Olympic medals (one gold, two silver). Frizzell also owned a freestyle win over 1977 NCAA national champion **Steve Barrett** (Oklahoma State) and a dual win by fall over two-time NCAA champ **Marty Kistler** of Iowa.

In 2012, J. Carl Guymon, legendary wrestling writer for the Daily Oklahoman, hosted a "Wrestling Rivalries" segment at the National Wrestling Hall of Fame in Stillwater, OK with Frizzell and Oklahoma State rival Kenny Monday prior to a Bedlam Series match at OSU. Here's what Guymon had to say about Frizzell:

"Roger might be the best collegiate wrestler I've seen in my 39 years of covering college wrestling to have never made it to the NCAA finals. I don't mean that to sound like a back-handed compliment. If he had been wrestling at that weight, at 150, a few years before or a few years after when he actually wrestled, I believe he would have won at least one NCAA title and maybe a couple. Because if you think about it, the two guys he lost to those last two years (Carr and Monday) combined for four NCAA titles, Olympic titles and world championships ... a couple of guys who were pound-for-pound about as good as (any) American wrestlers we've ever seen."

Frizzell was honored as an Outstanding American and inducted into the National Wrestling Hall of Fame in 2013 and chaired the 2014 marketing and public relations effort to return wrestling to the Olympic Games.

He currently is senior vice president and chief communications officer for Carnival Corporation. He continues to support wrestling by serving as a volunteer coach and clinician. He and his wife, Janna, split time between Miami, FL and Kingston, OK. They have five adult children (Sandra, Josh, Zack, Kyle and Andrea) and two granddaughters.

Mike Funk, Northwestern (1987, 1989-1991)
All-American Placements: 4th, 5th, 4th, 7th

Northwestern's first four-time all-American, Mike Funk also was named NU's Male Athlete of the Year for 1990-91. In 1991, he won the Big Ten championship at 190 and finished seventh at the NCAA Championships. That same year, he led NU in points, falls and net takedowns, sweeping the team's three major postseason awards. Funk finished his career with 122 wins, in the top ten for the school all-time, and participated in the 1991 East-West All-Star Tournament. Funk won a career-best 35 matches in 1990, which ranks among NU's top 10 for single season victories. He was inducted into the Northwestern Athletic Hall of Fame in 2004.

Joe Gibbons, Iowa State University (1982, 1984-1986)
All-American Placements: 4th, 4th, 1st, 3rd

Joe Gibbons was a four-time Iowa prep state champion at four different weights, compiling an impressive 105-5 record including a perfect 28-0 mark as a senior. He also won four state freestyle titles and four Greco-Roman state titles. He was named the number one recruit in the country his senior year, was captain of *Wrestling USA Magazine's* Dream Team in 1981 and was named outstanding wrestler of the 1981 USWF tournament.

He followed up his high school career by winning the prestigious Midlands Tournament at 126 pounds and placing fourth in the 1982 NCAA's his freshman year at Iowa State University. In 1984 he placed fourth at 142, then turned in his best season as a junior (1985) with a 53-3 record and a national championship. Gibbons edged **John Orr** of Princeton in the finals, 4-3, but had to survive a marathon 3-3, 1-1 criteria decision over fifth-seeded **Lew Sondgeroth** of Northern Iowa in the semifinals. His senior season, he placed third behind champion **Kevin Dresser** of Iowa and **Peter Yozzo** of Lehigh. Gibbons was a two-time big Eight champion and ended his career with a 124-20-3 record and owns the ISU record for most wins in a single season (53).

He was legendary coach **Dr. Harold Nichols'** last NCAA champion and served as an assistant coach for his brother, Jim, when the Cyclones won the 1987 NCAA team title. Joe was inducted into the Iowa Wrestling Hall of Fame with his brother Jim and uncle **Joe Frank** in 2003.

Duane Goldman, University of Iowa (1983-1986)
All-American Placements: 2nd, 2nd, 2nd, 1st

Wrestling at 177 and 190 in the NCAA's, Duane Goldman made the finals four consecutive years. In his first three trips to the championship match, he lost to three of the best upper weight wrestlers in history. In 1983, Oklahoma's **Mark Schultz** won his third straight title with a defensive 4-2 victory over Goldman. As the number one seed in his sophomore season, Goldman used a narrow 6-5 decision over Oklahoma's **Dan Chaid** in the semifinals to take a 31-0 mark into the finals against second-seeded **Jim Scherr** of Nebraska, but fell 3-2.

Top-seeded as a junior, Goldman took a 31-1 record into the finals against Chaid, but again fell short, 5-3. In his last shot at a title in 1986, he avenged the 1985 loss to Chaid with a narrow 5-4 decision, a national title and a perfect 36-0 record.

Goldman won four Big Ten Conference individual titles and finished with a 132-10 record (.930 winning percentage). In his final three seasons, Goldman was an astonishing 98-3 with two of those losses in the NCAA finals.

Steve Hamilton, Iowa State (1989-1992)
All-American Placements: 7th, 3rd, 2nd, 3rd

Wrestling at three different weights – 150, 158 and 167 – Steve Hamilton had three top-three finishes in the NCAA Tournament. He placed seventh at 158 in his freshman year (1989) and took a number two seed into the 1990 event. In the semifinals, Hamilton was extended into overtime by Navy's

Duane Goldman (Courtesy University of Iowa)

#3 **Scott Schleicher** and lost, 3-3, 3-2. He then beat fourth-seeded **Dan Russell** of Portland State, 10-5, to claim third place. In his junior campaign, Hamilton dropped to 150 and reached the finals, but lost a heart-breaking 4-3 decision to top-seeded **Matt Demaray** of Wisconsin. As a senior, Hamilton earned the top seed at 167 pounds but was upset in the semifinals by Oklahoma State's **Todd Chesbro**, 4-2. Hamilton scored a 5-3 decision over third-seeded **Dave Hart** of Penn State to claim his second third-place finish.

Hamilton was a member of the 1993 U.S. Freestyle Team after placing third at the World Team Trials. He also placed fifth at the U.S. Nationals in 1993 and eighth in 1994. He placed second and third at the Sunkist Open in 1993 and 1994, and placed fifth at the 1995 Grand Prix Slovakia. In 1996, he won titles at the Olympic Trials South and the Michigan International Open.

A native of Emmetsburg, Iowa, Hamilton received his Bachelor's in history from Iowa State in 1992. He and his wife, Erin, have one daughter, Avery.

Howard Harris, Oregon State University (1977-1980)
All-American Placements: 6th, 5th, 5th, 1st

Howard Harris was a four-time all-American at 190 and heavyweight, and holds the Oregon State school record for career wins (169) and single season pins (40 in 1980). He won the NCAA heavyweight crown in 1980, pinning future wrestling legend **Bruce Baumgartner** in the finals. He was named the tournament's Outstanding Wrestler – the first African-American to do so – and finished the season with a perfect 46-0 mark. He is one of only five wrestlers to pin every opponent in an NCAA tournament.

Harris announced he would sign with Oklahoma out of high school, but was convinced to stay in his home state by Oregon State Coach **Dale Thomas**. Had he gone to OU, he may have kept Sooner four-time all-American **Steve Williams** on the sidelines for his final two years. At a minimum, there would have been some titanic ranking matches in the OU wrestling room.

He was a member of the 1980 United States Olympic Team that didn't get to compete because of the political boycott. He did compete in the 1981 World Cup where he lost a close decision to Olympic champion **Sanasar Ognesyan**.

He lives in Portland, OR

Jim Heffernan, University of Iowa (1983, 1985-1987)
All-American Placements: 4th, 2nd, 1st, 2nd

A two-time state champion at St. Edward High School in Cleveland, OH, silver medalist in the Junior World Championships and three-time Midlands champion, Jim Heffernan was a member of three Iowa Hawkeye NCAA championship and four Big Ten championship teams. In his senior season (1987), Heffernan captained the Hawkeyes, was named Iowa's Male Athlete of the Year, Iowa Wrestling MVP and earned the Iowa Wrestling Leadership Award. He won four Big Ten individual titles.

Compiling a career record of 131-18-2, he had an exceptional NCAA Tournament career with a fourth, two seconds and a first. In 1983, he wrestled in the same weight class (150) as three-time champion **Nate Carr**, the incomparable **Kenny Monday** and four-time all-American **Roger Frizzell**, and came away with a fourth-place finish. As a second-seeded sophomore, he took a 35-4 record into the tournament and won five straight (including a pigtail match) to reach the finals against top-seeded **Eddie Urbano** of Arizona State. In a defensive struggle, Urbano prevailed, 4-1.

Heffernan's junior season proved magical as he powered his way into the finals and registered a 10-3 decision over fourth-seeded **Adam Cohen** of Arizona State to finish at 32-3-1. In 1987, he met top-seeded **Tim Krieger** of Iowa in the finals. The two four-time all-Americans hooked up in a classic defensive duel with Krieger earning a 1-1, 1-1 criteria decision for his first of two national titles. Heffernan finished at 36-3.

Heffernan and his wife, Rebecca, live in Champaign, IL with their son, Sean, and daughter, Alex.

Kevin Jackson, Louisiana State University/Iowa State University (1983-1985, 1987)
All-American Placements: 3rd, 3rd, 7th, 2nd

A native of Lansing, MI, Kevin Jackson won two state high school titles and was a Junior National Greco-Roman champion before signing with Louisiana State University. Following two third-place finishes at 158 behind the great **Jim Zalesky** of Iowa, Jackson moved up to 167 and earned the top seed in 1985. However, he suffered a huge upset in the first round to eventual fourth-place finisher **John Monaco** of Montclair State, and was beaten in the consolations by third-place finisher **John Laviolette** of Oklahoma.

When LSU dropped wrestling in 1986, Jackson transferred to Iowa State. In 1987, he had his best NCAA Tournament when he registered two technical falls and an 8-2 decision to reach the semifinals where he edged Penn State's third-seeded **Greg Elinsky** (a four-time all-American) by a 2-2, 1-1 criteria decision to reach the finals. However, Iowa's top-seeded **Royce Alger** prevailed, 10-4.

Jackson went on to international stardom, winning an Olympic freestyle gold medal in 1992 and World Games gold in 1991 and 1995. He placed fourth in the Worlds in 1993 and 11th in 1994. He also won three U.S. National titles (placing second five times) and took home two Pan American Games gold medals. Jackson also became the first American to win the prestigious Takhti Cup (1998) in Tehran, Iran.

Jackson's success earned him a number of major awards including the 1995 **John Smith** Award as National Freestyle Wrestler of the Year, 1992 *Amateur Wrestling News* Man of the Year and 1991 USA Wrestling and USOC Wrestler of the Year. Jackson is a member of the FILA International Wrestling Hall of Fame, the National Wrestling Hall of Fame (as a Distinguished Member) and the Iowa State University Athletics Hall of Fame. He became the head wrestling coach at Iowa State University in 2009.

Rob Koll, University of North Carolina (1985-1988)
All-American Placements: 8th, 3rd, 3rd, 1st

Rob Koll's road to four all-American finishes and three Atlantic Coast Conference titles began in 1985 with an eighth-place NCAA finish as an unseeded competitor at 150 pounds. Moving up to 158 as a sophomore, Koll took a number five seed into the 1986 NCAA Tournament and pushed national runner-up **Greg Elinsky** of Penn State to the limit in the semifinals before losing a 3-3, 5-1 overtime decision. Koll then knocked off fourth-seeded **Johnny Johnson** of Oklahoma in the battle for third place. Seeded number one in 1987, Koll lost in the quarterfinals to Iowa's **John Heffernan** and then stormed back to win five straight matches in the consolations to finish third again. In his senior season at 158, Koll lived up to his top seed by marching into the finals where he pinned sixth-seeded **Joe Pantaleo** of Michigan in 1:14, a finals record for the decade.

In 1989, Koll won the Pan-Am Games and was runner-up at the Olympic Festival; he won the U.S. national freestyle championship in 1990 and 1991; took first in the 1990 and 1993 World Cup; placed fifth in the 1991 World Championships; won the 1992 World Cup Grand Prix; and was an alternate for the 1992 Olympic Games.

He is the son of National Wrestling Hall of Fame member **Bill Koll**, a legendary three-time NCAA champion, fifth-place finisher at the 1948 London Olympic Games and Penn State coach. The elder Koll, who passed away in 2003, is one of just six wrestlers to pin every opponent in an NCAA Championship.

Tim Krieger, Iowa State University (1986-1989)
All-American Placements: 5th, 1st, 2nd, 1st

Tim Krieger was a three-time prep state champion with a remarkable 103-6-2 record at Mason City High School in four weight classes. As a senior, he pinned all opponents in the state tournament (winning the Outstanding Wrestler Award) wrapping up a streak of 83 wins in his final three seasons against just one loss.

At Iowa State, Krieger was the first wrestler in the history of the NCAA Championships to be seeded first in his weight class all four years of eligibility. As a freshman at 150 pounds he placed fifth, losing a tough 5-5, 1-0 overtime decision to **Scott Turner** of North Carolina State in the quarterfinals. As a sophomore (1987), he met second-seeded **Jim Heffernan** of Iowa in the finals and scored a criteria decision (1-1, 1-1) for his first championship. As a junior, Krieger again reached the finals only to run into Turner again with the same result, a narrow (1-1, 1-0) overtime loss.

A knee injury in the tournament required off-season surgeries, but Krieger powered his way back to the finals for the third straight year and came away with title number two by virtue of a 5-0 blanking of **Karl Monaco** of Montclair State who only lost two of 46 matches that season, both to Krieger.

Krieger received the prestigious 1988-89 Big Eight Conference Athlete of the Year Award after his fourth conference crown and second NCAA championship. Other accomplishments include winning the U.S. National Freestyle Tournament championship in 1984 after a third-place finish in 1983. He was inducted into the Iowa Wrestling Hall of Fame in 2002.

Randy Lewis, University of Iowa (1978-1981)
All-American Placements: 2nd, 1st, 1st, 7th

After winning three high school state titles in South Dakota, Lewis was a four-time all-American and two-time NCAA champion at the University of Iowa. He began his college career in 1978 with a runner-up finish at 126, losing to Iowa State's **Mike Land** 13-5 in the finals. As a sophomore, he lived up to his top seed with a rollicking 20-14 win over the sensational **John Azevedo** of Cal State-Bakersfield in the finals to complete an undefeated (36-0) season.

In 1980, Lewis moved up to 134, grabbed the top seed and won his second NCAA crown with a definitive 11-3 decision over second-seeded **Darryl Burley** of Lehigh to finish 40-1.

Suffering a horrendous elbow dislocation in his senior season, he wrestled virtually with one arm in the NCAA tourney and still placed seventh, losing to eventual champion **Jim Gibbons** of Iowa State in the quarterfinals.

Lewis was a member of the 1980 and 1984 U.S. Olympic Wrestling Teams, winning a gold medal in Los Angeles in 1984 at 136.5 pounds. He outscored his first four opponents 52-4 to advance to the final. In the highest scoring finals match in Olympic history, he easily defeated Japan's **Kosei Akaishi** 24-11 in 4:52. He was second in the 1988 Olympic trials to **John Smith** (who wound up winning a gold medal) and was 1990 Pan Am Games champion. He lives in Rapid City, SD.

One of the most exciting wrestlers in history, Randy Lewis of Iowa helped change the sport with his wide open, countering style. (Courtesy University of Iowa)

Mike Mann, Iowa State University (1979-1980, 1982-1983)
All-American Placements: 7th, 4th, 2nd, 2nd

Mike Mann was a state champion at Marshalltown (IA) High School and began his storied wrestling career at Iowa State University in 1979 with a seventh-place finish in one of the toughest weight divisions in the tournament, 190. In his sophomore season, the fourth-seeded Mann was beaten in the semifinals by eighth-seeded and eventual national champion **Noel Loban** of Clemson.

Mann's junior and senior seasons ended in the same place, the finals at 190. He lost a heart-breaking 3-3, 2-2 criteria decision to fourth-seeded **Pete Bush** of Iowa in 1982. As a senior, Mann was on a tear, beating two-time national champion **Ed Banach** of Iowa three times during the season including a rousing 13-8 victory in their dual match. Mann was a juggernaut in reaching the finals and Banach was waiting. In a very tough finals match, Banach escaped with a 4-3 win.

Mann also was a Big Eight champion in 1983 and a Midlands champion in 1981. He compiled 113 wins during his collegiate career.

Mike Mann, Iowa State, beat three-time national champion Ed Banach three of four times, only losing to the Hawkeye star in the 1983 NCAA finals (Courtesy Iowa State University)

Jim Martin, Penn State University (1986-1989)
All-American Placements: 4th, 2nd, 1st, 3rd

The most academically gifted wrestler of his generation, Jim Martin earned a 3.95 grade point average in pre-med at Penn State. He was equally adept on the mat with four top-four finishes and a national title at 126 in his junior season (1988). He was a two-year team captain, holds the Penn State record for most victories (155) and posted a 155-9-4 record (93.4%).

Following a fourth-place finish at 118 as a freshman, Martin powered his way into the finals in 1987 against top-seeded **Ricky Bonomo** of Bloomsburg, falling 8-4 to the three-time national champion. Martin moved up to 126 in his junior season and earned the #2 seed behind Iowa's **Brad Penrith**. The two stars battled down to the wire in the finals with Martin earning a 5-4 decision and his lone national championship. In 1989, Martin carried the top seed into the tournament but lost a difficult 2-2, 2-2 criteria decision to fifth-seeded **Michael Stokes** of North Carolina State in the semifinals. He then beat future three-time national champion and legend **Tom Brands** of Iowa, 6-5, for third place.

He was twice named GTE Academic All-American of the Year (1988 and 1989) and earned GTE Academic All-American honors all four years of college. He also was named 1989 Delta Scholar Athlete of the Year. After graduating with a Bachelor's from Penn State, he completed medical school at Penn State's Hershey Medical Center and is now a physician at University Orthopedics in State College, PA.

Joe McFarland, Michigan (1981-1982, 1984-1985)
All-American Placements: 5th, 6th, 2nd, 2nd

Joe McFarland is one of the best collegiate wrestlers to never win a championship. Twice he made it to the finals but lost very close matches to very exceptional wrestlers. In his freshman campaign at 118 in 1981, the unseeded McFarland upset fourth-seeded and future national champion (1983) **Adam Cuestas** 9-7 in the opening round. He reached the quarterfinals, but fell to North Carolina State's fifth-seeded **Chris Wentz**, 8-5. He won two consolation matches to place fifth.

In 1982, as the second seed, McFarland powered his way into the semifinals with two falls and an 8-3 decision over **Carl DeStefanis** of Penn State (future NCAA champion at 118 in 1984). In the semis, he pushed #3 **Kevin Darkus** of Iowa State (future NCAA champ at 126 in 1984) to the limit before falling, 5-3. In the consolations, he was beaten 13-4 by Lehigh's **Bobby Weaver** (two-time Olympian and Olympic gold medalist in 1984) to place sixth.

Redshirting in 1983, McFarland's junior season in 1984 saw him blow past four opponents (17-5, 13-5, 10-4 and 19-4) to set up a rematch with Darkus, this time in the 126-pound NCAA finals. Darkus registered a 9-6 win for the title. In 1985, McFarland won the Big Ten championship in his fourth trip to the finals and again roared into the NCAA finals against top-seeded two-time national champion **Barry Davis** of Iowa. Davis carved out an 8-4 win to deny him the championship. McFarland ended his career with a 166-24-4 record (No. 7 on the all-time list), but he wasn't done yet. Internationally, he was a World Games silver medalist in 1986, a World Cup bronze medalist and Tbilisi bronze medalist in 1987, and a World Cup champion in 1988.

Joe Melchiore, University of Oklahoma/University of Iowa (1985-1986, 1988-1989)
All-American Placements: 4ᵗʰ, 7ᵗʰ, 2ⁿᵈ, 3ʳᵈ

Joe Melchiore was a two-time all-American at Oklahoma (1985-86) wrestling at 118 pounds, placing fourth and seventh. In 1987, he transferred to Iowa and sat out the requisite one year. The year away from competition didn't hurt him, as he moved up to 134 and twice gained all-American status (1988 and 1989). In his freshman year at OU, the ninth-seeded Melchiore upset fourth-seeded **Tim Wright** of SIU-Edwardsville in the second round, 13-2, to reach the semifinals against eighth-seeded **Matt Egeland** of Iowa, a 9-8 upset winner over top-seeded **Mark Perry** of Oklahoma State. Egeland prevailed in a very tight match, 6-5, while Melchiore went on to place fourth. In his second season in Norman, Melchiore took a number three seed into the tournament. He was dropped in the quarterfinals by eventual runner-up **Al Palacio** of North Carolina, 9-6, and managed a disappointing seventh-place finish.

In 1988 at Iowa, the seventh-seeded Melchiore made it to the finals at 134 with an incredible run. He upset second-seeded **John Fisher** of Michigan, 14-4, in the quarterfinals and major-decisioned Northwestern's sixth-seeded **Joei Bales**, 10-2, in the semifinals. In the finals, he ran into the legendary **John Smith** of Oklahoma State and fell 9-2. In 1989, he took his #2 seed into the semifinals, but was beaten by eventual champion **Sean O'Day** of Edinboro. In a battle of four-time all-Americans, Melchiore pinned Fisher in 1:19 to earn third place.

Andre Metzger, University of Oklahoma (1979-1982)
All-American Placements: 5ᵗʰ, 2ⁿᵈ, 1ˢᵗ, 1ˢᵗ

Credited with wrestling and winning more matches than any amateur wrestler in history, Andre Metzger was a high school state champion at Cedar Springs, MI and the youngest World Championship medalist (bronze) at that time. He was named to *Wrestling USA Magazine's* High School All-American Dream Team in 1978. He won two NCAA championships at 142 pounds (1981 and 1982), was second in 1980 and placed fifth as a freshman in 1979.

In his first NCAA Tournament, the sixth-seeded Sooner scored a fall and a 16-3 superior decision before shocking third-seeded **Andy Rein** of Wisconsin, 17-4, in the quarterfinals. In the semifinals, **Scott Trizzino** of Iowa edged Metzger, 10-6. In the consolation bracket, he lost a 5-1 decision to **Lee Roy Smith** of Oklahoma State but beat Rein, 7-6, for fifth place. In 1980, Metzger took a number two seed into the event and plowed his way into the finals with wins of 17-5, 17-8, WBF 5:20 and an 11-7 decision over third-seeded **Bill Cripps** of Arizona State. In a rematch of the Big 8 finals won by Smith, 10-2, Metzger made it a match but fell 10-7 to the Cowboy superstar.

In his junior season, Big 8 champion Metzger cruised into the finals by pinning tenth-seeded **Shawn White** of Michigan State in 1:29. Top-seeded **Lennie Zalesky** of Iowa went toe-to-toe with Metzger in the finals, but the Oklahoma sensation prevailed, 10-6, for his first title. In 1982, second-seeded Metzger fell to #3 **Johnny Selmon** of Nebraska in the Big 8 finals, 15-11. Selmon racked up 62 points in three matches to reach the NCAA semifinals, but Metzger won a defensive rematch, 3-1. In the finals, a rematch with the top-seeded Zalesky, Metzger defended his crown with a 9-6 decision.

Internationally, Metzger won three Senior World Championship medals: silver (1986) and bronze (1979 and 1987), placed fourth in 1982 and qualified for the World Games but did not place in 1985.

Gene Mills, Syracuse University (1977-1979, 1981)
All-American Placements: 3rd, 4th, 1st, 1st

One of the greatest lightweights in history, "Mean Gene the Pinning Machine" was nominated for the NCAA 75th Anniversary Wrestling Team in 2005 and is a Distinguished Member of the National Wrestling Hall of Fame (2000). He compiled an incredible career record of 1356-46-1, with 886 wins coming by fall. A New Jersey state champion and high school national champion, Mills was Syracuse University's first four-time all-American (1977-79 and 1981) and owns the NCAA record for career pins, 107.

In his freshman season, the unseeded Mills pinned sixth-seeded **Steve Stalnaker** of Tennessee in 5:47 and scored an 18-5 superior decision in the second round. In the quarterfinals, third-seeded **Johnnie Jones** of Iowa State pinned Mills. In the consolations, Mills had two falls and a 9-2 decision before avenging his loss to Jones with a 6-4 win to take third. In 1978, Mills carried a #2 seed into the tourney and rolled into the semifinals, but unseeded **Andy Daniels** of Ohio University scored a 15-7 upset to drop him into the consolation bracket. Mills lost to **Dan Glenn** of Iowa, 12-8 to finish fourth. Daniels pinned future NCAA champ (1980) **John Azevedo** in just 30 seconds for the title.

Mills entered the 1979 event with the second seed and high hopes. He didn't disappoint. With three falls (a first-rounder over future national champion Adam Cuestas of Oregon) and a 17-2 superior decision, he roared into the finals against top-seeded **Joe Gonzales** of Cal State-Bakersfield. In a thriller, Mills won his first NCAA crown with a 16-13 decision over the future NCAA champion (1980) and National Wrestling Hall of Fame Distinguished Member (2015).

After taking a year off and making the U.S. Olympic Team in 1980 (boycott), a disappointed Mills returned for his senior season as a man on a mission. In a division that included future lightweight superstars **Barry Davis** of Iowa, **Joe McFarland** of Michigan and **Randy Willingham** of Oklahoma State, Mills came within a whisker of pinning every opponent. Only a 28-4 superior decision in the semifinals kept him from five consecutive pins. In the finals, Mills earned his second title by pinning **John Hartupee** of Central Michigan in 6:35, finishing second in the race for the Gorriaran Award. He was named the tournament's Outstanding Wrestler.

On the international scene, he was a 1980 Olympian, voted Athlete of the Year by the U.S. Olympic Committee, and was a three-time World Cup champion. In addition, he was the 1980 World Super champion in Japan; 1980 Tbilisi (U.S.S.R.) champion; **Roger Goulon** (France) champion; and Rokoczi Cup (Hungary) champion. He was named Outstanding Wrestler in all four of those tournaments.

Pat Santoro, University of Pittsburgh (1986-1989)
All-American Placements: 6th, 2nd, 1st, 1st

Santoro earned a third-place finish in the Pennsylvania state prep championships as a senior in 1984, then went on to win a National Prep title and Outstanding Wrestler award. He became the University of Pittsburgh's only four-time all-American and won two national championships, going 97-3 in his final two years at Pitt. He was 20-4 in NCAA tournament matches. His career win percentage of 92.78% (167-13) ranks in the top 50 all-time among all NCAA wrestlers with more than 100 bouts.

Following a sixth-place finish as an unseeded freshman in 1986, Santoro earned a number three seed the next year and edged second-seeded **Nick Neville** of Oklahoma, 8-6, in the semifinals. In the finals he met **Peter Yozzo** of Lehigh and was pinned at 3:52 by the three-time all-American. In his junior season, Santoro's top seed held up as he edged fourth-seeded **Karl Monaco** of Montclair State, 3-2, to reach the finals. He won his first championship with a back-and-forth 16-11 decision over third-seeded **Sean O'Day** of Edinboro. In 1989, Santoro appeared poised to win his second straight title in his senior campaign, cruising into the finals where he faced **Junior Saunders** (later to be known as **Townsend Saunders**) of Arizona State. Following a 6-6 deadlock in regulation, the two wrestlers each notched a point and remained tied, 1-1. Santoro won the match on the tenth criteria to end his college career and the decade with his second crown.

In the Olympic Trials, Santoro placed third in 1992, second in 1996 and fourth in 2000. He came within an eyelash of making the 1996 team, losing the third match in overtime to his last NCAA opponent, Townsend Saunders. Saunders won the Olympic silver medal that year.

Santoro was a four-time member of the U.S. National Team, serving as an alternate for the 1996 Olympic Team and the 1999 World Team. He is a member of the EWL and District XI Wrestling Halls of Fame.

His father, **Dick Santoro**, was an all-American at Lehigh (third in 1959) and his brother, **Rich Santoro**, was a three-time all-American for Lehigh (6th in 1980, 7th in 1983 and 5th in 1984).

Pittsburgh's Pat Santoro wins his second national title with a 6-6, 1-1 criteria decision over future two-time Olympian and 1996 silver medalist Townsend (Junior) Saunders. (Courtesy University of Pittsburgh)

Geno Savegnago, Eastern Illinois University (1979-1982)
All-American Placements: 8th, 5th, 3rd, 6th

A two-time high school state champion at Glenbard (IL) High School, Geno Savegnago is Eastern Illinois University's most successful wrestler in history earning four NCAA Division I and three Division II all-American honors. He captured a national championship in Division II in 1981 with a 42-3 record (21 falls). He holds the school record with 131 wins (131-25) and is second on the career pin list with 45.

In 1979, Savegnago was second in Division II and entered the Division I tournament unseeded. It was one of the toughest weight classes in the event with Oklahoma State's top-seeded **Eric Wais**, second-seeded and future national champion **Howard Harris** of Oregon State, and future four-time all-American **Mike Mann** of Iowa State. Following a first-round loss to eventual national champion Wais, he won two close consolation matches and finished eighth. In 1980, following a second-place finish in Div. II, #9 Savegnago lost to the fourth-seeded Mann. He then reeled off three consolation wins and placed fifth.

1981 proved to be his best season as he captured the Div. II national championship and reached the Div. I semifinals as the number five seed, losing a narrow 4-3 decision to eventual champion **Tom Martucci** of College of New Jersey. He then beat **Ryan Kelly** of Oregon for third place. As a senior, Savegnago was seeded sixth in a field that included top-seeded and soon-to-be three-time all-American **Colin Kilrain** of Lehigh, the second-seeded **Mann**, third-seeded and future NCAA champion (1984) **Bill Scherr** of Nebraska and fourth-seeded **Pete Bush** of Iowa, the eventual national champion. Savegnago registered two falls (6:24 and 1:01) before dropping a wild 13-9 decision to Scherr. He then won two consolation matches, but was edged 3-2 by Kilrain to finish sixth.

Mike Sheets, Oklahoma State University (1981-1984)
All-American Placements: 7th, 2nd, 1st, 1st

Mike Sheets is one of the best high school and college wrestlers this author ever saw in person. A state champion at Tahlequah (OK) High School, he provided the only blemish on **Kenny Monday's** high school record (140-0-1), an 8-8 tie in a dual their senior year. At Oklahoma State, Sheets ranks fifth all-time in victories (122). He went 74-0 in his final two seasons (third all-time at OSU behind **Pat Smith**, 98, and **John Smith**, 90), winning two NCAA titles in the process at 167. He narrowly missed a title in his sophomore season, falling to Oklahoma's **Dave Schultz** in the finals by criteria, 4-4, 1-1. Sheets had beaten Schultz in the Big 8 tourney, 4-3, and owned the top seed.

In 1981, his freshman season, Sheets entered the NCAA Tournament unseeded after a third-place finish in the Big 8 Tournament behind Iowa State's **Perry Hummell** (Big 8 champ) and Oklahoma's **Mark Schultz**. In the NCAA event, Sheets lost, 13-6, to Schultz in the opening round, but came back to win three consolation matches to finish seventh. In 1982, Sheets defeated Mark Schultz in the Big 8 finals, 4-3, and earned the top seed in the NCAA's. Both wrestlers reached the finals, and in an extremely close bout, Schultz edged the Cowboy star on criteria.

Sheets was unstoppable his junior season, going undefeated and rolling into the NCAA finals with wins of 29-2, 14-0, 6-0 and 5-1. In the finals, he shut out #2 **John Reich** of Navy, 14-0, for his first title. He also went undefeated in his senior year, blitzing his first three NCAA opponents 16-8, 12-0 and WBF 6:52, before slipping past fourth-seeded **Sylvester Carver** of Fresno State, 6-3, in the semis. For the second straight year, Sheets registered a shutout in the finals, this time blanking #2 **Lindley Kistler** of Iowa, 9-0.

He had some titanic qualifying battles with **Mark Schultz** in an effort to win membership on Olympic and World Teams, but was unable to beat the Sooner star who dominated the 82kg/180.5 pound division for six straight years, 1983-1988.

In Tahlequah, OK these days, people call him Dr. Sheets. He's a veterinarian.

Rick Stewart, Oklahoma State University (1979-1982)
All-American Placements: 7th, 1st, 1st, 3rd

As the sports editor at The Duncan Banner newspaper in the 1970s, I had the pleasure and privilege of watching Stewart roll to an undefeated high school career (88-0-1) and three consecutive state championships at 158 pounds under the tutelage of Coach **Mike Reding**, himself a three-time NCAA all-American at OSU. Stewart was named Oklahoma's Outstanding Wrestler, was a high school all-American, won the **Jim Thorpe** Award as the state's outstanding high school athlete (he also starred as a halfback in Duncan's wishbone attack) and was featured in *Sports Illustrated's Faces in the Crowd*.

Stewart won two NCAA national championships at 158 and finished with a 118-15 collegiate record. His 118 wins were the most by an OSU wrestler in history at that time. He also earned two Big 8 Conference championships and was the 1982 Big 8 Wrestler of the Year.

In 1979, the unseeded Stewart scored a pair of falls, but dropped a 7-2 decision to second-seeded **Dan Zilverberg** of Minnesota in the quarterfinals and placed seventh. In his sophomore year, the third-seeded Stewart had a terrific run, scoring a 19-5 superior decision and a fall before beating sixth-seeded **Fred Wortham** of Michigan State, 9-5. His semifinals opponent, seventh-seeded **Isreal Sheppard** of Oklahoma, had registered three straight falls, but Stewart edged his in-state rival, 8-6. In the finals, Stewart was in total control, besting fifth-seeded **William Smith** of Morgan State, 11-6, for his first NCAA title.

The 1981 semifinals at 158 featured future NCAA, World Games and Olympic champ **Dave Schultz** of Oklahoma, future three-time NCAA champ **Jim Zalesky** of Iowa, future NCAA runner-up **Perry Shea** of Cal State-Bakersfield and defending national champ Stewart. By virtue of two wins over Stewart during the season, Schultz earned the top seed. He narrowly edged Shea, 6-5, in the semifinals. Stewart beat then-freshman Zalesky, 8-4, to set up the finals. Trailing 3-1, Stewart caught Schultz with a near arm-far leg, put in the half-nelson and pinned the Sooner for his second straight championship. The following year, Stewart (No. 1), Zalesky (No. 2), Sheppard (No. 3) and Shea (No. 4) reached the semifinals. Shea upset Stewart, 8-4, dropping him into the consolations, where Stewart again beat Sheppard, 3-2, for third place.

Steve Williams, University of Oklahoma (1979-1982)
All-American Placements: 6th, 5th, 3rd, 2nd

Steve Williams attended Lakewood High School in Colorado, graduating in 1978. He was on the OU track team, played football (earned all-American status), and wrestled all four years. In 1979, the unseeded University of Oklahoma freshman knocked off number one seed and future Olympic Greco-Roman gold medalist (1984) **Jeff Blatnick** of Springfield (MA) College, 6-5, in the quarterfinals. Pinned in the semifinals by fifth-seeded **Dave**

Klemm of Eastern Illinois, Williams placed sixth. In 1980 as the seventh seed, he beat No. 2 **Harold Smith** of Kentucky, 6-2, in the quarterfinals, but was edged by future international superstar **Bruce Baumgartner** of Indiana State, 4-2, in the semifinals. In the battle for fourth, Williams was narrowly defeated by **Dean Phinney** of Iowa, 5-4.

His junior season, he was pinned by Baumgartner in the semifinals and by Arizona State's second-seeded **Dan Severn** in the consolations and had to settle for fourth. Williams' best tournament came in his senior year (1982) when he rolled into the semifinals and upset second-seeded and defending national champion **Lou Banach** of Iowa, 7-4. In a thrilling rematch with Baumgartner, Williams fell 4-2 in the finals and took second, his highest NCAA finish.

Williams, who had earned the nickname "Dr. Death" in junior high school when he had to wrestle in a hockey goalie's mask because of injury, became a professional wrestler. Sadly, Steve succumbed to cancer on Dec. 29, 2009.

Jim Zalesky, University of Iowa (1981-1984)
All-American Placements: 5th, 1st, 1st, 1st

Named the Wrestler of the Decade by *Amateur Wrestling News*, Zalesky dominated the 158-pound division for three years (1982-1984) by winning back-to-back-to-back national championships against tough competition including: two-time national champion and four-time all-American **Rick Stewart** of Oklahoma State; NCAA champ and Olympic and World gold medalist **Dave Schultz** of Oklahoma; four-time all-Americans **Kevin Jackson** of LSU and **Greg Elinsky** of Penn State; and two-time all-Americans **Isreal Sheppard** of Oklahoma; **Perry Shea** of Cal State-Bakersfield and **Bill Dykeman** of Oklahoma State.

As a freshman, the third-seeded Zalesky cruised through three bouts and into the semifinals against the second-seeded and defending national champion Stewart where he lost an 8-4 decision to the eventual champion and finished fifth. As a sophomore, Zalesky was seeded second behind Stewart and looking to avenge his 1981 loss. However, Stewart was upset by the fourth-seeded Shea in the semifinals. Zalesky held up his end of the bargain, edging Dykeman, 4-2, in the semis to set up a finals bout with Shea. Zalesky dominated, 10-3, for his first title.

Zalesky put together back-to-back undefeated seasons, going 89-0 as Iowa continued its national dominance by winning its sixth and seventh consecutive team titles. In 1983, he slipped past a determined Jackson in the semifinals, 9-7, and then decisioned **Lou Montano** of Cal Poly-San Luis Obispo, 7-4, for his second crown. Continuing his torrid streak, Zalesky cruised into the 1984 NCAA quarterfinals where he survived a 3-2 nail-biter over #8 Elinsky. His semifinal win over Oklahoma's fourth-seeded **Johnny Johnson** put him in the finals against sixth-seeded **Mark Schmitz** of Wisconsin who had bested the third-seeded Jackson. Zalesky maintained control and won, 9-5, to become a three-time champ and finish with a 132-7-1 career record. He was inducted into the National Wrestling Hall of Fame in 2004 as a Distinguished Member.

CHAPTER 14

All-Decade Wrestling Team, 1980-89

The list below is, obviously, subjective. However, I tried to establish certain criteria that would qualify a wrestler for the All-Decade Team. Wrestlers had to have competed at least one year in the decade. The number of wrestlers qualifying under the criteria is in parentheses.

(A) Being selected to or nominated for the NCAA 75th Anniversary Wrestling Team. (9)

(B) Being a four-time all-American and winning two or more NCAA titles. (7)

(C) Being a three-time all-American and winning two or more NCAA titles. (7)

(D) Being a two-time NCAA champion. (2)

(E) Being a four-time all-American and winning one NCAA title. (5)

(F) Being a three-time all-American and winning one NCAA title. (8)

(G) Being a two-time all-American and winning one NCAA title. (2)

(H) Being a four-time all-American with no NCAA titles. (3)

There are 49 wrestlers included on the team in 10 weight divisions. Almost half (24) earned high school all-American honors from *Wrestling USA Magazine* (indicated with a hashtag #). These outstanding student athletes accounted for 81 NCAA titles and 162 all-American designations in their careers. Twenty-two of these men (indicated with an asterisk*) are Distinguished Members of the National Wrestling Hall of Fame.

NCAA All-Decade Team (1980-1989)

118 – (1) *Gene Mills, Syracuse (2 NCAA titles; 4-time all-American; **NCAA 75**[th] **Anniversary Team Nominee**)

(2) *Ricky Bonomo, Bloomsburg (3 NCAA titles; 3-time all-American)

(3) #Jack Cuvo, East Stroudsburg (2 NCAA titles; 3-time all-American

(4) *Joe Gonzales, Cal State-Bakersfield (1 NCAA title; 2-time all-American)

126 – (1) *Barry Davis, Iowa (3 NCAA titles; 4-time all-American)

(2) *Terry Brands, Iowa (2 NCAA titles; 3-time all-American)

(3) #John Azevedo, Cal State-Bakersfield (1 NCAA title; 3-time all-American)

(T4) #Dan Cuestas, Cal State-Bakersfield (2 titles; 2-time all-American)

(T4) *Kendall Cross, Oklahoma State (1 NCAA Title; 3-time all-American)

134 – (T1) *Tom Brands, Iowa (3 NCAA titles; 4-time all-American; **NCAA 75**[th] **Anniversary Team Member**)

(T1) #*John Smith, Oklahoma State (2 NCAA titles; 3-time all-American; **NCAA 75**[th] **Anniversary Team Member**)

(T3) #*Randy Lewis, Iowa (2 NCAA titles; 4-time all-American; **NCAA 75**[th] **Anniversary Team Nominee**)

(T3) Darryl Burley, Lehigh (2 NCAA titles; 4-time all-American; **NCAA 75**[th] **Anniversary Team Nominee**)

(T5) Jim Jordan, Wisconsin (2 NCAA titles; 3-time all-American)

(T5) #Jim Gibbons, Iowa State (1 NCAA title; 3-time all-American)

142 – (1) #Andre Metzger, Oklahoma (2 NCAA titles; 4-time all-American)

(2) #Joe Gibbons, Iowa State (1 NCAA title; 4-time all-American)

(3) #Lee Roy Smith, Oklahoma State (1 NCAA title; 3-time all-American)

(T4) Pat Santoro, Pittsburgh (2 NCAA titles; 4-time all-American)

(T4) #Peter Yozzo, Lehigh (1 NCAA title; 3-time all-American)

150 – (1) #*Nate Carr, Iowa (3 NCAA titles; 3-time all-American; **NCAA 75**[th] **Anniversary Team Nominee**)

(2) *Kenny Monday, Oklahoma State (1 NCAA title; 3-time all-American)

(3) #Tim Krieger, Iowa State (2 NCAA titles; 4-time all-American)

(T4) #Andy Rein, Wisconsin (1 NCAA title; 3-time all-American)

(T4) #Jim Heffernan, Iowa (1 NCAA title; 4-time all-American)

(T4) #Roger Frizzell, Oklahoma (4-time all-American)

158 – (T1) *Jim Zalesky, Iowa (3 NCAA titles; 4-time all-American)

(T1) #Rick Stewart, Oklahoma State (2 NCAA titles; 4-time all-American)

(3) Dan St. John, Arizona State (2 NCAA titles; 3-time all-American)

(T4) Rob Koll, North Carolina (1 NCAA title; 4-time all-American)

(T4) #Greg Elinsky, Penn State (4-time all-American)

167 – (1) Mike Sheets, Oklahoma State (2 NCAA titles; 4-time all-American)

(2) #*Dave Schultz, Oklahoma (1 NCAA title; 3-time all-American)

(3) Marty Kistler, Iowa (2 NCAA titles; 3-time all-American)

(4) Royce Alger, Iowa (2 NCAA titles; 3-time all-American)

177 – (1) *Mark Schultz, Oklahoma (3 NCAA titles; 3-time all-American; **NCAA 75th Anniversary Team Nominee**)

(2) #Duane Goldman, Iowa (1 NCAA title; 4-time all-American)

(3) #*Melvin Douglas, Oklahoma (2 NCAA titles; 2-time all-American)

(4) #*Jim Scherr, Nebraska (1 NCAA title; 2-time all-American)

190 – (1) *Ed Banach, Iowa (3 NCAA titles; 4-time all-American; **NCAA 75th Anniversary Team Member**)

(2) Eric Voelker, Iowa State (2 NCAA titles; 3-time all-American)

(3) #Dan Chaid, Oklahoma (1 NCAA title; 4-time all-American)

(T4) #*Bill Scherr, Nebraska (1 NCAA title; 3-time all-American)

(T4) Mike Mann, Iowa State (4-time all-American)

HWT – (1) *Conrad Haselrig, Pittsburgh-Johnstown (3 NCAA titles; 3-time all-American; **NCAA 75th Anniversary Team Member**)

(2) *Lou Banach, Iowa (2 NCAA titles; 3-time all-American)

(3) *Bruce Baumgartner, Indiana State (1 NCAA title; 3-time all-American)

(T4) #Howard Harris, Oregon State (1 NCAA title; 4-time all-American)

(T4) *Kurt Angle, Clarion (1 NCAA title; 2-time all-American)

The No. 1 wrestlers on the list won 31 NCAA titles and earned all-American status 44 times in their legendary careers. The No. 2 wrestlers accounted for 13 championships and 26 all-American designations, while the third-ranked wrestlers won 16 titles and 32 all-American placements. Of note, 22 of the 24 members of the All-Decade Team who earned high school all-America honors won at least one NCAA championship. The other two, **Roger Frizzell** and **Greg Elinsky**, earned all-America status four times each.

At 118 pounds, Mills, Bonomo, Cuvo and Gonzales collected eight NCAA crowns and 12 all-American honors. The five wrestlers at 126 (Davis, **Terry Brands**, Azevedo, Cuestas and Cross) accounted for 9 NCAA titles and 15 all-American designations. Brands only wrestled one year in the decade (1989), but went on to claim two national titles.

Without a doubt, the toughest weight class in the 1980s was 134 pounds where the six superior wrestlers (**Tom Brands**, **John Smith**, Lewis, Burley, **Jim Jordan** of Wisconsin and **Jim Gibbons** of Iowa State) amassed 12 NCAA titles and 21 all-American awards. The top four selections (Brands, Smith, Lewis and Burley) were nominated for the NCAA 75th Anniversary Wrestling Team, with Smith and Brands making the team. While I placed Brands of Iowa and Smith of Oklahoma State at the top, as did the 75th Anniversary Wrestling Team committee, **Randy Lewis** of Iowa ("the toughest kid on the block") was equally dominant. Had he not suffered a devastating elbow dislocation in his senior season, he likely would have won three NCAA titles and been the number one seed on the team at 134. He places a fraction above **Darryl Burley** of Lehigh for the third slot by virtue of his head-to-head 11-3 major decision over Burley in the finals of the 1980 NCAA tourney … a great way to begin The Golden Era of Amateur Wrestling.

At 150, Carr, Krieger, Monday, Heffernan and Rein racked up seven individual titles. Adding Frizzell, the six wrestlers amassed 21 all-American designations. Frizzell still holds the record as the best consolation wrestler (4th, 3rd, 3rd, and 3rd) in NCAA history to never have wrestled in the finals. There were two reasons Frizzell didn't reach the finals: Hall of Famers Carr and Monday. Engaging in fierce dual, Big 8 Conference tournament and NCAA tournament matches, the three set the standard for the weight class in the decade. A 13-10 loss to Carr in 1982 and a narrow 7-5 loss to Monday in 1983 kept Frizzell out of the NCAA finals. The tie-breaker between Frizzell and Heffernan for the number four slot on the All-Decade Team at 150 would have come at the 1983 NCAA event, but Heffernan suffered an injury that kept him from wrestling Frizzell for third place. Frizzell and Rein traded victories throughout their collegiate and freestyle careers.

I put Iowa's **Jim Zalesky** and Oklahoma State's **Rick Stewart** together at the top of the 158-pound class, even though Zalesky won three NCAA titles to Stewart's two. It was Stewart's convincing 8-4 win over the Hawkeye in the 1981 semifinals that resulted in them sharing the No. 1 position.

The decade ended with five members of the All-Decade Team wrestling in the 1989 NCAA tourney: **Jack Cuvo** of East Stroudsburg, **Tom Brands** of Iowa, **Pat Santoro** of Pittsburgh, **Tim Krieger** of Iowa State and **Carlton Haselrig** of Pittsburgh-Johnstown. Cuvo (118), Santoro (142), Krieger (150) and Haselrig (275) won individual titles, with Krieger being named Outstanding Wrestler. Haselrig ended his storied career with his third NCAA Division I title (he also won three Division II titles) in the last year of the decade, while Brands was just beginning his career. Both were named to the 75th Anniversary Wrestling Team in 2005.

Twenty-nine of the 49 members of the All-Decade Team came from the Big Four: Iowa (12), Oklahoma (6), Oklahoma State (6) and Iowa State (5). Decade-dominant Iowa had five top-seeded wrestlers on the team, while Oklahoma State had three and Oklahoma had two. The team also included six sets of brothers: **Lou and Ed Banach** of Iowa; **Terry and Tom Brands** of Iowa; **Jim and Joe Gibbons** of Iowa State; **Jim and Bill Scherr** of Nebraska; **Dave and Mark Schultz** of Oklahoma; and **Lee Roy and John Smith**, Oklahoma State – fitting that the decade-dominating Big Four were so family-friendly.

With my All-Decade Team selected, I circulated a list of the top 20 collegiate wrestlers in the 1980s to dozens of wrestlers and coaches from the era and asked them to rank their top 10. Many of them expressed difficulty in ranking the wrestlers because there were so many great wrestlers from which to choose. Do you pick them strictly on national championships won? All-American designations? Overall record? Victories over other superstars? Though not easy, they finally were able to make their selections. There was only one wrestler from the decade who was named on every ballot submitted: Oklahoma's incomparable **Mark Schulz**. He earned the top ranking in a close race with Iowa's **Ed Banach**, whom Schultz defeated in the 1982 NCAA finals to derail Banach's attempt at becoming the first wrestler to win four straight titles. Here's how wrestlers and coaches of the 1980s ranked the top 10:

Top 10 Wrestlers, Decade of the 1980s
1. Mark Schultz, Oklahoma
2. Ed Banach, Iowa
3. Barry Davis, Iowa
4. John Smith, Oklahoma State
5. Nate Carr, Iowa State
6. Randy Lewis, Iowa
7. Tom Brands, Iowa
8. Jim Zalesky, Iowa
9. Carlton Haselrig, Pittsburgh-Johnstown
10. Dave Schultz, Oklahoma

Representation by the Big Four reflected the dominance of those programs in the '80s, with Iowa claiming five of the top 10, Oklahoma two, and Oklahoma State and Iowa State one each. Only Haselrig of the University of Pittsburgh-Johnstown spoiled a clean sweep. All 10 wrestlers are Distinguished Members of the National Wrestling Hall of Fame, with Haselrig to be inducted in 2016.

CHAPTER 15

Band of Brothers

It is fairly common for brothers to participate in wrestling. Some of the best matches in history occurred on the living room floors and basements of homes across America. The 1980-89 All-Decade Team includes six sets of brothers: **Lou and Ed Banach** of Iowa, **Terry and Tom Brands** of Iowa and **Jim and Bill Scherr** of Nebraska are twins. The other brother pairs are: **Jim and Joe Gibbons**, Iowa State; **Dave and Mark Schultz**, Oklahoma; and **Lee Roy and John Smith**, Oklahoma State.

These 12 amazing wrestlers accounted for 21 NCAA individual championships and all-American status 38 times. The Banach and Brands brothers led the way with five combined titles and seven all-American designations for each. Ed Banach and Tom Brands won three titles and four all-American designations, while Lou Banach and Terry Brands each won two NCAA crowns and made all-American three times. The Schultz brothers were right behind with four titles and six all-American honors, with Mark winning three consecutive championships (1981-1983). Following were the Smith brothers with three titles and six all-American honors; the Gibbons brothers with two titles and seven all-America honors; and the Scherr brothers (two and five). Of note, **Jeff Gibbons** also wrestled at Iowa State in the decade and earned all-American status twice.

Internationally, four sets of brothers on the All-Decade Team won seven Olympic medals and 20 World Championship medals. The Schultz brothers won two Olympic gold medals and eight World medals (three gold, three silver and two bronze). The Scherrs won an Olympic bronze along with seven World medals (one gold, four silver and two bronze). The Smiths accounted for two Olympic golds, four World golds and one silver, while each Banach brother took home an Olympic gold.

John Smith dominated international wrestling like no other U.S. wrestler in history. During a six-year period (1987-1992), he won two Olympic gold medals and four World Championship gold medals, an accomplishment never equaled.

Other outstanding brother combinations in the NCAA tournament in the 1980s were: twins **Ricky and Rocky Bonomo** of Bloomsburg (three titles; five all-American designations); **Nate** (Iowa State) and **Mike** (West Virginia) **Carr** (three titles, four A-A); **Dan and Adam Cuestas** of Cal State-Bakersfield (three titles; three A-A); **Greg** (Penn State) and **Mike** (North Carolina) **Elinsky** (five A-A); **Jim and John Heffernan** of Iowa (one title; six

A-A); **Jim and Jeff Jordan** of Wisconsin (two titles; five A-A); **Jerry** (Oklahoma State) and **Bill** (Iowa State) **Kelly** (one title; three A-A); **Marty, Harlan and Lindley Kistler** of Iowa (two titles; five A-A); **John** and **Karl Monaco** of Montclair State (three A-A); **Dave, Dan and Rod Severn** of Arizona State (six A-A); **Luke, Matt** (Oklahoma State) and **Jude** (Ohio State) **Skove** (one title; five A-A); **Scott** and **Mark Trizzino** of Iowa (four A-A); and **Jim and Lennie Zalesky** of Iowa (three titles; seven A-A).

* * *

The Banach Brothers: Ed and Lou

Many wrestling fans know the heart-rending story of the Banach brothers – Steve and twins Ed and Lou – who were separated from their large family (14 children) follow-

ing a fire that destroyed their Newton, NJ home when they were toddlers. Their recent (2014) outstanding book *Uncommon Bonds: A Journey in Optimism* chronicles their abandonment by their parents, adoption by Alan and Stephanie Tooley, their love affair with wrestling and their rise to the pinnacle of the sport.

The Banach brothers (L-R: Steve, Lou and Ed) with current Iowa Coach Tom Brands. (Courtesy University of Iowa)

"Mom and Dad channeled our energy into sports," said Ed. "Wrestling was instrumental in our development in junior high and high school in Port Jervis, NY. In 1972, I watched **Dan Gable**, **Wayne Wells** and **John Peterson** win gold medals and **Ben Peterson** win a silver medal in the Olympics. I was 12 years old. I told my coach I was going to be an Olympic champion. Four years later, my high school coach (**Mark Faller**) encouraged me to compete in the 1976 Olympic District Trials. I went 2-2 but didn't qualify for the finals. The experience exposed me to the type of training I needed to reach my Olympic goal I set at 12. Now I knew it was possible."

At the state wrestling tournament in Steve's senior year, he was wrestling and winning on one mat, while Ed was on the next mat struggling in his match. Ed was taken down at the buzzer to send his match into overtime and Steve, still wrestling, was yelling encouragement at Ed. The momentary lapse allowed his opponent to take him down and win the match over Steve.

Steve went to Clemson on a wrestling scholarship. That year, Ed competed in the Junior Nationals in Iowa City and was impressed by the fieldhouse and the wrestling atmosphere. That's why the twins chose to wrestle at the University of Iowa.

"It was a big culture shock, coming from New York to Iowa," said Ed. "One day, Lou was watching TV and said 'hey, there are pigs on TV! You don't see that every day.' I said not in New York, but maybe that's normal in Iowa."

After two years, Steve transferred from Clemson to Iowa to be with his brothers.

"We three brothers understood each other's ambitions and dreams," said Lou. "We lifted each other up. We formed a dynamic, positive, stable environment at Iowa. We were united."

The situation, however, was not without its problems.

"There were a few things that happened along the way," said Ed. "When it comes to brothers, you learn how to push their buttons. We became very good at pushing each other's buttons."

Ed Banach pinning an opponent was a familiar sight for Iowa fans from 1980-1983. (Courtesy University of Iowa)

In Lou's first season, trouble arose. Following a series of injuries, trying to make weight and a particularly stinging loss to defending national champion **Eric Wais** of Oklahoma State at 190, Lou told Ed he needed a break. "I told Lou he needed to drill with me. So we got in the wrestling room and were drilling. But he started slamming me around. I said 'that's not how you drill. This is how you drill.' I hit him with a high crotch and took him to the mat. When I was getting up, he slugged me in the stomach and knocked the wind out of me. I saw red and chased after him. He jumped over a stair railing, so I grabbed a trash can full of water cups and tossed it over the railing and then jumped over. The can is crashing down the stairs between me and Lou, water cups flying all over the place. At the bottom of the stairs stood Athletic Director **Bump Elliott**. 'What's going on, boys?' he asked. Lou said something like the can fell down the stairs and he was trying to stop it. I think Bump and Gable had a good laugh over that incident."

Lou Banach won two NCAA championships at heavyweight for the Hawkeyes and an Olympic gold medal in 1984. (Courtesy University of Iowa)

Lou eventually quit the team that season, while Ed went on to win a national championship with a 16-5 major decision over Iowa State's **Dave Allen** in the finals at 177. Lou returned for his sophomore season and both brothers won NCAA titles, Ed at 177 and Lou at heavyweight with a fall over future legend **Bruce Baumgartner** of Indiana State. That same year (1980), Ed qualified for the Olympic Trials Finals. He faced **Chris Campbell** and **John Peterson** in the final round robin, beating both wrestlers in their first matches, but losing the next two to each.

In 1984, all three brothers wrestled in the Olympic Trials Qualifier in Iowa City, with Ed and Lou advancing to the finals and eventually making the U.S. team. Steve began his career in the U.S. Army after the qualifying tournament and when Ed and Lou won their gold medals in Los Angeles, Steve was on the live-fire range at Ft. Bragg, NC.

"Winning a gold medal was very satisfying. It was part of my bucket list," said Lou. "It also was very humbling. It was an honor to represent the United States. But you have to put it into perspective. We were provided that opportunity by the men and women who protect our nation and freedoms. Steve was in the military and wasn't there to share that with us. The rope is strongest when all strands are there. One of our strands was missing. His leadership and sponsorship as our older brother is one of the key characteristics in our lives. You can't talk about the Banach brothers without talking about all three of us. What Ed and I did, winning Olympic gold, pales in comparison to what Steve did in service to this country. He stood on the tip of the spear for 20 years."

In 1991, as American troops stormed into Kuwait to drive Saddam Hussein's troops from the country, Steve was a captain of the 1st Ranger Battalion. He was a lieutenant colonel of the 3rd Ranger Battalion and led the first boots on the ground for the war in Afghanistan after 9/11. In 2003, he led the Ranger parachute assault into Iraq. For his heroism and leadership, he was awarded the Bronze Star.

In 2010, Steve retired as a colonel in the U.S. Army Rangers and now is a leadership speaker. Ed still works for the athletic department at ISU and Lou is head of commercial banking for Associated Bank in Green Bay, WI.

* * *

The Brands Brothers: Terry and Tom

Tom Brands is five minutes older than twin brother Terry. "I beat him out," says Tom. "I pushed him out," responds Terry. Their competitive natures were already established in the womb.

"We were very competitive. Everything was a contest," said Terry. "Wrestling was the next brutal thing for us to compete against each other. We had a great environment to grow up in."

Tom remembers playing football, baseball, basketball and wrestling in their small basement room, 12 feet by 8 feet. It was one-on-one without rules no matter the sport.

"You had to fight your way through the other guy," said Tom. "If we were playing football, you had to drive and push your way past the competition. If it was basketball, there were no lane violations. No traveling. It was full contact. If someone made a good move in checkers, the battle was on. Civility went out the window."

"We put an old wrestling mat in our house and we beat the tar out of the walls," said Terry. "It was a brawl that never stopped until both parties got the best of each other. If it ended and I thought Tom had gotten the best of me, I would go right back at him. If he thought I ended getting the better of him, he came right back at me. Sometimes it didn't stop until both guys swung and landed a punch."

Neither Tom nor Terry ever submitted or gave in. They were a pair of alpha males, unusual for twins. "The couch legs were broken pretty early on," said Tom. "We had to secretly haul bricks into the house from outside to use as legs. We couldn't let the neighbors see us because that would have been a social faux pas."

The boys learned about having a strong work ethic from their father, a hardworking man in the auto body business. Tom says they weren't raised to be shortcut people.

"We learned to do things the right way. If we had to organize the mowing shed, we did it the right way. If we didn't, we were yanked back in there by our ears. That established a strong work ethic early on."

"Dad's strong work ethic was present in our house," said Terry. "We were taught about values and that if you didn't toe the line, you'd get your tail beat. It didn't matter what you were doing, all that mattered was that you did your best at all times. Dad didn't hold us back as kids. He would grab us and wrap us in a blanket and hold us down saying 'sea kelp, sea kelp.' I had horrible claustrophobia so I learned to fight my way out. The number one thing was to fight. If you want something bad enough, fight for it."

When Terry and Tom started wrestling in the fifth grade, they didn't know anything about international wrestling or the Olympics.

"All we knew about the Olympics was track and field and swimming. We knew **Bruce Jenner** was the decathlon champion. His picture was on the Wheaties box," said Tom. "But when we started wrestling, we were hooked immediately. Eight months later, we went to our first AAU development camp and **Chris Campbell** was the featured clinician. We heard about the 1980 boycott and the politics involved from Chris with absolute pain in his voice. And we learned how good you needed to be in order to be the best in the world."

The first college season the Brands brothers watched closely was 1981-82 and they learned the big difference between Iowa and Iowa State in how they wrestled and competed.

"There was a mystique about Iowa and its dominance at that time. My heroes were **Chris Campbell** and the Kistler brothers," said Tom. "For our birthday present in 1986, we got tickets to the nationals at Carver Hawkeye and we watched Iowa set a scoring record with **Brad Penrith**, **Kevin Dresser**, **Jim Heffernan**, **Marty Kistler** and **Duane Goldman** winning championships. **Greg Randall**, **Royce Alger** and **Rico Chiapparelli** were all-Americans, too. Marty had unbelievable hand-fighting skills and was very explosive. His wins were all lopsided in '86. At a clinic later that summer, he taught me more about wrestling in one week than I had learned in the previous five years. The Iowa wrestlers all were very giving and caring. They shared information and answered my questions. At the clinic, Iowa Assistant Coach **Mark Johnson** took us over and introduced us to **Dan Gable**. He said 'Hi, I'm Dan Gable' and we blurted out "I know!"

Their high school careers were fairly comparable, with Terry winning two state championships and Tom winning one at Sheldon (IA) High School. High placements in the Junior Nationals made them top recruits on Gable's radar.

"It was awesome to be recruited by Iowa," said Tom. "Dan's a nervous kind of guy. It's like he knows he's good and he knows you know that he's good and that makes him uncomfortable. But he didn't have to sell us. We were going to Iowa. We were hooked. But Terry and I took other visits, even though we always wanted to go to Iowa.

"When Gable and **Jim Zalesky** drove to Sheldon to sign us, they got lost and made a tour of Northwest Iowa," continued Tom. "They didn't get to our house until around 10:30 at night. I said 'I'm ready to sign' and did. But Terry didn't sign. He had promised **J Robinson** at Minnesota that he would call J before he signed. Terry is a man of his word, so he tried to call J but he didn't answer. The next morning, J still hadn't answered, so Terry signed, too. So, we ended up signing on two different days."

According to Tom, what makes Gable unique is his ability to see what each individual needs to improve and helping them do just that.

"In the 1988 Olympic Trials I got whipped by **Pete Schuyler** 1-0 and pinned by **Randy Lewis** and **Charlie Heard** beat Terry," remembers Tom. "Gable grabbed us by our collars and shoved us against a wall and he's yelling at us 'Don't you know you are the future of Iowa wrestling? You need to weld yourself to these guys' legs and learn how to finish!' Our eyes got big as saucers. I was thinking 'He's relying on us?' Man, that got me fired up."

Tom and Terry became the linchpins of the Hawkeye teams from 1989 through 1992, with Tom winning three national titles and Terry two. As a freshman, Terry had a very good season going but lost a late season ranking match to **Steve Martin** and didn't make it to the NCAA Championships.

"I had beaten several nationally-ranked guys and things were going well. But I lost a wrestle-off match to Steve Martin at the end of the year and didn't make it into the NCAA Championships," re-

Terry Brands (left) won two high school state championships and two NCAA titles. (Courtesy University of Iowa)

calls Terry. "When I evaluated that season, I realized I just wasn't good enough yet. Martin was busy preparing to wrestle me, while I was busy preparing to wrestle opponents. He got me on my heels and beat me. Lesson learned."

Tough losses also made brother Tom a better wrestler.

"I learned more about how to be competitive by wrestling **John Smith** and **Randy Lewis**. In a match with John Smith, he ankle-laced me and was scoring a bunch. It hurt like crazy. He beat me easily and after the match I kicked a chair in frustration. Smith came over yelling at the coach "Why the hell is he kicking a chair? He thinks he can beat me? He can't beat me!' Then I wrestled Lewis in a tournament qualifier and he was on top of me telling me what he was going to do and laughing about it. Then he would do it. Later, we met in the tournament and he was all business and pinned me in about a minute. He and Smith were just so focused and so locked in, it taught me a lot about what it takes to be a champion."

Another lesson learned for Tom came in a loss to Oklahoma State's **Kendall Cross** in the NCAA semifinals. "I beat him in our dual at Carver Hawkeye 19-9 in 1989. But in the NCAA semifinals, he beat me 1-0," said Tom. "I didn't get to my offense and he had a strategy. He found a way to beat me. I wasn't smart and kept doing the same things I had done in the dual. But he and his coaches strategized. You have to use your imagination to get ahead of the other guy. You have to be more ready than your opponent. I didn't use my imagination enough. He was really slippery and hard to handle from the top. I kind of felt like I was having to chase him because he was so slippery. He had a better game plan and won."

Cross's path crossed the Brands brothers again in 1991 when Terry won the national championship at 126 and Cross placed third. They met again in the 1996 Olympic Trials. "Those matches are hazy for me, but I know I beat him in the first one, but he came back and beat me in the last two (7-6 and 8-7)," said Terry. "Wrestling Kendall made me better and made him better, too. I had done the proper things. I had trained right. But sometimes, you're just not the better guy. Kendall was one of the best in the world and the top American in my weight class."

In 1993, Tom and Terry qualified for the World Championships in Toronto – Terry at 57 kilograms (125.5 pounds) and Tom at 62 kilograms (136.5). Terry dispatched **Shim Sang-ho** of South Korea in the gold medal match and Tom followed with his own gold medal performance.

"I had great expectations to win and I did," said Tom. "I was very relaxed. **Bruce Bennett** was in his first year as Team USA coach and he let us go home for a few days after training camp before we had to fly to Toronto for the tournament. That was great to be at home for a few days. I came in very relaxed and wrestled well, winning some close matches. In the finals against **Lázaro Reinoso** of Cuba, I avoided a disaster when he ankle-laced me and I ended up beating him."

The following year was a disaster for both brothers at the World Championships in Istanbul, Turkey. They both placed eleventh.

"It takes an incredible focus to become a World or Olympic champion. I know the years I didn't perform well, I had distractions and distractions derail," said Terry. "It might be hunting, playing paintball or a hobby. Distractions were catastrophic. But on the other side of that, even if you trained right, you still better be on when you walk on that mat. One small mental

Tom Brands was a three-time national champion, four-time all-American, 1993 World Champion and 1996 Olympic gold medalist. (Courtesy University of Iowa)

mistake can cost you a match. My weight was a little high and I was drinking cranberry juice after training, putting in calories that I didn't need. I didn't train my body to rely on water for rehydration and it cost me. The average person may read that and say 'What? Cranberry juice is bad?' They can't relate to the focus required to train for high-level competition or to maintain a competitive weight."

Tom is in agreement. "We had to give up a lot to train and stay focused on our goal. We were asked to be best men at friends' weddings and had to say 'no thank you.' We missed a family funeral. People were asking where we were and they weren't happy with us. We were so driven to attain our goal. You have to be selfish to dedicate yourself like that. Personal relationships suffer because of what we were going after. But my wife was awesome. We got married in 1996 before the Olympics. You have to have a partner who doesn't keep score. Our eight-day honeymoon was cut to four and a half so I could get back to training. She just said to me 'All you have to do is stay two nights in one place and we'll be fine.' What a saint."

In the 1996 Olympic Trials, Tom won the 62 kilogram weight class. Terry ran into arch-nemesis **Kendall Cross** and didn't qualify. Nevertheless, Terry was in Tom's corner at the Atlanta Games.

"I was very relaxed because Terry was my training partner and scout," said Tom. "Terry had given me the scouting report, so when I walked on the mat I had a strategy. I was 0-2 against my opponent, but I had beaten three world champions **Abbas Hajkenari** (Iran),3-0; **Sergey Smal** (Belarus), 5-0; and **Magomed Azizov** (Russia), 4-1, to get to the finals. I took care of business, was tuned in and focused. I beat **Jang Jae-sung** of South Korea 7-0 in the finals and had my gold medal."

Tom's gold medal motivated Terry to continue his career in quest of gold at the 2000 Olympics in Sydney, Australia. However, he had to settle for the bronze behind Iran's **Alireza Debir** and **Yevhen Buslovych** of Ukraine.

Both brothers chose the coaching profession, serving as assistants to Gable until the legendary coach retired in 1997. Assistant Coach **Jim Zalesky** was elevated to the head coaching position, with the Brands brothers remaining as assistants. In 2000, Terry left Iowa for Nebraska and after one season with the Huskers moved to Montana State-Northern for a year before getting a head coaching position with the University of Tennessee-Chattanooga. Three years later, Terry became the USA Wrestling National Freestyle Resident Coach in Colorado Springs, CO.

Tom left Iowa after the 2005 season to become the head coach at Virginia Tech.

"I wanted to be a head coach and I had to go to Virginia Tech to get that first job," said Tom. "I was there 22 months and turned a lot of heads in what we were able to accomplish. The year I came to Iowa (2007) I had two other offers, one from Oregon State and one from Ohio State. But Iowa was my dream job."

Terry joined Tom in Iowa City in 2008 as his assistant and today is the Hawkeye's associate head coach. He turned down the Iowa State head coaching position in 2009. Under Tom, the Hawkeyes have won three national championships (2008, 2009 and 2010) and had four top-four finishes. Iowa wrestling is still a big deal in the Hawkeye State.

"Iowa doesn't have a professional sports team," said Terry. "The people love their Hawkeye wrestling and basketball and football, too. Iowa sports have become a brand and the University of Iowa has marketed that brand very well. This is a unique situation and Tom and I know how important the athletic program is to the great people of Iowa."

* * *

The Gibbons Brothers: Jeff, Jim, Joe and Tim

"We grew up in an exciting time for wrestling and Ames, IA was the epicenter. **Dan Gable** had just graduated from high school as an undefeated champion and started his remarkable career at Iowa State. He was already a hero and we all wanted to be like him," said Joe Gibbons. "My mom's two brothers – **Joe** and **Omer Frank** – were state champions at Cresco (IA) High School and they both wrestled for **Dr. Harold Nichols** at Iowa State, who also was from Cresco."

All of the boys – Jim, Tim, Joe and Jeff – were involved in football, baseball, basketball and wrestling. They competed in Punt, Pass & Kick competitions and dreamed of playing for their favorite NFL teams. But given their smaller stature, their father, Bill, steered them to wrestling even though he never wrestled himself. "Dad, who was 5-6 ½, said 'We're not big people. You need to find something you can excel at'," said Joe.

The boys watched the great Iowa State wrestling teams win and received photocopies of wrestling technique books from Bill. He bought a wrestling mat and put it in the house and the boys worked on their moves constantly.

"We practiced and lifted weights. I remember we had a TV we put in the doorway to where the wrestling mat was and watched Monday Night Football while we worked on moves," said Joe.

Jim says his Dad was instrumental in putting a process together of what the boys needed to do to be successful. "We watched **Dan Gable**. We were exposed to good wrestling and how to do the right things like drilling and strength training," said Jim. "If you did the right things, you would be successful. We wrestled each other a lot. It was obvious that Joe was going to be a very good wrestler. He started at a young age. I didn't start wrestling until the sixth or seventh grade. Jeff started a little later, but he learned very quickly."

"I grew up crying a lot because I couldn't beat them. And I couldn't wrestle Jeff because he was the youngest," said Joe said with a chuckle. "Mom was like 'don't mess with the baby.' But battling with Jim and Tim made me tough. And I ended up winning more state titles than they did, so that was a bit of revenge."

Jim and Tim's first wrestling tournament was in Corning, IA. They were a year apart in school. "I'm three years younger than Tim and Jeff is three years younger than me," said Joe. "I was in the third grade and I saw kids my size who were wrestling. The next year I started going to kid tournaments and I was ready to go. I had practiced every night, did a lot of repetition on drills. Wrestling in Iowa really took off with the growth of the kids programs in the 1970s. Every small town had a kids program. We would travel around to tournaments and we were welcomed in people's homes because there weren't any motels."

Joe was the first wrestler in Iowa prep history to win four state titles in the state's largest class. He finished 105-5, did not allow a single takedown his senior season and shut out every opponent in the state tournament as a senior. He also won four state freestyle championships and four state Greco-Roman titles and was the nation's number-one recruit.

"We grew up around the university and Jim was recruited by **Coach Nichols**. Tim followed him there the next year, but just wrestled one season before focusing on his veterinary studies. He's the smart one. After graduating from veterinary school, he went to med school and now is an orthopedic surgeon in Mason City, IA," said Joe.

Jim won three state titles at Ames High School (1975-77) and was a three-time all-American at Iowa State, winning a national championship at 134 pounds in 1981. After college, he was an uncompensated coach under Nichols and then became the recruiting coordinator.

"I got a lot of experience in talking about our program and selling myself to recruits and their families," said Jim. "I learned a lot about training from **Chris Campbell**, about how to get guys in the best shape. Chris had a deep understanding of conditioning. I learned a lot about instruction, how to teach wrestlers, from **Russ Anderson**. So I was around great mentors and leaders."

As an assistant coach, Jim had a natural curiosity. He asked a lot of questions of other coaches such as **Tom Chesbro** (Oklahoma State), **Stan Abel** (Oklahoma) and **Dan Gable** (Iowa).

"I was fed the right information on how to run a successful program at an early age," said Jim. "I was asked to apply for the Iowa State head coaching position because I had been a successful recruiter and my brothers were really good people who projected a positive brand. Joe was a national champion in 1985. Fortunately, I had a bunch of guys my first year as head coach (1985-86) that bought into what I was all about – nobody's bigger than the program. The guys in the program were tired of not having success as a team and were willing to do what it took to be national champions."

Jim's first year was big. The Cyclones beat Iowa in a dual and his charges beat some national champions during the season. With a 19-1 dual record and a fourth-place national finish, he was named Rookie Coach of the Year. (Author's Note: Gibbons was the second-youngest head coach to win a national title at 26. The

Jim Gibbons was a three-time high school state champion, three-time all-American, 1981 NCAA champion and coached the Cyclones to their only national team championship (1987) in the decade. (Courtesy Iowa State University)

Four-time all-American and 1985 NCAA champion Joe Gibbons also served as an assistant coach under brother Jim. (Courtesy Iowa State University)

youngest was the late legendary **Myron Roderick** – 23 years of age – of Oklahoma State in 1958).

"Our time together at Iowa State was a lot of fun. I wrestled as a true freshman. Jim was a fifth-year senior and the defending national champion at 134, so I had to cut to 126 and that was very tough for me," said Joe. "We had a team of weight cutters back then, but we got into great shape first and then cut. There was a lot of competition in that wrestling room. Coach Nick didn't spare on recruits. He brought in the best wrestlers he could find, believing that steel sharpens steel."

In 1982, ISU won the Big 8 tournament over Oklahoma and swept the lower weights. Joe won at 126 over Oklahoma's **Mark Zimmer**, while Jim beat **Clar Anderson** of Oklahoma State at 134 and **Kevin Darkus** edged **Randy Willingham** of Oklahoma State at 118. According to Joe, that tournament may have had the greatest accumulation of wrestling talent in history.

"You had Darkus and Willingham at 118, me and Zimmer at 126, my brother Jim and Anderson at 134, **Andre Metzger** and **Johnnie Selmon** at 142, **Kenny Monday**, **Nate Carr**, **Roger Frizzell** and **Wes Roper** at 150, **Ricky Stewart** and **Isreal Sheppard** at 158, **Mike Sheets** and **Dave Schultz** at 167, **Mark Schultz**, **Perry Hummel** and **Jim Scherr** at 177, **Bill Scherr** and **Mike Mann** at 190 and **Steve Williams**, **Gary Albright** and **Wayne Cole** at heavyweight."

(Author's note: 25 Big 8 wrestlers earned all-American status in the 1982 NCAA Championships, the most by any conference in the decade, with four winning national titles – Metzger, Carr and the Schultz brothers – and five others making the finals. Six of those wrestlers are enshrined as Distinguished Members in the National Wrestling Hall of Fame: Carr, Monday, Bill Scherr, Jim Scherr, Dave Schultz and Mark Schultz).

The 1986-87season (Jim's second as head coach with Joe serving as a volunteer assistant) would prove to be historic for the program as they ended Iowa's nine-year reign as NCAA champions.

"We were fired up to win after not wrestling well at nationals. Even though we lost four duals, we never lost more than five matches. We wrestled at Arizona State, at Iowa and at Oklahoma State and that experience made us better," said Jim. "At nationals, we performed at or above our ability in every weight. I remember that the officials juggled the finals lineup to provide the stage for an Iowa comeback and a tenth straight title. The finals were in the afternoon. We had five guys in the finals and four of them won. We scored significant points in the consolations to pull away, but when **Bill Kelly** (No. 2 seed at 126) pinned top-seeded **Brad Penrith** of Iowa, I knew we were going to win. **Dan Gable** wrote me a congratulatory letter that I still have. That showed me what a class act he is."

In 2014, the Gibbons family received the Family Legacy Award from the Iowa Wrestling Hall of Fame. Bill and Bea Gibbons and their four wrestling sons were honored for their exceptional contribution to the sport in the state. Jim and Joe also are members of the **Glen Brand** Wrestling Hall of Fame of Iowa.

Jeff was a state champion for Ames High School in 1983 and 1984, and a second place finisher in 1982. He was a two-time all-American for Iowa State, placing third at the 1987

NCAA tournament and sixth at the 1988 NCAA tournament. Tim was a state champion for Ames in 1976. He wrestled at Iowa State for one season.

* * *

The Scherr Brothers: Bill and Jim

Three words best describe Bill and Jim Scherr: Champions. Leaders. Involved. And all three words carry multiple meanings for two of the most successful wrestlers from the 1980s.

Born in Eureka, SD on July 27, 1961, the twin brothers have been intimately involved in wrestling since their early days of battling each other around their family home and their prep days at Mobridge High School, hard by the Missouri River, just south of the North Dakota border. In 1980, the two brothers set a precedent by each winning a state championship, leading Mobridge to its first-ever state championship. That year, Bill also won the Junior Nationals.

At the University of Nebraska, the brothers continued their winning ways and the precedent set at Mobridge when each won an NCAA championship in 1984. Jim (35-2-1) won his title at 177 just minutes before Bill (36-1) captured the 190-pound crown. Their performance helped Nebraska register a school-record fourth-place finish in the team race behind Iowa, Oklahoma State and Penn State. It remains the second-highest NCAA placement in school history behind the 1993 team's third-place finish.

Bill was a three-time all-American finishing fourth in 1982 and third in 1983 along with his title, while Jim was a two-time all-American with a sixth-place finish in 1982 to accompany his '84 championship. In 1983, Jim (seeded second behind defending champion **Mark Schultz**) was upset in the second round and wasn't pulled through into the consolations and did not place.

Bill Scherr was a three-time all-American and 1984 NCAA champion at Nebraska and was the 1985 World champion and bronze medalist in the 1988 Olympics. (Courtesy University of Nebraska)

With their college careers behind them, the Scherrs stepped into the world of international freestyle. Continuing their excellence on the mat, they earned nine international medals including Bill's gold medal performance in the 1985 World Championships in

Budapest, Hungary. Bill added two silver medals and a bronze medal in the Worlds, while winning a bronze medal in the 1988 Olympics in Seoul, South Korea. Jim also competed in the '88 Games, placing fifth. He collected two silver medals and a bronze in the World Championships.

They continued the precedent of ascending the medal podium in the same events three times: 1986, 1987 and 1989. Their last World Championship appearance in Martigny, Switzerland in 1989 saw the brothers each battle their way to silver medals. Bill's five consecutive years of earning a medal in the World Championships and Olympics is one of the longest streaks in the annals of USA wrestling.

Bill won a gold medal in the Pan American Games in 1987 and was World Grand Champion in 1989. He won a key match in the dual meet against the Soviet Union to help lead the USA to team title at the 1990 Goodwill Games. He also won six national championships in freestyle and one in Greco-Roman.

Among the most successful wrestling siblings in history, the brothers went on to earn success in business, gaining leadership roles and involvement in the wrestling community that truly bettered the sport.

Jim Scherr captured an NCAA crown the same year as his brother (1984), had three top-three placements in the World Games and finished fifth in the 1988 Olympics. (Courtesy University of Nebraska)

Jim became executive director of USA Wrestling in 1990 and held that position until 2000. In 2003, he joined the U.S. Olympic Committee and became CEO in 2005, the only former wrestler to hold that exalted role. In 2013, he became the CEO of the inaugural European Games and in 2015 he took on the role of interim executive director of the National Wheelchair Basketball Association.

Bill served as an assistant wrestling coach at Indiana University following graduation. Later, he settled in Chicago, joining Goldman Sachs where he became a vice president and served the firm for 21 years. In 2012, he became Managing Director and Head of West Region at Barclays Wealth.

He served as Director of Sport of Chicago's 2016 Olympic Bid and president of World Sport Chicago, and was the logical choice to take the reins of the Committee for the Preservation of Olympic Wrestling (CPOW) when the sport was targeted for elimination from the 2016 and 2020 Games. Jim joined his brother to lead the lobbying effort on behalf of wrestling worldwide. The two built a strong organization of former wrestlers, businessmen and leaders that convinced the incredibly short-sighted International Olympic Committee to retain wrestling, one of the original Olympic sports, for the next two Olympiads. For their efforts, the Scherrs were named the 2012-2013 **Mike Chapman** Impact Award winners presented annually by *Wrestling Insider News* magazine (WIN).

Other honors earned by both brothers include: USA Wrestling Man of the Year (Jim in

1994, Bill in 2013) and induction into the National Wrestling Hall of Fame as Distinguished Members (Bill in 1998, Jim in 2003). Jim also was named to the NWHOF's Order of Merit in 1997.

Champions on and off the mat. Leaders on and off the mat. And the Midwest Distributors of Wrestling Involvement throughout their storied careers, Bill and Jim Scherr are two shining examples of wrestlers who starred during The Golden Era of Amateur Wrestling.

* * *

The Schultz Brothers: Dave and Mark

Much has been written about **Dave** and **Mark Schultz**, their wrestling prowess and Dave's senseless, tragic death at the hands of a mentally unstable millionaire. For the millions of people who only know what they saw in the movie Foxcatcher, please know the movie does not tell the whole (or correct) story. For instance, Dave and Mark were never at Foxcatcher at the same time as the movie depicts. The scenes involving Dave and Mark were mostly incidents between Mark and former Oklahoma teammate **Andre Metzger**, a coach at Foxcatcher. For more insight into the brothers, one should read the **David Thomas**/Mark Schultz book *Foxcatcher: The True Story of My Brother's Murder, John du Pont's Madness, and the Quest for Olympic Gold.* Told from Mark's perspective, the book, unfortunately, doesn't tell the whole story either.

Anyway, my interest is not in the Foxcatcher story. It's in the NCAA and international careers of the Schultz brothers, who grew up in poverty in California and through hard work and discipline became two of the most highly-regarded wrestlers in U.S. history. And both wrestled collegiately during the decade of the eighties.

Overweight, dyslexic and bullied as a youngster, Dave found solace – and his calling – in wrestling. In his high school senior season, he pinned two-time NCAA champion **Chuck Yagla** in the Great Plains Tournament, then traveled to the Soviet Union with the U.S. contingent to compete in the Tbilisi Tournament, considered by most to be the toughest tournament in the world. He won a silver medal, then returned to California for the state tournament. Because he had missed part of the season, he had to petition the state coaches association to allow him to compete. Wrestling up two weight classes, he pinned his way into the finals and registered a lopsided 12-1 win to earn a state championship. Later that year, he won his first national title by winning the U.S. Open Greco-Roman Championships. Dave's senior year is regarded as the best ever high school season in the sport of wrestling.

Mark Schultz derailed Ed Banach's chance to become the first-ever four-time NCAA champion with a thrilling 16-8 decision in the 1982 tournament. (Courtesy Mark Schultz)

Recruited by Oklahoma State, Schultz spent one season with the Cowboys. He placed third at 150 pounds in the 1978 NCAA Championships, falling in the semifinals to defending champion **Mark Churella** of Michigan, 13-10. Schultz transferred from OSU to join his brother at UCLA the next year and sat out. When UCLA dropped its program, the Schultz brothers transferred to Oklahoma. In 1981, Dave won the Big Eight title over defending NCAA champion **Rick**

Stewart of Oklahoma State and carried the number one seed into the NCAA's. In the finals, Stewart hit Dave with a near-arm, far-leg, inserted a half-nelson and pinned the Sooner star. Motivated by the loss, Schultz returned for the 1982 season and won his lone NCAA title at 167 pounds over OSU'S **Mike Sheets**, 4-4, 1-1 criteria 5.

Dave (left) and Mark Schultz each won the 1984 Olympic Trials (above) and went on to win gold medals in the Los Angeles Games. (Courtesy Mark Schultz)

While Dave was defeated by Stewart in 1981, Mark won his first of three consecutive NCAA titles with a 10-4 decision over Iowa's **Mike DeAnna** in the finals at 167. The following year, Mark moved up to 177 and upset **Ed Banach** of Iowa in one of the greatest finals matches in history, 16-8. His win kept Banach from winning his third straight crown. In his senior season, Schultz ground out a 4-2 win over Iowa's **Duane Goldman** for his third consecutive NCAA title.

In the 1984 Los Angeles Games, the Schultz brothers became the first U.S. brothers to win gold medals at the same Olympics just minutes before the Banach brothers did the same – the only time that has occurred. Internationally, the Schultz brothers earned more NCAA and international medals than any other brother tandem in history and are the only brothers to both win World and Olympic titles.

Dave won the World Championships in 1983 and also placed in the event seven times including silver medals in 1985, 1987 and 1993. Mark won World titles in 1985 and 1987 and placed another two times.

Mark was inducted into the National Wrestling Hall of Fame as a Distinguished Member in 1995. Dave received the same honor posthumously in 1997.

* * *

Lee Roy Smith's reaction to the inclusion of the above photo in this book: "Who said there's no Kung Fu in wrestling?" (Courtesy Oklahoma State University)

The Smith Brothers: Lee Roy and John

The Smiths are recognized as the first family of wrestling. The four brothers won seven NCAA championships (Lee Roy one, John two and **Pat** four) and, with **Mark's** three NCAA placements, earned all-American status 13 times. They also collected 10 high school state championships at Del City, OK, and five junior national freestyle titles.

Lee Roy Smith, an NCAA champion, three-time all-American and four-time Big 8 Conference champion, went on to coach the Martigny Club de Lutte in Martigny, Switzerland, served as U.S. National Freestyle Team coach and was head coach at Arizona State from 1993-2001. Today, he is the executive director of the National Wrestling Hall of Fame in Stillwater, OK.

John Smith became the most successful international wrestler in U.S. history with a stunning six-year run (1987-92) atop the world rankings. He won two Olympic gold medals (1988 in Seoul, South Korea and 1992 in Barcelona, Spain) and four World Games gold medals (1987, 1989, 1990 and 1991).

"In training for the Worlds and Olympics, the greatest part wasn't winning, as strange as that may sound. It was the daily lifestyle of focusing on being the best and not compromising in any way," said John. "There was no room for compromise. Everything was very serious. You can't make mental mistakes. Going through that time, preparing over seven years, I realized how tough it was to stay that focused. There aren't very many people who can do that. I couldn't imagine anyone working as hard as I was. I blocked everything out that didn't fit my purpose of being the best in the world. It tested my will power on a daily basis. It was the challenge to not settle for less. It was a very deep process that I wouldn't change for anything. It has made me strong when times are tough and helped me gather strength and courage to push through."

John became the head coach at Oklahoma State in 1991while still wrestling internationally and currently guides the Cowboys' wrestling fortunes. Through the 2015 championships, his teams have won five national championships and 16 conference team titles. He has coached 29 NCAA champions, 95 conference champions and 111 all-Americans. In 2005, both John and Pat were named to the prestigious NCAA 75th Anniversary Wrestling Team. John was inducted into the National Wrestling Hall of Fame in 1997, while Pat was elected in 2006.

Pat Smith, who is one of the few freshmen to win a national title, became the first wrestler ever to win four NCAA titles (1990-92 and 1994). Following his historic career guided by brother John, he served as an assistant coach at Oklahoma State. Currently, Pat runs and coaches the Arkansas Wrestling Academy in Little Rock. **Mark Smith** was a three-time all-American at OSU, placing fourth in 1997 at 177, fourth in 1998 at 167 and fifth in 1999 at 177.

Amateur Wrestling News picked the Smiths as the "Family of the Decade" in 1999 for their unprecedented accomplishments.

"When you're the first to engage in a sport and have some success, it influences your brothers," said Lee Roy. "The more success I had, the more passion I had and I shared that with John, Pat and Mark. My mom and dad embraced wrestling. It was a good fit for our particular family culture. My Dad didn't have the opportunity to wrestle because his school didn't offer

Over a six-year period, John Smith won two Olympic gold medals (displayed above) and four World Games gold medals, an unprecedented accomplishment. (Courtesy Oklahoma State University)

it. But he was a good athlete, playing baseball, basketball and football. He got a scholarship to play baseball in college. My mother starred in softball and basketball. They exposed the kids to all sports."

John remembers just how competitive the Smith household was.

"There is a daily competitive nature that exists in a household with 10 kids," said John. "Everything from food to getting a hot shower or finding a clean pair of underwear. Socks were definitely at a premium. I have really good memories of growing up in a large family. But it was very competitive. If you wanted cereal, you had to get up early enough to get cereal or you got oatmeal. If you didn't get home for dinner on time, you were stuck with a bologna sandwich. Very competitive environment."

In that environment, the kids developed self-reliance, and learned the difference between right and wrong and the value of hard work. Taking on his older brother on the mat truly was hard work.

"Lee Roy was a tough older brother. He didn't take it easy on me. He was a workout partner, but I didn't belong on the mat with him," said John. "He had a wrestler's mentality that he forced on me very early. It's amazing that I didn't go south. Just the opposite. I embraced it. The beatings helped me develop a competitive edge and made me really love competition. I was seldom fearful because of that and sometimes fear can be a great hurdle."

"We wrestled at home. Inside, outside, upstairs, downstairs," said Lee Roy. "John got into the play of wrestling as soon as he could get on his knees and crawl. He could wrestle well at a very young age. There was a seven-year gap between me and John, so I always had the physical advantage. However, we did match up well with our sisters. They could really wrestle. I would show John moves, but I was tough on him. He would get frustrated, but he learned. I could handle him until I became an assistant coach at OSU. John was a junior when he caught up with me. One day, we were wrestling and he put me on my back and wouldn't let me up. I was so mad, but realized just how good he was and would be."

Lee Roy and John credit their father, **Lee Roy Smith, Jr.,** with their early commitment to the sport. "Dad was like a coach. He guided and mentored us," said Lee Roy. "He navigated us toward doing the right things. I cannot undervalue the importance of his guidance. He sought other coaches to help us develop. The Mid-Del schools (Midwest City, Del City) had some really good coaches."

Lee Roy, Jr. received the Lifetime Service to Wrestling Award (Oklahoma) from the National Wrestling Hall of Fame in 2013.

Joseph Smith (Courtesy Oklahoma State University)

"When you have success, you begin to realize as you get older that you could have a chance at a college scholarship," said Lee Roy. "As that started to resonate with me, and the reality set in that I wasn't going to be a superstar in football, my Dad steered me toward wrestling. You have to narrow your focus if you want a college scholarship. Our parents encouraged us to think that way. They exposed us to college sports, attending OU football games and even attending bowl games. I saw the Sooners wrestling team, too. We were all OU fans back then."

John recalls watching the 1972 Munich Olympics on TV as a seven-year-old. "I saw **Wayne Wells** win a gold medal and he was from Oklahoma. Suddenly, it became very real that it was possible to be an Olympic champion."

Once Lee Roy selected OSU, the Smith clan gave up the crimson-and-cream for the orange-and-black and became ardent fans and supporters of Cowboy athletics. Since his debut in an OSU singlet in 1977, a steady stream of Smiths (Lee Roy, John, Pat and Mark) and cousins (**Mark Perry,** Jr. and

Chris Perry) have claimed national titles. The most recent came in 2015 when John's son **Joseph Smith** captured the 160-pound crown at the ASICS/Vaughan Freestyle National Championships in Fargo, ND, by outpointing his opponents, 72-0. Joe began his collegiate career in the 2015-2016 season at (where else?) Oklahoma State and earned all-American honors at 157 pounds.

That leaves little doubt that the Smith family wrestling legacy will continue to grow.

CHAPTER 16

Four-time NCAA Champions

In the storied history of the NCAA Wrestling Championships, begun in 1928, only four wrestlers have won four individual national championships: **Pat Smith**, Oklahoma State; **Cael Sanderson**, Penn State; **Kyle Dake**, Cornell; and **Logan Steiber**, Ohio State. No four-time champions existed before 1972 because freshmen were not allowed to wrestle. Still, it took 22 years for anyone to accomplish that feat. While none of these wrestlers competed in the 1980s, I thought it was important to recognize their incredible accomplishment.

Pat Smith, Oklahoma State (1990-92, 1994)

Wrestling collegiately on the cusp of The Golden Era of Amateur Wrestling, Pat, the third youngest of the Smith Brothers Wrestling Dynasty, became the first-ever four-time champion in NCAA history in 1994 and helped OSU to its 30th national crown. He also won four Big 8 tournament titles and reeled off an amazing streak of 98 consecutive matches without a loss during his career. He was named to the NCAA 75th Anniversary Team in 2005.

Pat Smith, first-ever NCAA Division 1 four-time champion. (Courtesy Oklahoma State University)

1990 (158): Smith rolled through his first four opponents 19-7, fall in 4:42, 16-6 over eighth-seeded **Chauncey Wynn** of Morgan State and 16-7 over #4 **Dan Russell** of Portland State. In the finals, Smith outlasted #3 **Scott Schleicher** of Navy, 11-7.

1991 (158): Easy wins in the first three rounds (16-10, TF 17-2 and 16-5 over #8 **Torrae Jackson** of Iowa State) put Smith in the semifinals against fourth-seeded **Scott Hovan** of Pittsburgh. Smith edged the Panther star 5-4, setting up his finals match against #2 **Tom Ryan** of Iowa. Ryan had powered his way into the semifinals, but had to squeak out a 4-3 win over #3 **Ray Miller** of Arizona State to face Smith for the title. In a true battle of all-Americans, Smith held on for a 7-6 win over the Hawkeye and his second crown.

1992 (158): Four relatively easy wins, including 8-3 over #8 **Mike Schyck** of Ohio State in the quarterfinals and 13-2 over Pitt's **Scott Hovan** again in the semis, put him into the finals against the rugged third-seeded **Ray Miller** from ASU. In a defensive struggle, Smith prevailed 3-1.

1994 (158): After missing the 1993 season, Smith came back with a vengeance as he sought to become the first four-time champ in history. With 23-8, 26-10 and 14-3 victories, he faced #5 **Earl Walker** of Boston University in the semis and came away with a 6-2 win. In the finals, Smith was pushed to the limit by **Sean Bormet** of Michigan and hit with a one-point stalling penalty, but captured a 5-3 win and his unprecedented fourth crown. Smith had defeated Bormet in the finals of the Junior Nationals by technical fall when they were high school seniors.

Cael Sanderson, Penn State (1999-2002)

Undefeated in his collegiate career at 159-0, he is the only wrestler in NCAA Division I history with more than 100 wins to go undefeated. *Sports Illustrated* named his career as the second most impressive college sports feat behind the setting of four world records by **Jesse Owens** in a single hour at the 1935 Big Ten track and field championships. Sanderson was seeded #1 in all four NCAA tournaments in which he competed and won four Outstanding Wrestler Awards, the only wrestler in history to accomplish that feat. He is, without doubt, the most dominant collegiate wrestler in history.

Cael Sanderson (top) won his first NCAA crown in 1999. (Courtesy Iowa State University)

1999 (184): As a freshman, Sanderson obliterated the field with three pins and an 18-6 superior decision to reach the finals. Second-seeded **Brandon Eggum** of the University of Minnesota put up a tough fight, but Sanderson prevailed 6-1.

2000 (184): Once again, Sanderson mowed down the competition (WBF 3:51; TF 21-6; TF 20-5; MD 16-5) to reach the finals. He scored a convincing 19-6 superior decision over #2 **Vertus Jones** of West Virginia University, the most points scored in NCAA finals history.

2001 (184): Another romp through the field (TF 24-9; WBF 1:37; TF 21-6; SD 21-7) set up a finals match against Oklahoma State's third-seeded **Daniel Cormier**. In his toughest finals battle ever, Sanderson scored a solid 8-4 decision.

2002 (197): Looking to become only the second four-time champion in history, Sanderson was a man on a mission as he moved up to 197. He scored falls in the first two rounds, then dominated the eighth seed 23-8 and the fourth seed 18-7. In the finals, he registered a 12-4 major decision over #2 **Jon Trenge** of Lehigh to complete the greatest NCAA wrestling career in history.

Kyle Dake, Cornell (2010-2013)

Dake accomplished what no wrestler had ever accomplished when he won his fourth national title (without a redshirt season) at a fourth different weight. His toughest roads to the title were in his freshman and senior years.

Kyle Dake celebrates after winning his third straight NCAA title in 2012. (Courtesy Lindsey Mechalik)

2010 (141): Top-seeded, Dake survived a 4-1 decision in the first round and a 3-2 tie-breaker overtime heart-stopper in the semifinals against **Reese Humphrey** of Ohio State University. In the finals, Dake fought his way to a 7-3 win over #6 **Montell Marion** of Iowa.

2011 (149): Moving up a weight pushed Dake down to a No. 4 seed, with **Darrion Caldwell** of North Carolina State earning the top seed. Unfortunately, the 1 vs. 4 match never materialized as Caldwell suffered an injury in his second-round match and was out of the event. Dake did not allow a point in his first four matches, dispatching #5 **Jamal Parks** of Oklahoma State 3-0 in the quarterfinals and #8 **Ganbayar Sanjaa** of American University 4-0 in the semis. In the finals, Dake gave up his first point but rolled to an 8-1 victory over second-seeded **Frank Molinaro** of Penn State. Molinaro would win the 149-pound title in 2012 and become a four-time all-American.

2012 (157): Registering falls (1:13, 1:31 and 4:10) in his first three matches, top-seeded Dake replicated his tough 2011 4-0 victory over Sanjaa in the semifinals. In the finals, second-seeded **Derek St. John** of Iowa, who would win a national title in 2013 and earn all-American honors four times, pushed Dake to the limit before falling 4-1.

2013 (165): Intense pressure. That's what Dake felt as he sought to become the first NCAA wrestler to win four titles at four different weights. A narrow 3-0 first-round win over unseeded **Mark Martin** of Ohio State was followed by three more shutouts including a tense 2-0 victory over fourth-seeded **Tyler Caldwell** of Oklahoma State. Defending 165-pound champion **David Taylor** of Penn State stood as Dake's biggest roadblock to becoming a four-time champion. In one of the best finals matches in history, Dake edged the talented Taylor, 5-4. Taylor would win a second title at 165 in 2014 and finish his career as a two-time champ, two-time runner-up and four-time all-American.

Logan Steiber, Ohio State (2012-15)

While Dake was grabbing his final two titles, Steiber was racking up his first two at 133 pounds. His final victory in 2015 at 141 helped Ohio State claim the national championship, breaking the run of four straight by Penn State, coached by **Cael Sanderson**.

2012 (133): The second-seeded Steiber scored a pair of falls followed by a narrow 7-4 decision over tenth-seeded **Chris Dardanes** of Minnesota. In the semifinals, Steiber ran into Iowa's tough third-seeded **Tony Ramos** and survived a 4-2 struggle. Oklahoma State's top-seeded **Jordan Oliver** had three falls and an 8-2 semifinals win over **Bernard Futrell** of Illinois. In the toughest finals match of his career, Steiber escaped with a 4-3 decision over Oliver to win the national championship.

Logan Steiber of Ohio State (top) rides Edinboro's Mitchell Port in the 2015 NCAA finals at 141 on his way to his fourth consecutive championship. (Courtesy Ohio State University)

2013 (133): Steiber registered two falls and two technical falls en route to the finals. Waiting for him with revenge in mind for 2012 was Iowa's second-seeded Ramos. In a tense match, Steiber held on for a 7-4 win and his second title.

2014 (141): Moving up to 141 was a success for second-seeded Steiber as he rolled into the semifinals with two falls and a technical fall. In the semis, he registered a 7-3 win over third-seeded **Zain Retherford** of Penn State and moved to the title bout against #4 **Devin Carter** of Virginia Tech instead of top-seeded **Mitchell Port** of Edinboro who had fallen in the quarterfinals. Steiber was at his finals best with a 10-1 convincing win over Carter and title number three.

2015 (141): THE story of the tournament was top-seeded Steiber's quest to become the fourth four-time NCAA champion. He breezed into the semifinals scoring an 18-1 technical fall, a fall in 2:19 and a 16-1 superior decision, then dispatched unseeded **Kevin Jack** of North Carolina State, 12-2.

Jack had knocked off fourth-seeded Carter of Virginia Tech, 10-8, in the quarterfinals. Second-seeded **Mitchell Port** of Edinboro made sure the anticipated finals battle with Steiber that fell through in 2014 would be a reality in 2015 as he was untested on his way to the title bout. Steiber built an early lead in the long-anticipated match, but took his foot off the gas pedal after Port suffered a knee injury. Steiber won 11-5 and stepped into history with his fourth NCAA championship.

CHAPTER 17

The Olympians

The 1980s also were a golden age for U.S. wrestlers at the Olympics, with eleven American athletes claiming the ultimate prize during the decade – the gold medal. Members of the All-Decade Team for the 1980s are indicated with **boldface type** and an asterisk (*).

1980 Olympics (Moscow, USSR)

The U.S. boycotted the 1980 Olympics – held in Moscow – to protest the Soviet invasion of Afghanistan. Members of that team who were denied a chance to fulfill their childhood dreams were:

Freestyle

Bobby Weaver, 105.5 lbs.; *Gene Mills, 114.5 lbs.; *John Azevedo, 125.5 lbs.; *Randy Lewis, 136.5 lbs.; Chuck Yagla, 149.5 lbs.; Lee Kemp, 163 lbs.; Chris Campbell, 180.5 lbs.; Ben Peterson, 198 lbs.; Russ Hellickson, 220 lbs.; Greg Wojciechowski, HWT

Greco-Roman

Mark Fuller, 105.5 lbs.; Bruce Thompson, 114.5 lbs.; Brian Gust, 125.5 lbs.; Dan Mello, 136.5 lbs.; Tom Minkel, 149.5 lbs.; John Matthews, 163 lbs.; Dan Chandler, 180.5 lbs.; Mark Johnson, 198 lbs.; Brad Rheingans, 220 lbs.; Jeff Blatnick, HWT

1984 Olympics (Los Angeles, CA)

Andy Rein on his way to defeating Zsigmond Kelevitz of Australia, 4-0, in the 1984 Olympics. (Courtesy Dennis Bronte)

The 1984 Olympics returned to Los Angeles, 52 years after hosting the 1932 Games. Soviet nations boycotted the L.A. Olympics. Of the 20 U.S. wrestlers who competed, 13 won medals, including nine who won gold (seven Freestyle, two Greco-Roman).

Freestyle

Bobby Weaver, 105.5 lbs., GOLD; *Joe Gonzales, 114.5 lbs., DNP; *Barry Davis, 125.5 lbs., SILVER; *Randy Lewis, 136.5 lbs., GOLD; *Andy Rein, 149.5

lbs., SILVER; *Dave Schultz, 163 lbs., GOLD; *Mark Schultz, 180.5 lbs., GOLD; *Ed Banach, 198 lbs., GOLD; *Lou Banach, 220 lbs., GOLD; *Bruce Baumgartner, HWT, GOLD

Greco-Roman

Mark Fuller, 105.5 lbs., DNP; Bert Govig, 114.5 lbs., DNP; Frank Famiano, 125.5 lbs., 5TH; Abdurrahim Kuzu, 136.5 lbs., 4TH; Jim Martinez, 149.5 lbs., 3RD; Chris Catalfo, 163 lbs., DNP; Dan Chandler, 180.5 lbs., DNP; Steve Fraser, 198 lbs., GOLD; Greg Gibson, 220 lbs., SILVER; Jeff Blatnick, HWT, GOLD

Freestyle GOLD
Bobby Weaver, 48 kg/105.5 pounds
Round 1: WBF 2:56 over Reiner Heugabel (FRG)
Round 2: Won by Decision 13-0 over Gao Wenhe (China)
Finals: WBF 2:58 over Takashi Irie (Japan)

Weaver, a member of the 1980 U.S. Olympic team, won the silver medal at the 1979 World championships. A Pennsylvania native, Weaver was a 1982 NCAA all-American at Lehigh. He was inducted into the National Wrestling Hall of Fame as a Distinguished Member in 2008.

*Randy Lewis, 62 kg/136.5 pounds
Round 1: Won by Decision, 12-0 over Mark Dunbar (Great Britain)
Round 2: Won by Decision 13-1 over Chris Brown (Australia)
Round 3: Won by Decision 12-0 over Gian Singh (India)
Round 4: Won by Decision 15-3 over Antonio LaBruna (Italy)
Finals: Won by Decision 24-11over Kosei Akaishi (Japan)

Lewis, a member of the 1980 Olympic team, was a three-time South Dakota high school state champ, two-time NCAA champion (1979, 1980) and four-time all-American for the University of Iowa. He entered the National Wrestling Hall of Fame as a Distinguished Member in 1998.

*Dave Schultz, 76 kg/163 pounds.
Round 1: Won by Decision 9-1 over Pekka Rauhala (Finland)
Round 2: Won by Decision 12-0 over Zane Coleman (New Zealand)
Round 3: Won by Decision 12-0 over Romelio Salas (Columbia)
Round 4: WBF 1:46 over Saban Sejdi (Yugoslavia)
Round 5: Bye
Round 6: Won by Decision 5-0 over Han Myung-Woo (Korea)
Finals: Won by Decision 4-1 over Martin Knosp (West Germany)

In his senior high school season, Schultz won a California state championship for Palo Alto High; defeated two-time NCAA champion **Chuck Yagla** in the Great Plains Tournament; and was a silver medalist in the World Championships – the greatest senior season in U.S. high school history. Schultz was a three-time all-American, first at Oklahoma State, then at the University of Oklahoma, where he won the 167-pound title at the 1982 NCAAs. The National Wrestling Hall of Fame welcomed Dave Schultz posthumously as a Distinguished Member in 1997.

*Mark Schultz, 82 kg/180.5 pounds.
Round 1: Won by Disqualification (injury) 0:30 over Resit Karabacak (Turkey)
Round 2: Won by Decision 16-7 over Kenneth Reinsfield (New Zealand)
Round 3: Won by Decision 5-3 over Christopher Rinke (Canada)
Round 4: WBF 1:36 over Luciano Ortelli (Italy)
Finals: Won by Decision 13-0 over Hideyuki Nagashima (Japan)

The younger brother of Dave, Mark Schultz was a three-time NCAA champ for the Oklahoma Sooners, earning Outstanding Wrestler honors as a senior. After the Los Angeles Games, Mark won two World championships (1985 and 1987). He was inducted into the National Wrestling Hall of Fame as a Distinguished Member in 1995.

*Ed Banach, 90 kg/190 pounds.
Round 1: Won by Decision 15-2 over Edwin Lins (Austria)
Round 2: Won by Decision 11-0 over Ismail Temiz (Turkey)
Round 3: Won by Decision 11-2 over Clark Davis (Canada)
Round 4: WBF 0:48 over Abdul Majeed Maruwala (Pakistan)
Finals: Won by Decision 15-3 over Akira Ota (Japan)

Banach was a four-time Big Ten champ and three-time NCAA title winner for the University of Iowa and twin brother of Olympic and Hawkeye teammate Lou Banach. Ed joined the National Wrestling Hall of Fame as a Distinguished Member in 1993.

*Lou Banach, 100 kg/220 pounds.
Round 1: WBF 1:14 over Hayri Sezgin (Turkey)

Round 2: WBF 1:45 Ambroise Sarr (Senegal)
Round 3: Won by Decision 11-1 over Wayne Brightwell (Canada)
Round 4: WBF 1:56 over Tamon Honda (Japan)
Finals: WBF 1:01 over Joseph Atiyeh (Syria)

A New York high school state champ, Banach wrestled at Iowa, winning two Big Ten titles, and the NCAA heavyweight crown in 1981 and 1983. He served as a coach at West Point and Penn State. The National Wrestling Hall of Fame welcomed Lou as a Distinguished Member in 1994.

Bruce Baumgartner displays his four Olympic medals. (Courtesy National Wrestling Hall of Fame)

*Bruce Baumgartner, Super-heavyweight.
Round 1: WBF 1:58 over Vasile Andrei (Poland)
Round 2: WBF over Ayhan Taskin (Turkey)
Finals: Won by Decision 10-2 over Robert Molle (Canada)

A three-time NCAA all-American at Indiana State, Baumgartner won the NCAA heavyweight title in 1982. The New Jersey native won a total of four Olympic medals: gold in 1984 and 1992, silver in 1988, and bronze in 1996. He also won a total of nine World medals. He was inducted into the National Wrestling Hall of Fame as a Distinguished Member in 2002.

Greco-Roman GOLD

Steve Fraser, 90 kg/198 pounds.

Finals: Won by Decision 1-1 criteria over Ilie Matei (Romania)

A Michigan high school state champ, **Steve Fraser** was a two-time NCAA all-American at the University of Michigan. He became the first American to win a gold medal in Greco-Roman competition in the Modern Olympics. Fraser, an Olympic Greco coach, was inducted into the National Wrestling Hall of Fame as a Distinguished Member in 1994.

Jeff Blatnick, Super-heavyweight.

Finals: Won by Decision 2-0 over Thomas Johansson (Sweden)

A New York high school state champ, **Jeff Blatnick** was a two-time NCAA Division II heavyweight champ for Springfield College. The National Wrestling Hall of Fame honored Blatnick as a Distinguished Member in 1999.

1988 Olympics (Seoul, South Korea)

The 1984 Olympics were held in Seoul, South Korea. Of the 20 U.S. wrestlers who competed, six won medals, including two gold medals in Freestyle.

Freestyle

Tim Vanni, 105.5 lbs., 4TH; Ken Chertow, 114.5 lbs., DNP; *Barry Davis, 125.5 lbs., DNP ; *John Smith, 136.5 lbs., GOLD; *Nate Carr, 149.5 lbs., BRONZE; *Kenny Monday, 163 lbs., GOLD; *Mark Schultz, 180.5 lbs., 6TH; *Jim Scherr, 198 lbs., 5TH; *Bill Scherr, 220 lbs., BRONZE; *Bruce Baumgartner, HWT, SILVER

Greco-Roman

Mark Fuller, 105.5 lbs., DNP; Shawn Sheldon, 114.5 lbs., DNP; Anthony Amado, 125.5 lbs., DNP; Ike Anderson, 136.5 lbs., 6TH; Andy Seras, 149.5 lbs., DNP; David Butler, 163 lbs., DNP; John Morgan, 180.5 lbs., 7TH; Michial Foy, 198 lbs., DNP; Dennis Koslowski, 220 lbs., BRONZE; Duane Koslowski, HWT, 8TH

1988 U.S. Olympic Wrestling Team. Back, L-R: Mark Schultz, Bill Scherr, Bruce Baumgartner, Jim Scherr, Kenny Monday. Front, L-R: John Smith, Ken Chertow, Tim Vanni, Barry Davis, Nate Carr. (Courtesy Tim Vanni)

Freestyle GOLD

*John Smith, 62 kg/136.5 pounds.

Round 1: Won by Decision 11-4 over Jozsef Orban (Hungary)

Round 2: Won by Decision 6-3 over Simeon Shterev (Bulgaria)

Round 3: Won by Decision 4-2 over Marian Skubacz (Poland)

Round 4: Won by Decision 16-6 over Mike Lehto (Finland)

Round 5: WBF 5:54 over Giovanni Schillaci (Italy)

Round 6: Won by Decision 12-7 over Avirmediin Enkher (Mongolia)

Finals: Won by Decision 4-0 over Stepan Sarkisyan (Russia)

A two-time NCAA champ at Oklahoma State University, John Smith's true success was on the international stage, as a two-time Olympic gold medalist (1988, 1992), four-time World champion, and two-time Pan Am gold medal winner. Over a six-year period (1987-1992), Smith was the number one 136.5 pound wrestler in the world with two Olympic golds and four World Championships. Since 1991, Smith has served as head coach at Oklahoma State. He joined the National Wrestling Hall of Fame as a Distinguished Member in 1997.

*Kenny Monday, 74 kg/163 pounds.

Round 1: Won by Decision 12-0 over Fitzlloyd Walker (Great Britain)

Round 2: WBF 2:00 over Alfonso Jessel (Mexico)

Round 3: Won by Decision 3-2 over Janos Nagy (Hungary)

Round 4: Won by Decision 4-0 over Sahan Sejdi (Yugoslavia)

Round 5: Won by Decision 6-0 over Gary Holmes (Canada)

Round 6: Won by Decision 2-0 over Lodoyn Enkhbayar (Mongolia)

Round 7: Won by Decision 7-0 over Pekka Rauhala (Finland)

Finals: Won by Decision 5-2 over Adlan Varayev (Russia)

Monday was an undefeated (140-0-1) four-time Oklahoma high school state champ at Tulsa Washington High School. In 1984, he captured the 150-pound NCAA title for Oklahoma State, while placing second in 1982 and 1983. He became the first African-American wrestler to win an Olympic gold and earned a silver medal in Barcelona in 1992. Monday was welcomed into the National Wrestling Hall of Fame as a Distinguished Member in 2001.

Olympics 1992 - Barcelona, Spain

The 1992 Olympic Games were held in Barcelona, Spain. Of the 20 U.S. wrestlers who competed, eight won medals, including three Freestyle golds.

Freestyle

Tim Vanni, 105.5 lbs., 5TH; Zeke Jones, 114.5 lbs., SILVER; ***Kendall Cross, 125.5 lbs., 6TH**; ***John Smith, 136.5 lbs., GOLD**; Townsend Saunders, 149.5 lbs., 7TH; ***Kenny Monday, 163 lbs., SILVER**; Kevin Jackson, 180.5 lbs., GOLD; Chris Campbell, 198 lbs., BRONZE; Mark Coleman, 220 lbs., 7TH; ***Bruce Baumgartner, HWT, GOLD**

Greco-Roman

Mark Fuller, 105.5 lbs., DNP; Shawn Sheldon, 114.5 lbs., 4TH; Dennis Hall, 125.5 lbs., 8TH; Buddy Lee, 136.5 lbs., 6TH; Rodney Smith, 149.5 lbs., BRONZE; Travis West, 163 lbs., DNP; Dan Henderson, 180.5 lbs., 10TH; Michial Foy, 198 lbs., 6TH; Dennis Koslowski, 220 lbs., SILVER; Matt Ghaffari, HWT, DNP

Freestyle GOLD

*John Smith, 62 kg/136.5 pounds
Round 1: Won by Decision 3-2 over Ismail Faikoglu (Turkey)
Round 2: Won by Decision 2-1 over Kim Gwang-choi (North Korea)
Round 3: Won by Decision 8-0 over Karsten Polky (Germany)
Round 4: Won by Decision 17-1 over Magomed Azizov (Russia)
Round 5: Lost by Decision 3-1 to Lazaro Reinoso (Cuba)
Finals: Won by Decision 6-0 over Askari Mohammadian (Iran)

John Smith became the first U.S. freestyle wrestler to win two gold medals, earning his title just over an hour before Baumgartner won his second. Smith and Reinoso each had one loss, but Smith had 14 classification points and 31 technical points to Reinoso's 13 classification points and 28 technical points and advanced to the finals, which he dominated. The Freestyle Wrestler of the Year Award by USA Wrestling is named in his honor.

Kevin Jackson, 82kg/180.5 pounds
Round 1: Won by Decision 1-0 over Sabahattin Ozturk (Turkey)
Round 2: Won by Decision 4-3 over Robert Kostecki (Poland)
Round 3: Won by Decision 3-2 over David Hohl (Canada)
Round 4: Won by Decision 8-0 over Francisco Iglesias (Spain)
Round 5: Won by Decision 3-1 over Rasoul Khadem (Iran)
Finals: Won by Decision 1-0 over Elmadi Jabrailov (Russia)

Kevin Jackson was a four-time NCAA Division I all-American at LSU and Iowa State, placing second in 1987 when the Cyclones won the NCAA title. He won two World titles (1993, 1995), two Pan Am Games championships, three U.S. Freestyle titles and was the first American to win the Takhti Cup (1998) in Iran. The 1995 **John Smith** Award winner served as national freestyle coach for USA Wrestling for eight years (2001-2008) and became head coach at Iowa State in 2009. He was inducted into the National Wrestling Hall of Fame as a Distinguished Member in 2003.

*Bruce Baumgartner, Super-heavyweight.
Round 1: Won by Decision 9-1 over Kiril Barburton (Bulgaria)
Round 2: Won by Decision 8-0 over Zsolt Gombos (Hungary)
Round 3: Won by Decision 3-0 over David Gobezhishvili (Russia)
Round 4: Won by Decision 5-0 over Wang Chunguang (China)
Round 5: Won by Decision 7-0 over Andreas Schroder (Germany)
Finals: Won by Decision 8-0 over Jeffrey Thue (Canada)

Bruce Baumgartner became the second American to win two Olympic wrestling gold medals, sharing that accomplishment with Olympic teammate **John Smith** on the same night. He allowed a single point in his opening match and then went on to shut out five consecutive opponents in a display of dominance rarely seen in the Olympics.

Olympics 1996 - Atlanta, Georgia

Atlanta hosted the 1996 Olympic Games. Of the 20 U.S. wrestlers who competed, eight won medals, including three Freestyle gold medals.

Freestyle

Rob Eiter, 105.5 lbs., 8TH; Lou Rosselli, 114.5 lbs., DNP; *Kendall Cross, 125.5 lbs., GOLD; *Tom Brands, 136.5 lbs., GOLD; Townsend Saunders, 149.5 lbs., SILVER; *Kenny Monday, 163 lbs., 6TH; Les Gutches, 180.5 lbs., 7TH; *Melvin Douglas, 198 lbs., 7TH; *Kurt Angle, 220 lbs., GOLD; *Bruce Baumgartner, HWT, BRONZE

Greco-Roman

Brandon Paulson, 114.5 lbs., SILVER; Dennis Hall, 125.5 lbs., SILVER; David Zuniga, 136.5 lbs., 10TH; Rodney Smith, 149.5 lbs., 9TH; Gordy Morgan, 163 lbs., 9TH; Dan Henderson, 180.5 lbs., DNP; Derrick Waldroup, 198 lbs., 7TH; Jason Gleasman, 220 lbs., DNP; Matt Ghaffari, 286 lbs., SILVER

Freestyle GOLD

*Kendall Cross 57kg/125.5

Round 1: Won by Decision 10-0 over Talata Embalo (GBS)

Round 2: Won by Decision 4-2 over Sanshiro Abe (Japan)

Round 3: Bye

Round 4: Won by Decision 12-2 over Ri Yong-sam (North Korea)

Finals: Won by Decision over Magomed Azizov (Russia)

Kendall Cross was a three-time all-American at Oklahoma State University including an NCAA title at 126 pounds in his junior year (1989). Cross placed sixth at the Barcelona Olympics in 1992. He was inducted into the National Wrestling Hall of Fame as a Distinguished Member in 2002.

*Tom Brands 62kg/136.5 pounds

Round 1: Won by Decision 3-0 over Abbas HajKenari (Iran)

Round 2: Won by Decision 5-0 over Sergey Smal (Belarus)

Round 3: Bye

Finals: Won by Decision 4-1 over Magomed Azizov (Russia)

Tom Brands was a three-time NCAA champion and four-time all-American at Iowa and was named Outstanding Wrestler in the 1991 NCAA tournament. Brands won four U.S. Freestyle Championships, was a gold medalist in the 1993 World Championships and won two golds in the World Cup and a gold in the Pan Am Games. As head coach at Iowa since

2006, he has led the Hawkeyes to three national championships. He was inducted into the National Wrestling Hall of Fame as a Distinguished Member in 2001.

*Kurt Angle 100kg/220 pounds
Round 1: Won by Decision 4-0 over Dolgorsuren Sumyaabazar (Mongolia)
Round 2: Won by Decision 2-0 over Wilfredo Morales (Cuba)
Round 3: Won by Decision 4-3 over Sagid Murtazaliev (UKR)
Round 4: Won by Decision 4-01 over Konstantin Aleksandrov (KGZ)
Finals: Won by Decision 1-1 criteria over Abbas Jadidi (Iran)

Kurt Angle was a two-time NCAA Division I champion (1990, 1992) at Clarion University of Pennsylvania and a 1995 World Games champion. He is one of just four wrestlers to win the Grand Slam of amateur wrestling: Junior Nationals, NCAA, World and Olympic Games. He was named the greatest shoot wrestler and one of the top 15 college wrestlers in history by USA Wrestling. He was inducted into the National Wrestling Hall of Fame as a Distinguished Member in 2001.

CHAPTER 18

International Tournaments and Hall of Fame

To further establish the case for the 1980s being The Golden Era of Amateur Wrestling, I compared – by decades in which they wrestled collegiately – the Olympic and World Championship placements of wrestlers (Freestyle and Greco-Roman) who are **Distinguished Members of the National Wrestling Hall of Fame.** Some wrestlers' results were included in two decades. By decade, the numbers of Distinguished Members who wrestled collegiately are: 2000-2009 (1); 1990-1999 (13); 1980-89 (29); 1970-1979 (17); 1960-1969 (23); 1950-59 (30); 1940-1949 (20); 1930-39 (18); 1920-1929 (16); 1900-1919 (2). As you will quickly see in the list to follow, National Wrestling Hall of Fame wrestlers from the 1980s are, by far, the most decorated international wrestlers in U.S. history.

Joe Gonzales (left) of the U.S. triumphs over Anatoli Beloglazov of the Soviet Union in the 1988 World Cup. (Courtesy Joe Gonzales)

In the Olympic Games, the National Wrestling Hall of Fame Distinguished Members from the '80s won 27 medals (17 gold, six silver and four bronze) and had an additional six placements. Two gold and two silver medals were earned in Greco-Roman. Bunched closely together were the wrestlers from the '50's, '60's, '70's and '90's. The 1970s grapplers earned five gold, five silver and three bronze; the 50's Hall of Famers won four gold, two silver and two bronze; the '60's wrestlers won four gold and four silver; and the '90's competitors won four gold, one silver and three bronze. Olympic medal counts for wrestlers from the 1970s and 1980s would have been higher had the U.S. not boycotted the 1980 Olympic Games in Moscow, and probably a bit lower had the Eastern Bloc countries not boycotted the 1984 Olympics in Los Angeles.

In the World Championships, NWHOF Distinguished Members from the '80s accounted for 50 medals: 22 gold, 15 silver and 13 bronze, along with 28 placements. Of those, two gold, one silver and one bronze were earned in Greco-Roman. The 1960s wrestlers were a distant second with 17 medals (four gold, nine silver and four bronze) and an additional nine placements, all in Freestyle.

Combining Olympic and World medal counts, NWHOF members who wrestled collegiately in the '80s collected **39 gold medals, 21 silver medals, 17 bronze medals and earned placements 34 times.** The next closest decade was the 1970s with 11 gold medals, 10 silver, seven bronze and nine placements. **In total medals earned, the 1980s had 77, followed by the '70's with 28 medals; the '60's with 25; the '90's with 20; and the '50's with nine.**

Further evidence that the decade of the 1980s was The Golden Era of Amateur Wrestling in the U.S. comes from the beginning of women's international freestyle competition in 1987. Although the U.S. did not compete in the initial 1987 World Games in Lorenskog, Norway (featuring teams from Europe and Japan), American female wrestlers finally had the opportunity to challenge the world's best two years later. In 1989, women's wrestling received a huge boost when the International Wrestling Federation (FILA) added the women's division to the World Wrestling Championships in Martigny, Switzerland. The U.S. team competed for the first time internationally and won three medals: **Asia DeWeese** (50 kg) and **Leia Kawaii** (70 kg) captured silver medals and **Afsoon Roshanzamir** (47 kg) took home a bronze.

After winning a pair of silver medals in 1990 (**Marie Ziegler** at 44 kg and Roshanzamir at 47 kg) and 1991 (Ziegler at 44 kg and **Shannon Williams** at 50 kg), America's first women's international gold medal came in 1992 when **Tricia Saunders** was crowned in the 50 kg division at the World Games in Villeurbanne, France, and was named the event's Outstanding Wrestler. Saunders, who began wrestling competitively in the late 1980s, went on to win a silver in 1993 and three more gold medals (1996, 1998 and 1999) to become America's only female wrestler to win more than two gold medals in World Games competition. She won 11 U.S. Freestyle Championships and 11 World Games

Tricia Saunders (right) won America's first women's international gold medal at the 1992 World Games. (Courtesy National Wrestling Hall of Fame)

trials, never losing to an American wrestler. Saunders was duly inducted into the National Wrestling Hall of Fame as a Distinguished Member in 2006.

Without a doubt, the 1980s produced the best wrestlers – male and female – in U.S. history. Here's a look at U.S. international success by decade in which they wrestled collegiately.

2000-2009 Wrestlers: 1 Gold, 1 Silver

Olympic Freestyle
2004 Cael Sanderson 1st

World Freestyle

2003 Cael Sanderson 2nd

Greco-Roman

None

1990-1999 Wrestlers: 9 Gold, 3 Silver, 7 Bronze, 16 placements

Olympic Freestyle

1996 Tom Brands 1st; Kendall Cross, 1st; Les Gutches 7th; 2000 Brandon Slay, 1st; Sammie Henson 2nd; Terry Brands 3rd; Lincoln McIlravy 3rd; Kerry McCoy 5th; 2004 Kerry McCoy 7th; Eric Guerrero 16th

Olympic Greco-Roman

2000 Rulon Gardner, 1st; 2004 Rulon Gardner, 3rd

World Freestyle

1993 Terry Brands, 1st; Tom Brands, 1st; 1994 Terry Brands, 11th; Tom Brands, 11th; 1995 Terry Brands, 1st; Tom Brands, 9th; 1997 Les Gutches, 1st; Lincoln McIlravy, 12th; 1998 Sammie Henson, 1st; Lincoln McIlravy, 3rd; Kerry McCoy, 4th; Les Gutches, 7th; 1999 Lincoln McIlravy, 2nd; Les Gutches, 3rd; Eric Guerrero, 7th; 2001 Kerry McCoy, 4th; Eric Guerrero, 13th; **2002 USA did not compete**; 2003 Kerry McCoy, 2nd; Eric Guerrero, 10th; 2005 Sammie Henson, 14th; 2006 Sammie Henson, 3rd

World Greco-Roman

1994 Dennis Hall, 3rd; 2001 Rulon Gardner, 1st

1989 World Games Team. Front (L-R): John Smith, Melvin Douglas. Back (L-R) Brad Penrith, Bruce Baumgartner, Tim Vanni, Kenny Monday, Zeke Jones, Jim Scherr, John Giura, Bill Scherr. (Courtesy Tim Vanni)

1980-1989 Wrestlers: 39 Gold, 21 Silver, 17 Bronze, 34 Placements

Olympic Freestyle

1980 USA did not compete. Team members: John Azevedo, Randy Lewis, Gene Mills, Bobby Weaver
1984 Bobby Weaver, 1st ; Randy Lewis, 1st; Ed Banach, 1st; Lou Banach, 1st; Bruce Baumgartner, 1st; Dave Schultz, 1st; Mark Schultz, 1st; Barry Davis, 2nd; **1988** Kenny Monday, 1st; John Smith, 1st; Bruce Baumgartner, 2nd ; Nate Carr, 3rd; Bill Scherr, 3rd; Jim Scherr, 5th; Mark Schultz, 6th; **1992** Bruce Baumgartner, 1st; Kevin Jackson, 1st; John Smith, 1st; Kenny Monday, 2nd; Zeke Jones, 2nd; Kendall Cross, 6th; **1996** Kurt Angle, 1st; Tom Brands, 1st; Kendall Cross, 1st; Bruce Baumgartner, 3rd; Terry Brands, 3rd; Kenny Monday, 6th; Melvin Douglas, 7th; 2000 Melvin Douglas, 18th

Olympic Greco-Roman

1984 Jeff Blatnick, 1st; Steve Fraser, 1st; Greg Gibson, 2nd; 1996 Matt Ghaffari, 2nd

World Freestyle

1981 Joe Gonzales, 5th; 1982 Joe Gonzales, 3rd; Dave Schultz, 3rd; Randy Lewis, 4th; Bruce Baumgartner, 7th; **1982** Joe Gonzales, 3rd; Dave Schultz, 3rd; Randy Lewis, 4th; Bruce Baumgartner, 7th; **1983** Dave Schultz, 1st; Bruce Baumgartner, 3rd; Bobby Weaver, 5th; Ed Banach, 7th; Mark Schultz, 7th; Nate Carr, 8th; Joe Gonzales, 9th; Barry Davis, 12th; **1985** Bill Scherr, 1st; Mark Schultz, 1st; Dave Schultz, 2nd; **1986** Bruce Baumgartner, 1st; Barry Davis, 2nd; Bill Scherr, 2nd; Jim Scherr, 3rd; Dave Schultz, 3rd; Mark Schultz, 7th; **1987** John Smith, 1st; Mark Schultz, 1st; Barry Davis 2nd; Jim Scherr, 2nd; Dave Schultz, 2nd; Bruce Baumgartner, 3rd; Bill Scherr, 3rd; **1989** Kenny Monday, 1st; John Smith, 1st; Bruce Baumgartner, 2nd; Melvin Douglas, 2nd; Bill Scherr, 2nd; Jim Scherr, 2nd; Zeke Jones, 7th; **1990** John Smith, 1st; Bruce Baumgartner, 2nd; Zeke Jones, 4th; Nate Carr, 5th; **1991** Kevin Jackson, 1st; Zeke Jones, 1st; John Smith, 1st; Kenny Monday, 2nd; Bruce Baumgartner, 7th; **1993** Bruce Baumgartner, 1st; Terry Brands, 1st; Tom Brands, 1st; Melvin Douglas, 1st; Dave Schultz, 2nd; Kevin Jackson, 4th; Zeke Jones, 4th; **1994** Bruce Baumgartner, 2nd; Melvin Douglas, 3rd; Dave Schultz, 7th; Kevin Jackson, 7th; Terry Brands, 11th; Tom Brands, 11th; Zeke Jones, 11th; **1995** Kurt Angle, 1st; Bruce Baumgartner, 1st; Terry Brands, 1st; Kevin Jackson, 1st; Melvin Douglas, 3rd; Zeke Jones, 3rd; Dave Schultz, 5th; Tom Brands, 9th; **1997** Melvin, Douglas, 9th; Zeke Jones, 11th; **1998** Melvin Douglas, 5th

World Greco-Roman

1985 Mike Houck, 1st; 1995 Dennis Hall, 1st; Matt Ghaffari, 3rd; 1998 Matt Ghaffari, 2nd

1970-1979 Wrestlers: 11 Gold, 10 Silver, 7 Bronze, 9 Placements

Olympic Freestyle

1972 Ben Peterson, 1st; John Peterson, 2nd; Chris Taylor, 3rd; 1976 John Peterson, 1st; Russ Hellickson, 2nd; Ben Peterson, 2nd; 1976 John Peterson, 1st; Russ Hellickson, 2nd; Ben Peterson, 2nd; Stan Dziedzic, 3rd; 1980 (Boycott) Chris Campbell, Russ Hellickson, Lee Kemp; Randy Lewis, Gene Mills, Ben Peterson, Greg Wojciechowski, Chuck Yagla; 1984 Dave Schultz, 1st; Mark Schultz, 1st; 1988 Mark Schultz, 6th; 1992 Chris Campbell, 3rd

Olympic Greco-Roman

None

World Freestyle

1973 Ben Peterson, 3rd; 1974 Stan Dziedzic, 5th; 1975 Ben Peterson, 4th; 1977 Stan Dziedzic, 1st; Chris Campbell, 5th; 1978 Lee Kemp, 1st; John Peterson, 3rd; Ben Peterson, 5th; 1979 Lee Kemp, 1st; John Peterson, 2nd; Bobby Weaver, 2nd; 1981 Chris Campbell, 1st; Lee Kemp, 3rd; 1982 Lee Kemp, 1st; Dave Schultz, 3rd; 1983 Mark Schultz, 7th; 1985 Mark Schultz, 1st; Dave

Schultz, 2nd; 1987 Dave Schultz, 2nd; 1990 Chris Campbell, 2nd; 1991 Chris Campbell, 5th; 1993 Dave Schultz, 2nd; 1994 Dave Schultz, 7th; 1995 Dave Schultz, 5th

World Greco-Roman
None

1960-1969 Wrestlers: 8 Gold, 13 Silver, 4 Bronze, 14 Placements

Olympic Freestyle
1964 Yojiro Uetake, 1st; Bobby Douglas, 4th; Larry Kristoff, 7th; 1968 Yojiro Uetake, 1; Don Behm, 2nd; Rick Sanders, 2nd; Wayne Wells, 4th; Larry Kristoff, 5th; Steve Combs, 7th; 1972 Dan Gable, 1st; Wayne Wells, 1st; Rick Sanders, 2nd; 1976 Russ Hellickson, 2nd; 1980 Russ Hellickson (Boycott)

Olympic Greco-Roman
None

World Freestyle
1963 Dean Lahr, 4th; 1965 Larry Kristoff, 3rd; Rick Sanders, 3rd; Wayne Baughman, 5th; 1966 Bobby Douglas, 2nd; Larry Kristoff, 2nd; Dean Lahr, 5th; 1967 Rick Sanders, 2nd; Larry Kristoff. 3rd; Wayne Baughman, 6th; 1969 Fred Fozzard, 1st; Rick Sanders, 1st; Don Behm, 2nd; Larry Kristoff, 2nd; Wayne Wells, 2nd; Bobby Douglas, 4th; 1970 Wayne Wells, 1st; Larry Kristoff, 2nd; Don Behm, 5th; Fred Fozzard, 5th; 1971 Dan Gable, 1st; Don Behm, 2nd; Russ Hellickson, 3rd; Gene Davis, 4th; 1975 Russ Hellickson, 4th; 1979 Russ Hellickson, 2nd

World Greco-Roman
None

1950-1959 Wrestlers: 4 Gold, 2 Silver, 3 Bronze, 16 Placements

Olympic Freestyle
1952 William Smith, 1st; Jay Thomas (Tommy) Evans, 2nd; Bill Kerslake, 5th; 1956 Dan Hodge, 2nd; Peter Blair, 3rd; Myron Roderick, 4th; Richard Delgado, 5th; Jay Thomas (Tommy) Evans, 5th; Bill Kerslake, 7th; 1960 Douglas Blubaugh, 1st; Terry McCann, 1st; Shelby Wilson, 1st; Daniel Brand, 5th; Gray Simons, 5th; Bill Kerslake, 8th; 1964 Daniel Brand, 3rd; Dave Auble, 4th; Gray Simons, 7th

Olympic Greco-Roman
None

World Freestyle

1954 Richard Delgado, 5th; Alan Rice, 5th; 1961 Daniel Brand, 4th; 1962 Daniel Brand, 3rd; Dave Auble, 4th; 1963 Russ Camilleri, 6th; 1966 Werner Holzer, 4th

World Greco-Roman

None

1940-1949 Wrestlers: 1 Gold, 1 Bronze, 1 Placement

Olympic Freestyle

1948 Glen Brand, 1st; Bill Koll, 5th; 1952 Josiah Henson, 3rd

Olympic Greco-Roman

None

World Freestyle

No Events

World Greco-Roman

No Events

1930-1939 Wrestlers: 3 Gold, 3 Silver

Olympic Freestyle

1932 Jack Van Bebber, 1st; 1936 Frank Lewis, 1st; Ross Flood, 2nd; Richard Voliva, 2nd; 1948 Henry Wittenberg, 1st; 1952 Henry Wittenberg, 2nd

Olympic Greco-Roman

None

World Freestyle

No Events

World Greco-Roman

No Events

1900-1929 Wrestlers: 4 Gold, 1 Placement

Olympic Freestyle

1904 George Mehnert, 1st; 1908 George Dole, 1st; George Mehnert, 1st; 1924 Russell Vis, 1st; Guy Lookabaugh, 4th

Olympic Greco-Roman
No Events

World Freestyle
No Events

World Greco-Roman
No Events

Distinguished Members of the National Wrestling Hall of Fame

Joe Gonzales (center), Cal State-Bakersfield legend, was inducted into the National Wrestling Hall of Fame in 2015. Sharing the moment were CSUB teammates John Azevedo (left) and Tim Vanni. (Courtesy Larry Slater)

Twenty-three members of my **All-Decade Team** for the 1980s have been inducted into the National Wrestling Hall of Fame in Stillwater, OK as Distinguished Members (induction year in parentheses):

Ed Banach, Iowa (1993)
Lou Banach, Iowa (1994)
Mark Schultz, Oklahoma (1995)
Dave Schultz, Oklahoma (1997)
John Smith, Oklahoma State (1997)
Randy Lewis, Iowa (1998)
Bill Scherr, Nebraska (1998)
Gene Mills, Syracuse (2000)
Tom Brands, Iowa (2001)
Kenny Monday, Oklahoma State (2001)
Kurt Angle, Clarion (2001)
Bruce Baumgartner, Indiana State (2002)
Kendall Cross, Oklahoma State (2002)
Jim Scherr, Nebraska (2002)*
Nate Carr, Iowa State (2003)
Jim Zalesky, Iowa (2004)
Zeke Jones, Arizona State (2005)
Terry Brands, Iowa (2006)
Barry Davis, Iowa (2007)
Ricky Bonomo, Bloomsburg (2008)
Melvin Douglas, Oklahoma (2013)
Joe Gonzales, California State-Bakersfield (2015)
Carlton Haselrig, Pittsburgh-Johnstown (2016)

* Also selected to the NWHOF's Order of Merit in 1997

Other Distinguished Members of the National Hall of Fame who wrestled in the 1980s (induction date in parentheses) are:

Ben Peterson, Iowa State (1986)

John Peterson, University of Wisconsin-Stoudt (1986)

Russ Hellickson, Wisconsin (1989)

Steve Fraser, Michigan (1994)

Jeff Blatnick, Springfield College (1999)

Kevin Jackson, LSU and Iowa (2003)

Chris Campbell, Iowa (2005)

Greg Gibson, Oregon (2007)

Bobby Weaver, Lehigh (2008)

Mike Houck, Maranatha Baptist Bible College (2008)

Matt Ghaffari, Cleveland State (2013)

CHAPTER 19

Mean Gene the Pinning Machine

Gene Mills, two-time NCAA champion (1979 and 1981) and Syracuse University's first four-time all-American, is recognized as one of the greatest pinners of all-time. He holds the NCAA record for most career falls at 107. He was also known for his take-no-prisoners aggressive style and his killer half-nelson he learned from his father that earned him the nickname "Mean Gene the Pinning Machine."

Gene Mills demonstrating his patented half-nelson. (Courtesy Gene Mills)

In high school, Mills was a New Jersey state champion and a national prep champion. In 1976 while still in high school, he was a spectator at the Montreal Olympics and saw six Americans win medals: **John Peterson** (gold), **Ben Peterson**, **Russ Hellickson** and **Lloyd Keaser** (silver) and **Gene Davis** and Mills' future international coach **Stan Dziedzic** (bronze).

"Right then and there, I said I can do that in four years," said Mills. "I began my plan to win an Olympic gold medal."

Further motivation to seek an Olympic medal came in 1979 when he wrestled five-time World champion **Yuji Takada** of Japan in the 1979 World Championships, but lost. "That really motivated me. I wanted to beat him so bad," remembers Mills.

In 1980, Mills redshirted to focus on his quest for Olympic gold. In training camp for the Tbilisi tournament in January 1980, the U.S. team was preparing to travel to Russia.

"The movie Midnight Express came out the year or so before, where an American guy was imprisoned in Turkey," said Mills. "The Russians were invading Afghanistan. President Carter didn't want Americans traveling to that region. Tbilisi was 125 miles from the border of Iran. The Iranians were holding hostages in Tehran."

That started Mills thinking that he really didn't want to go to Tbilisi.

"I called my mom and dad and they said 'don't go.' I talked to my high school coach and my college coach, and they both said 'don't go.' So I decided I wouldn't go," said Mills. "I told Coach **Stan Dziedzic** that I wasn't going. He started yelling and screaming at me saying 'I've been there. It will be safe!' He got choked with tears and said 'You don't understand. Only four Americans have won the Tbilisi tournament in 22 years. I believe you can kill those commies!' I said, 'What? Kill commies? OK, I'm in.' I had two goals at that point. One, kill commies. Two, set a pinning record there by pinning everyone. I felt like I was going to war. I wanted to set a record, not just beat them."

At the weigh-in at Tbilisi, an ugly bearded guy walked up to Mills and smacked him in the chest.

"The guy said 'Usa! Usa!' It took a minute, but I figured out he meant USA," said Mills. "I asked him where he was from. He finally understood what I was asking and said Iran. He kept pestering me, but I kind of waved him off. I said 'I'm here to kill commies. I'm not interested in you.'"

At the opening ceremonies, the Iranian team had a huge picture of the Ayatollah Khomeini and they looked over at the USA team and yelled "We have your hostages!"

After the ceremony, Dziedzic broke the bad news to Mills: there wasn't a Russian at his weight.

"I went ballistic. I said 'I fly here to kill commies and I don't have one to wrestle?' I was so mad," recalls Mills as if it were yesterday. "Then, just before my first match, assistant coach **Bill Wick** walked up wearing a big smile. He started shaking out my arms. He said 'I have a present for you. Look over there.' I looked across the mat and that ugly bearded Iranian was standing there. I ran out on the mat and told him I was going to kick his ass. It was 5-5 when I put him on his back. He tried to gouge my eyes and grabbed me by my boys. I flipped out. Started kicking at him, trying to rip his face off and I went ahead 27-5. I was getting ready to pin him and he tried to bite my face. So, I see his ugly little beard and I start biting out patches of it. He's screaming and his teammates are screaming from the sidelines. I looked up at the ref and he was chuckling and giving me two more points."

Mills wrestled nine matches on that tour and was winning by more than 20 points in each match before he pinned every opponent except one.

"I wrestled **Yurali Shugaev** who had beaten **Sergei Beloglazov** (1979 World runner-up and eventual 1980 Olympic champion). In the second period, I was up like 18-0 and he gets disqualified for stalling. He was the only one I didn't pin," said Mills.

In the 1980 World Cup in the University of Toledo's Centennial Hall, Mills beat Shugaev 16-11 to help lead the U.S. Team (coached by **Dan Gable** and Dziedzic) to a victory over the Russians, 7-3. In the 1980 World Super Tournament, he pinned everyone again, including three-time world champion **Toshio Asakura** of Japan.

"I was up 15-2 when I pinned him in the first period. I was on a mission," said Mills. "That 1980 trip, **Jim Humphrey**, Dziedzic, **Chris Campbell** and **Dave Schultz** told me time and time again that my performance was

1985 World Games Team. Front, L-R: Dave Schultz, Andre Metzger, Gene Mills, Kevin Darkus, Joe Gonzales, Tim Vanni. Back, L-R: Coach Jim Humphrey, Bruce Baumgartner, Dan Severn, Bill Scherr, Mark Schultz, Coach Joe Seay. (Courtesy Gene Mills)

the most dominant human performance on a wrestling mat they had ever seen, me beating the daylights out of everybody."

At the 1980 Olympic Trials finals in Brockport, NY, he pinned all opponents at 114.5 pounds to become a member of the U.S. Olympic Team. At Olympic training camp, Dziedzic told the team they were still going to the Moscow Olympics despite the looming boycott.

"He said we would travel to Germany for training and then fly to Russia and there would be nothing the U.S. could do," remembers Mills. "So I trained my ass off. I worked so hard. Then Stan came to us and said we had to support President Carter and we weren't going to Moscow. I was devastated. I had worked so hard and it was all for nothing."

As a consolation, the U.S. Olympic wrestlers were invited to The White House to be honored for making the Olympic team.

"I didn't want to go. But I did," said Mills. "One of the Secret Service guys, one of Carter's bodyguards, was a former wrestling coach from Virginia. He told Carter to compliment me on my half-nelson when he met me. So Carter shakes my hand and says, 'Mills. I've heard about your half-wilson.' I just chuckled. I wanted to pin him right there. But I just kept walking through the reception line."

Back at Syracuse University for his senior year (1980-81), Mills was on a mission to win a second NCAA Championship. Ron Good, editor of *Amateur Wrestling News*, called Mills early in 1981.

"He said 'you have possibly 26 matches left,'" remembers Mills. "I said so? He said, 'do you realize that if you pin 25 of those 26 you will beat the NCAA record of 106 pins?' I said 'I can do that.'"

Before the NCAA Championships, the Princeton (NJ) daily newspaper interviewed Mills. The article also appeared in the *New York Times*.

"The reporter asked me who my toughest opponent would be in the tournament. I said 'Joe Scale from Toledo.' They printed that. Of course, I was saying that if I made weight, those other poor bastards were dead." They were. Mills racked up three falls and a 28-4 semifinal romp before pinning Central Michigan's **John Hartupee** at 6:35 in the finals for the pin record and his second NCAA crown.

As Mills traveled around the country to teach at wrestling camps, he worked out with two University of Oklahoma wrestlers, **Andre Metzger** and **Dave Schultz**.

"We would stay after the camp and work on stuff," said Mills. "We were constantly trying to innovate, to create scoring situations from everywhere. We'd say, 'what if we did this or what if we did that?' We worked to refine our moves over and over."

In an interview, **Mark Schultz** said "I consider myself among the top five or ten wrestlers of all-time. I was dominant. But the most dominant person ever to step on the mat was Gene Mills."

Mills was nominated for the NCAA 75th Anniversary Wrestling Team in 2005 and was inducted into the National Wrestling Hall of Fame as a Distinguished Member in 2000. He compiled an incredible career record of 1356-46-1, with 886 wins coming by fall. If that's not a pinning machine, I don't know what is.

CHAPTER 20

Tim Vanni, Perseverance Personified

Open a dictionary – Cambridge, Merriam-Webster or Oxford – and turn to the letter P. Look up Perseverance. Accompanying that word should be a picture of Tim Vanni. Take the time to paste his picture into your dictionary, for Vanni personifies the word like no other wrestler in history. The new entry will look like this:

PERSEVERANCE (see Vanni, Tim)

noun: **perseverance** per·se·ver·ance

        steadfastness in doing something despite difficulty or delay in achieving success.

        "his **perseverance with** the technique illustrates his single- mindedness."

              persistence, tenacity, determination, staying power, indefatigability, stead-
              fastness, purposefulness; Morepatience, endurance, application, diligence,
              dedication, commitment, doggedness, assiduity, tirelessness, stamina;

synonyms: intransigence, obstinacy;

        informal: stick-to-it-iveness;

        formal: pertinacity

        "in a competitive environment, perseverance is an invaluable asset"

Is Vanni really the personification of perseverance? Let's look closely at the definitions and synonyms. Steadfastness? Check. Single-mindedness? Check. Persistence, tenacity, staying power?

Check. Check. Check. Indefatigability, purposefulness, Morepatience, endurance, diligence, dedication, commitment, doggedness, tirelessness, stamina? All in the affirmative. And then some.

How many wrestlers would continue their wrestling careers after losing a state championship on a nightmarish scoring error that wasn't corrected? How many would stay on a wrestling team when they didn't get a single takedown in the wrestling room for the first two months of their collegiate career? How many would continue to get beaten day after day by superior teammates, knowing they would never earn a starting spot on the team for four years? How many would refuse to gain weight

Tim Vanni (Courtesy Tim Vanni)

123

(to improve their chances to make the team) in order to stay at the lowest weight for international competition? The answer to all those questions: very few.

Despite facing insurmountable odds, Vanni never quit. He worked harder. He made himself into one of the most prolific international wrestlers in U.S. history.

Vanni's wrestling career began on the carpets of his boyhood home, going up against his older and bigger brothers, **Vince** and **Danny**. "I got into wrestling because of my older brothers. They tormented me at home," said Vanni. "We had some knock-down, drag-out fights that would tear up the house. Vince got us into wrestling and taught me how to wrestle and compete."

Vince was a California state qualifier in the 1970s and wrestled at Porterville Junior College and in the Marines. Danny wrestled throughout high school.

Tim compiled a 36-3 record his junior year and reached the state finals his senior year. In that two-year period, Vanni was never taken down. In the state finals, he lost a controversial 4-3 decision to **Bruce Terry** of Loara High School in Anaheim, the defending state champion and 1979 Dream Team member of *Wrestling USA Magazine's* High School all-Americans. Leading 3-2 late in the match, Vanni fought off a turn attempt by Terry and escaped. Terry immediately shot in at the buzzer but didn't score. However, officials awarded Terry back points after the match and disallowed Vanni's escape calling it no loss of control by Terry. Cal State-Bakersfield Coach **Joe Seay** (future Oklahoma State head coach and National Wrestling Hall of Fame inductee as a Distinguished Member in 1998) was at the match and was incredulous the officials didn't correct the error. The loss haunted Vanni.

"I had nightmares about that match. I didn't go to the state meet for six years. Then when I did, I saw my nemesis Bruce Terry. He wasn't the guy I wanted to see right then."

Tim Vanni, Cal State-Bakersfield.
(Courtesy Tim Vanni)

At Cal State-Bakersfield

Heavily recruited by Fresno State Coach **Dick Francis**, Vanni opted for a late scholarship offer from Cal State-Bakersfield after the Roadrunners' **Joe Gonzales** helped recruit him and because his dream was to make the Olympic team.

"I helped recruit Tim out of Porterville Monache High School. He was a little guy and I thought 'Oh, my gosh, he's gonna get his butt whipped, and he did," said Gonzales. "He never made the varsity lineup. He would challenge for a spot on the team at 118 and he was barely a buck ten. And other guys were coming down from 134. But he stuck it out and started going to and placing in freestyle tournaments and started beating national 105-pounders that were already rated in the U.S. Before you knew it, he was a national 105-pound champion in freestyle. He took his lickings, but he never quit. He didn't just say 'I'm outta here, college wrestling isn't for me.' Or that he was going somewhere else. He didn't make it at the college level, but he made it internationally as a U.S. Freestyle champion, two-time Olympian and three-time Pan Am Games medalist."

In 1979-80, no school in America had a tougher wrestling room in the two lower weights than CSUB. Headliners were senior all-Americans **John Azevedo** (126) and Gonzales (118). Both wrestlers won NCAA Division I and Division II titles that season and both went undefeated: Gonzales was 55-0 and Azevedo went 53-0. Also on the team were **Dan Cuestas** (126), who would win two titles (1982 and 1983) and his brother **Adam Cuestas**, who would capture a crown in 1983 at 118. Gonzales still has the highest career winning percentage at CSUB, .990 (98-1), while Azevedo is second (121-2, .984). Gonzales (118), Azevedo (126) and Dan Cuestas (126) are all members of the All-Decade Team (see Chapter 14).

"I walked into that wrestling room as a freshman and got the living daylights beaten out of me from day one. I didn't get a takedown for the first two months," said Vanni. "That wrestling room had just one mat so it got pretty crowded and you were always bumping into other guys. There were a few fisticuffs. **Adam Cuestas** and I got into it once.

"After getting pounded on for two months, I finally got a takedown and built on that and started getting a takedown a week. It was a huge challenge. It was my Mount Everest. And it was a rough climb. But I kept chipping away at it. I worked on my skills over and over and worked hard to get better. I weighed 112 as a freshman and the guys told me I should lift weights and get bigger to compete at 118, but I was worried that I would get too big for international competition at 105.5 pounds."

His first year, Vanni attached himself to Gonzales. He wanted to stay in Joe's shadow and do what he did and learn all he could. Vanni credits Gonzales for making him a better wrestler.

"It was a bunch of rag-tag guys that were never state champions in their state, especially California, and **Joe Seay** was able to get these guys who were still hungry to achieve something in wrestling," said Gonzales at his June 2015 induction into the National Wrestling Hall of Fame. "He gave us the belief that we could be NCAA champions. He never said 'I can make you an all-American.' He said 'I can make you a national champion.' So we always had that mentality in the room. It was a small room. No air conditioning. No heat. It was one 45-foot mat. Coach Seay ran a loose practice. We'd warm up and start drilling hard and we just beat up each other. That's how we made each other national champions. We would get on each other's case if a guy was slacking in practice. We kind of pushed each other."

Because of their exposure to international competition, Gonzales, Azevedo and Vanni shared techniques they learned abroad.

"We taught each other techniques," said Gonzales. "Tim traveled the world. I traveled the world. John traveled the world. We'd say, 'hey, I learned this from the Russians. I learned this from the Japanese. Let's drill it.' So we taught each other our techniques and we kind of combined them, sort of a hybrid system. Everyone had different techniques. We were able to establish ourselves and started making a name for ourselves in the country. We were a Division II school. Small college. I remember all the cotton fields and the corn fields around Bakersfield and yet we were beating up these huge Division I schools. If it wasn't for John,

I wouldn't have been a national champion. We would beat each other up every day. I hated practicing with him. But he made me better."

Azevedo's first impression of Vanni: "He was tiny. I thought to myself, 'I hope he grows.' He was there training every day. He never complained. I didn't wrestle him a lot, but we did wrestle some. He was game and that's what made him tough. He just kept going. He had great people to train with. We all helped each other with technique. We all got better in the process. Tim was very determined. He kept coming back day after day, week after week. When someone is willing to do that, you know they will get better. And he kept getting better and we all got better together. Joe got better and he made me better. And we had the Cuestas brothers, too."

That wrestling room was unique. CSUB wrestlers won NCAA titles at 126 pounds for three straight years (**John Azevedo** in 1980; **Dan Cuestas** in 1981 and 1982) and two out of four at 118 (**Joe Gonzales** in 1980 and **Adam Cuestas** in 1983)., and **Jesse Reyes** was the Division I kingpin at 142 in 1984 and took down two Div. II titles (1983, 1984).

"There were 18 wrestlers at 118 when I was a freshman," remembers Vanni. "But that number was down to just six by the end of the year because some guys couldn't take it. CSUB was the place to be if you wanted to be successful. We attracted a lot of great wrestlers. It's why I went there. Fresno State and Cal Poly didn't have the international mystique that I wanted."

According to Azevedo, "wrestlers who wanted to be international champions came here. The ones that stayed got better and many became successful on the international level."

Tim Vanni scores a victory over his New Zealand opponent in the 1982 World Games in Edmonton, AB, Canada. (Courtesy Tim Vanni)

Azevedo, Gonzales and Vanni are shining examples of international success. Gonzales was an alternate on the 1980 Olympic team and was on the 1984 team, but did not place due to injury. He also had one bronze medal placement, plus two fourth-place and one fifth-place finish in four World Games appearances (1981, 1982, 1983 and 1985). In addition, he won three gold medals in the World Cup and was a five-time USA Freestyle champion (1980, 1982, 1983, 1985 and 1988). Azevedo made the 1980 Olympic team but didn't get to wrestle because of the boycott, then was an alternate on the 1984 team. He also placed fourth in the 1982 World Games and won two USA Freestyle championships (1977 and 1981).

While he wrestled in the large shadows of his well-known teammates at CSUB, Vanni moved out of those shadows and became one of the most prolific wrestlers in U.S. history.

His best memory as a wrestler? "Winning the 1988 Olympic Trials. I had an incredible opponent in **Rich Salamone** as we competed in the U.S. Freestyle Championships and the Olympic Trials,"said Vanni. "Rich won freestyle titles in 1983 and 1984, then I beat him in 1985, but he came back and won again in 1986. But in 1988 I won the U.S. Freestyle Championship and then faced Rich in the Olympic Trials. I beat him twice to become an Olympian for the first time. I had a shot at my dream of becoming an Olympic champion."

At the 1988 Olympics: Seoul, South Korea

"The 1988 Olympics in Seoul was pretty special. It was my first time there and my eyes were wide open. It was phenomenal," said Vanni. "It is difficult to express in words. Just standing outside the stadium waiting to go in for the opening ceremonies with crowds all around was amazing. The experience of walking into the stadium was incredible. We were there 10 days before wrestling started. I remember Coach **Dan Gable** coming by our rooms the first day at 6 a.m. saying 'Let's go run' to my roommate Barry Davis. I said no way. It was time for rest and recovery from the long trip."

Vanni also remembers hearing the USA baseball team playing catch outside his window, hearing the pop of the ball in the glove. "I looked out and saw **Jim Abbot** (1987 **James E. Sullivan** Award winner) playing catch. That was cool," said Vanni. "It was difficult to stay focused for those 10 days."

Incredibly, there were two other future Sullivan Award winners in the Olympic village in 1988: **John Smith** (1990, the first wrestler so honored) and **Bruce Baumgartner** (1995).

Vanni remembers Smith and the awesome atmosphere in the Olympic Village. "I remember walking into the food court that was open 23 hours a day. I was in awe as I looked around at all the great athletes and realized that I was one of them. When we went outside one day I was with John and it was like paparazzi with movie stars. John was the star. Everyone was yelling 'John, John!' It was incredible."

"My greatest memory at the Olympics was winning my first match and having my hand raised in victory. Looking up into the crowd, I realized this was it. I'm an Olympic wrestler. This is awesome. I felt very fortunate to obtain my goal. But I blew it in my match against the Japanese wrestler (**Takashi Kobayashi**) in the second round and got pinned. Of course, that's the picture that was in *USA Today*. I wrestled **Sergey Karamchakov** for the bronze medal and lost, 3-1. He was the best wrestler I ever faced. I wrestled him a dozen times in my career and only beat him twice."

One of those wins came in the 1989 World Cup, five months after the Olympic Games, when Vanni beat Karamchakov, 5-2.

Another tough Soviet wrestler Vanni faced was four-time World Champion and Olympic bronze medalist **Sergei Kornilayev**. "I wrestled him in a dual in Moscow and he beat me 10-0 in 1982," said Vanni. "I celebrated my 21st birthday in Siberia. In the 1986 World Cup I lost to him 11-4. He was much more mature physically than I was. But in 1988, he only beat me 8-7 in the World Cup. I continued to get better."

In 1992, Vanni went to the finals in the Olympic Trials against **Rob Eiter**, an opponent he knew extremely well. Vanni and Eiter (at 105.5 pounds) and **Joe Gonzales** (at 115) were teammates and workout partners on the Sunkist Kids Wrestling Club coached by National Wrestling Hall of Fame Distinguished Member **Bobby Douglas**. Like Vanni at CSUB, Eiter was too small to make the Arizona State starting lineup (future World Champion, Olympic silver medalist and three-time all-American **Zeke Jones** was ASU's lightweight at that time). Like Vanni, Eiter focused on freestyle and never gave up on his dream of an Olympic medal. And like Vanni, Eiter became a coach. He was head coach at the University of Pennsylvania from 2008 to 2014.

The two lightweights battled each other for 105.5 pound supremacy throughout the late 1980s and early '90's. For the nine years from 1988 through 1996, Vanni and Eiter dominated the weight class by winning every title. In addition to a championship in 1985 when Eiter wasn't in the field, Vanni won four more U.S. Open titles (1988, 1989, 1991 and 1994). Eiter won five titles (1990, 1992, 1993, 1995 and 1996).

As the top two wrestlers at 105.5 pounds (48 kilograms) for 12 years, you would think there would be an intense rivalry between the two. That couldn't be farther from the truth.

Tim Vanni vs. Russian nemesis Sergey Karamchakov in the 1986 World Cup. (Courtesy Tim Vanni)

"I first met Tim when I was a freshman at ASU in 1985 at the Sunkist Open Tournament," said Eiter. "In all honesty, it was never a rivalry. He was the guy I wanted to be like at the weight class. **Joe Gonzales**, too. Tim was my mentor and my idol. I looked up to him because I never wrestled freestyle until I got to college. Through high school, I was a hockey player. When I got to ASU, Zeke Jones was there. I trained with Zeke and Tim and Joe. They were my coaches and training partners. I credit all my success to Coach **Bobby Douglas** and Timmy for taking me under his wing. At our size, it was hard to find training partners. He taught me everything. And I knew if I got better I could push him and he would get better. He'd be doing camps and clinics and I would go along with him and we would train in between sessions. I told people I was his luggage."

The two trained together beginning in 1987, the year Vanni won his second national championship.

"I tried out for the 1988 Olympic team, but I was rooting for Timmy," said Eiter. "I was more excited that he made the team and was thrilled at how well he did in Seoul. Our relationship was more of big brother-little brother or teacher-student. He would beat me pretty easily when we first started. I didn't think I was supposed to beat my coach. After 1988, it was more competitive. In 1990, I won the U.S. Open but Tim wasn't in the field. But he was so excited for me. He won in 1991 and then I won in '92 when he wasn't in the field again. Things changed after that. I was much more confident."

In the 1992 Olympic Trials mini-tournament in Philadelphia, Vanni was in Eiter's corner when he beat former Oklahoma State all-American **Cory Baze**. That put Eiter into the final head-to-head, best-of-three match against Vanni in Pittsburgh two weeks later. To get ready for that match-up, the two did not train together. Vanni trained with **Joe Gonzales** and Eiter trained with **Zeke Jones**.

"Timmy thought of me as a good training partner. He was all about loyalty and friendship. And legacy," said Eiter. "He put the seed in the back of my head that I would be the one to take over at 48 kilos. **Billy Rosado** had trained Tim and passed the crown to him. Tim would say 'when I'm done, you can take over. Keep the crown with the Sunkist Kids.'

Without Tim I wouldn't have gotten to where I got. He showed me how to train, diet, run and live as a wrestler. He turned me from a weekend wrestler into an international champion."

What made Tim Vanni so great?

"Planning and strategy. He had a plan and he stuck to that plan," said Eiter. "At the end of the day, it was his mental strength that was the key. He believed he would win every match. His preparation, watching tape, planning an attack was second to none. Only a couple of wrestlers gave him trouble. **Sergey Karamchakov** of Russia was unorthodox and had long arms. He was tough for Timmy."

"Tim preached being prepared, covering all your bases," Eiter continued. "Having a good mindset. I was like his protégé. I helped him get ready to compete and we made each other better. He just put his nose down, pushed through everything and grinded it out. He led by example. You couldn't ask for a better person in that respect. The worst thing he ever did was ride a motorcycle. He is such a good guy. His high school wrestlers love him."

At the 1992 Olympic Trials

The 1992 Olympic Trials were held at the A. J. Palumbo Center on the campus of Duquesne University in Pittsburgh. Vanni faced his protégé Eiter and intense pressure to make his second Olympic team.

"I won the first match 3-2 and I thought 'that's not supposed to happen.' He was my coach," said Eiter.

"I had been wrestling for years, but I was totally frozen without the ability to move. That was serious pressure," said Vanni. "Rob was a great training partner, an outstanding individual and a great friend. He made me a better wrestler. He's the one who helped me every step of the way in my career."

Vanni had only lost to one other American since his 1986 U.S. Nationals loss to **Rich Salamone** and that was **Cory Baze** during the 1990 World Team Trials 20 days after knee surgery.

"Following that first match everyone came up to me trying to find out what went wrong or with an answer to solve the unknown problem. I knew the problem. I was scared to death I would lose," said Vanni. "Hearing coaches **Tadaaki Hatta**, **Joe Seay** and **Bobby Douglas** and teammates telling me what I should do, I just screamed at them to leave me alone and I would be alright. I had been to the Olympics and having experienced the village life and competition, I understood what it had taken to get there."

Vanni focused on two things following that loss.

"First was the end of my first match in Seoul in 1988 as my hand was raised in victory, that I had accomplished a portion of my goal of making it to the Olympic Games saying to myself, 'If I never get another chance to do this again it has been awesome'. My second thought was how I experienced this situation during the 1988 Olympic Trials down in Pensacola when my good friend and roommate, Joe Gonzales, lost his first match to **Kenny Chertow**. Many coaches, friends and family came by the room telling Joe 'its ok you'll get it back', or fix this and that. Nerves and the pressure of being so close to your dreams and goals can make you lose your focus and totally drain the life out of you. I was there with my loss to Rob. I do not mean to take anything away from Rob or Kenny. They did rise to the occasion and executed a good game plan."

In their second match, Vanni shook off the nerves and rolled to a 13-4 decision over Eiter. In the rubber match, the two friends and training partners battled closely, with Vanni registering a narrow 3-1 win to earn a spot on his second U.S. Olympic Team.

Wanting to compete at least once prior to the Olympics, Vanni powered his way into the finals of the Canada Cup Championships in Toronto to face old rival **Aldo Martinez** of Cuba. With Vanni leading, Martinez countered a solid single leg with a cutback, sweeping Vanni's legs. Unfortunately, Vanni suffered a ligament tear in his left ankle and was forced to default the match – the only time he defaulted in his career.

"It was not the default or loss that concerned me, but the fast approaching Olympic Games I worried about," said Vanni. "I basically had five weeks to be ready to win Olympic gold."

Rob Eiter was there to help Vanni recover.

"He was a tremendous help. We would only do drill matches for 15-20 minutes at a time, keeping my ankle stable. I was forced to use an old lace up brace over the ankle tape," said Vanni. "It wasn't until a week before our departure to Barcelona that I was asked to test my ankle. Coach **Bobby Douglas** wanted to see me wrestle one live match. I told him I didn't think my ankle was ready yet but at his insistence I would give it a go. I tweaked it. Not bad, but it was a setback. As the final week closed and we made our way to Barcelona, Olympic Village and Opening Ceremonies, I would continue vigilant therapy sessions. I would even ice it on the plane. Ready or not I was coming for gold."

At the 1992 Olympic Games: Barcelona, Spain

U.S. wrestlers were housed in a second-floor, five-room apartment with two assigned to each room. Vanni's roommate was the most decorated U.S. wrestler in history, **Bruce Baumgartner**. The pair made quite a sight together, with the massive Baumgartner (275 pounds) towering over the diminutive Vanni. Baumgartner had earned the honor of being the U.S. flag bearer for the opening ceremonies. In the apartment below were professional U.S. tennis players including **Pete Sampras**, **Michael Chang** and **Jim Courier**. The pros didn't stay long in the apartment house, moving into the plush Hilton Hotel the next day.

U.S. heavyweight Bruce Baumgartner (275) and lightweight Tim Vanni (105.5) at the 1992 Olympic opening ceremonies. (Courtesy Tim Vanni)

"At the opening ceremonies, it seemed as though every participant began searching out **Magic Johnson** and other Dream Team members," Vanni recalls. "As teams mingled on the field, I happened to run into **Karl Malone** and **John Stockton** of the Utah Jazz. I spent 45 minutes looking straight up at Malone talking to him about a mutual friend, **Les Roh**, we had in Idaho Falls. My neck was sore the next day."

Vanni says the anticipation of waiting to compete is the toughest part of the Games. "We all had gold on our minds 24/7. We were ready to get going," he said.

He stormed out of the gate with a 16-0 domination of his first-round opponent and a narrow 3-2 win in the second round. In his third match, Vanni trailed Iran's **Nader Rahmati**, 7-5, with just eight seconds left. He shot a single leg and when Rahmati locked him around his waist, Vanni grabbed his wrist and rolled the Iranian to his back and scrambled for a winning gut wrench turn to win at the buzzer, 9-7.

In the next round, Vanni registered a 5-0 shutout to set up a rematch with Romanian nemesis **Romica Rasovan** who had broken Vanni's nose with a head butt in the 1987 World Championships. The two gladiators went back and forth, exchanging leads. As Vanni was trying to turn a double leg into a backward throw, he reinjured his ankle. Vanni lost a barn-burner, 11-9, and was incensed that Rasovan had hit him in the face with several uppercuts during the match.

"I was pissed as I came off the mat and I was heading over to punch my cheating opponent," Vanni said. "**Joe Seay** and **Tadaaki Hatta** restrained me long enough to cool me down saying I would be kicked out of the Games. Later the Romanian lost and all I had to do to get in the gold medal match was to beat **Kim Jona-shin** of South Korea."

In the U.S. locker room, Vanni asked **Linda Baumgartner** (Bruce's wife) to re-tape his ankle as tight as possible so he did not have to wear a brace. The weak ankle limited his offense and he lost a 5-2 decision.

"I was completely distraught and had no interest in wrestling for fifth place. I was done. I left the arena and went down to a square where there were tables and chairs with lots of big televisions," he said. "I sat by myself for two to three hours asking myself why I should continue. I concluded that the only saving grace would be to go out with a win to complete my Olympic experience. In the Seoul Olympics I lost my last match finishing with a 5-2 record and fourth place finish. I rationalized that even though I could not medal I could go out with a victory matching my 5-2 finish four years before."

Vanni's match for fifth place was against **Reiner Heugabel** from West Germany.

"Reiner was truly the dirtiest opponent I ever faced in all my years of wrestling," said Vanni. "He would always lead out with multiple head butts. He also put this Burma Shave stuff in his hair so it would burn your eyes in a tie-up. When he wasn't head butting or keeping his head ground into your face, he would be gouging at your eyes and clawing your face."

Vanni likened the bout to a six-minute cat fight. "This was not a shoving match, but more like a street fight brawl. It was the kind of match where people see your battle scars and say 'You won? I'd hate to see the other guy.' I would love to see this match on video. I know the fans were very entertained and got their moneys' worth. I got a 1-0 win and my 5-2 finish."

On International Wrestling

"It was a phenomenal experience, traveling the world to do what I loved most – wrestle," said Vanni. "In 1989 I placed third at Tbilisi even though I tore up my knee in a car accident before the event. But I wasn't going to miss that trip. **Joe Gonzales** went with me and it was a crazy trip with plane delays and bomb scares. We had to stay over in Paris and got to the tournament a day late. I was a kilo over weight, but I lost it pretty easily. Then the Russians beat the hell out of us. Gonzo was the only one to win in the first dual.

"There were a lot of great people on those trips in the eighties, like **Ed** and **Lou Banach, Dave** and **Mark Schultz, Bruce Baumgartner,** the Scherr brothers and **Lee Kemp**. International matches were six minutes and we worked hard on conditioning. We outperformed the competition with endurance. Freestyle wrestling was evolving in the U.S. with the influence of **Dave Schultz** and the Oklahoma Underdogs wrestling team. Dave was a freestyle guru. Mark was, too. Adapting to the rules became our specialty. We owe a large debt to Dave because he was so innovative."

What It Takes to be a Champion

"You can't just tell a kid what it takes to be a champion. Most of the things come through experience. You are not going to be a good weight cutter until someone teaches you how," said Vanni. "To compete at the highest level took perseverance. Perseverance drove me to be my best. Fear of losing drives you somewhat, but you can't get caught up in thinking about the outcome. You have to think about performing. You did the drills, you're well trained. So use what you've learned."

Vanni sees the importance in never giving up. His message to his wrestlers each year: "Wrestle hard. Execute your techniques and when you walk off the mat, it's important that you know you gave it your best shot. You can't think about winning or losing – only about performing your best. It's hard to focus if you're thinking about winning. You must stay focused every second on the mat and execute throughout the match. Then you'll know the outcome when it's over. You can't get lost in other things. You need to stay focused in the match. Do not care about the outcome. You need to execute better than your opponent, stay focused and you need to think 'I'm not going to let you score.' If your opponent can't score, you can't lose."

Vanni's wrestling mantra has always been deny, deny, deny … something he learned from his international coach, **Tadaaki Hatta**. "Don't let anyone take you down," he said. "In my matches, I always told myself 'I'm down by one, I'm down by one.' It helped me to stay aggressive and, as a lightweight, I had to be. I learned from Joe Gonzales how to keep people off balance, create an opening and score. Joe's takedown record is phenomenal.

"Another thing that helps champions stay on top is to say to yourself 'I am the best'. I used to say it to myself a thousand times a day. I use that phrase to help kids start believing in themselves. You can ask any kid who has wrestled for me 'Who is the best?' A rookie will reply 'you are coach.' The rest know the answer is 'I'm the best'.

The dictionary uses the following sentence for the word perseverance: "In a competitive environment, perseverance is an invaluable asset." Tim Vanni's career more than proves that.

<u>Olympics</u>
1984 – Alternate; 1988 – 4th; 1992 – 5th; 1996 – Alternate

1988 Olympics, Seoul, South Korea, 48kg, Tim Vanni (USA)
Round 1: Beat **Alfredo Marcuno** (Spain), 16-0
Round 2: Lost by Fall to **Takashi Kobayashi** (Japan), 1:48
Round 3: Beat **Mohamed El-Messouti** (Syria), 13-1
Round 4: Won by Fall over **Nasser Zeinalnia** (Iran), 4:25
Round 5: Beat **Ilyas Sukriioglu** (Turkey), 5-3
Round 6: Bye
Medal Round: Lost to **Sergey Karamchakov** (Russia), 3-1

1992 Olympics, Barcelona, Spain, 48kg, Tim Vanni (USA)
Round 1: Beat **Vincent Pangelinan** (Guam), 16-0
Round 2: Beat **Chen Zhengbin** (China), 3-2
Round 3: Beat **Nader Rahmati**, (Iran), 9-7
Round 4: Beat **Tom Petryshen** (Canada), 5-0
Round 5: Lost to **Romica Rasovan** (Romania), 10-7
Round 6: Lost to **Kim Jona-shin** (Korea), 5-2
Round 7: Beat **Reiner Heugabel** (Germany), 1-0

World Games
1982 – 6th; 1985 – 10th; 1986 – 6th; 1987 – 5th; 1989 – 5th; 1991 – 11th

World Cup
1986 – 3rd; 1988 – 3rd; 1989 – 4th; 1990 – 2nd; 1995 – 5th

Pan American Games
1987 – 2nd; 1992 – 2nd; 1995 – 3rd

Goodwill Games
1994 – DNP

U.S. Freestyle Championships
1981 – 2nd; 1982 – 4th; 1983 – 2nd; 1984 – 4th; **1985 – 1st**; 1986 – 2nd; **1988 – 1st**; **1989 – 1st**; **1991 – 1st**; 1993 – 2nd; **1994 – 1st**; 1995 – 2nd; 1996 – 2nd

CHAPTER 21

Most Prolific Wrestlers in U.S. History

Additional evidence that the 1980s produced the greatest amateur wrestlers in history can be found in the list of the most prolific U.S. wrestlers in history, all of whom were collegiate wrestlers in The Golden Era of Amateur Wrestling: **Bruce Baumgartner,** Indiana State; **Dave Schultz,** Oklahoma State/Oklahoma; **Melvin Douglas,** Oklahoma; **Andre Metzger,** Oklahoma; **and Kenny Monday,** Oklahoma State.

1. **Bruce Baumgartner (17 years: 1980-1996; 51 top-three placements)**
   NCAA: 1980 (2nd), 1981 (2nd), **1982 (1st)**
   Olympics: 1980 (Alternate), **1984 (1st)**, 1988 (2nd), **1992 (1st)**, 1996 (3rd)
   World Games: 1982 (7th), 1983 (3rd), 1985 (3rd), **1986 (1st)**, 1987 (3rd), 1989 (2nd), 1990 (2nd), 1991 (7th), **1993 (1st)**, 1994 (2nd), **1995 (1st)**
   World Cup: 1983 (2nd), **1984 (1st)**, **1985 (1st)**, **1986 (1st)**, 1988 (2nd), **1989 (1st)**, **1990 (1st)**, **1991 (1st)**, 1993 (2nd), **1994 (1st)**, 1995 (2nd)
   Pan American Games: 1983 (2nd), **1987 (1st)**, **1991 (1st)**, **1995 (1st)**

Bruce Baumgartner (Courtesy Indiana State University)

U.S. Freestyle Championships: 1980 (1st), 1981 (1st), 1982 (1st), 1983 (1st), 1984 (1st), 1985 (1st), 1986 (1st), 1987 (1st), 1988 (1st), 1989 (1st), 1990 (1st), 1991 (1st), 1992 (1st), 1993 (1st), 1994 (1st), 1995 (1st), 1996 (1st)

Goodwill Games: 1986 (1st), 1990 (2nd), 1994 (3rd)

Without question, Baumgartner is the most decorated wrestler in history. Period. His longevity and success are unmatched in the annals of amateur wrestling. He is the only U.S. wrestler to medal in four Olympics (1984, 1988, 1992 and 1996). He holds the world record for the most World Games and Olympic medals (13) and shares the U.S. record for most Olympic gold medals in wrestling with **John Smith** (2). He is one of just eight U.S.

athletes to medal in four Olympiads. From 1981 to 1997 he never lost a match to a U.S. wrestler and won **17 consecutive** U.S. Freestyle titles. Baumgartner's two most incredible seasons were 1984 when he won the Olympics, World Cup, Tbilisi, AAU, Midlands and U.S. Freestyle titles and 1986 when he won World Games, Goodwill Games, World Cup, Sports Festival, Midlands and U.S. Freestyle championships. In the NCAA, Olympics, World Games, World Cup, Pan American Games, U.S. Freestyle Championships and Goodwill Games, he placed in the top three in 51 of 53 events. Astonishing!

Baumgartner won the 1995 **James E. Sullivan** Award as the top amateur athlete in the U.S. (only the second wrestler to do so at the time) and was inducted into the National Wrestling Hall of Fame as a Distinguished Member in 2002.

2. **Dave Schultz (19 years: 1977-1995; 30 top-three placements)**
   NCAA: 1978 (3rd), 1981 (2nd), **1982 (1st)**
   Olympics: 1984 (1st)
   World Games: 1982 (3rd), **1983 (1st)**, 1985 (2nd), 1986 (3rd), 1987 (2nd), 1993 (2nd), 1994 (7th), 1995 (5th)
   World Cup: 1978 (2nd), **1980 (1st)**, 1981 (2nd), **1982 (1st)**, 1983 (2nd), **1985 (1st), 1994 (1st), 1995 (1st)**
   Pan American Games: 1987 (1st)
   U.S. Freestyle Championships: 1977 (1st, Greco-Roman), **1983 (1st), 1984 (1st), 1986 (1st), 1987 (1st), 1988 (1st), 1993 (1st), 1994 (1st), 1995 (1st)**
   Goodwill Games: 1986 (1st), 1994 (2nd)

Dave Schultz (Courtesy University of Oklahoma)

One of wrestling's greatest technicians and ambassadors, Schultz excelled on every level winning a high school state championship (1978), NCAA championship (1982), World Games gold medal (1983) and Olympic gold medal (1984). Beginning with a Greco-Roman championship in the U.S. Open in 1977, Schultz wrestled and promoted amateur wrestling around the world for nearly 20 years. He was a seven-time U.S. Freestyle champion, five-time World Cup champion and won six medals in the World Games. Combining Greco-Roman, folkstyle and freestyle techniques into his repertoire, Schultz was the ultimate technician and teacher, sharing his knowledge with teammates and competitors throughout his career. His focus was always on making the sport of wrestling better.

3. Melvin Douglas (17 years: 1985-2000; 2004; 19 top-three placements)

Melvin Douglas, Oklahoma vs. Mike Sheets, Oklahoma State in 1984. (Courtesy Oklahoma State University)

NCAA: 1985 (1ˢᵗ), 1986 (1ˢᵗ)
Olympics: 1996 (7ᵗʰ), 2000 (18ᵗʰ)
World Games: 1989 (2ⁿᵈ), **1993 (1ˢᵗ)**, 1994 (3ʳᵈ), 1995 (3ʳᵈ), 1997 (9ᵗʰ), 1998 (5ᵗʰ)
World Cup: 1994 (1ˢᵗ)
Pan American Games: 1995 (1ˢᵗ)
U.S. Freestyle Championships: 1986 (6ᵗʰ), 1987 (2ⁿᵈ), **1988 (1ˢᵗ)**, 1991 (2ⁿᵈ), 1992 (2ⁿᵈ), **1993 (1ˢᵗ), 1994 (1ˢᵗ), 1995 (1ˢᵗ), 1996 (1ˢᵗ), 1997 (1ˢᵗ), 1998 (1ˢᵗ)**
Goodwill Games: 1994 (2ⁿᵈ)

A two-time NCAA champion at 177 for the Oklahoma Sooners, Douglas was the World freestyle champion in 1993, and won a silver medal in 1989 and a bronze in 1995. He was a two-time Olympian, placing seventh in 1996 and 18ᵗʰ in 2000. After a short retirement, he attempted a comeback in the 2000 Olympic Trials, but fell short. The Douglas resume shows seven U.S. Freestyle championships – including six in a row from 1993 to 1998 – a World Cup gold medal (1994), a Pan Am Games championship (1995), a silver medal in the 1994 Goodwill Games and two U.S. Open Grand Prix championships (1992-93). He also won the prestigious Tbilisi tournament in Russia in 1989.

4. Andre Metzger (15 years: 1979-1992; 2012; 19 top-three placements)

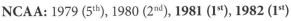

Andre Metzger (Courtesy University of Oklahoma)

NCAA: 1979 (5ᵗʰ), 1980 (2ⁿᵈ), **1981 (1ˢᵗ), 1982 (1ˢᵗ)**
Olympics: None
World Games: 1979 (3ʳᵈ), 1982 (4ᵗʰ), 1986 (2ⁿᵈ), 1987 (3ʳᵈ)
World Cup: 1980 (2ⁿᵈ), 1981 (3ʳᵈ), 1986 (2ⁿᵈ), 1988 (2ⁿᵈ)
Pan American Games: 1979 (1ˢᵗ), 1987 (1ˢᵗ)
U.S. Freestyle Championships: 1979 (1ˢᵗ), 1980 (2ⁿᵈ), **1982 (1ˢᵗ), 1984 (1ˢᵗ), 1986 (1ˢᵗ), 1987 (1ˢᵗ)**
Goodwill Games: 1986 (2ⁿᵈ)

One of the fiercest competitors and greatest technicians in amateur wrestling history, Andre Metzger is credited by many of his peers with melding a variety of disciplines to create the exciting high-scoring matches of the 1980s. A judo, freestyle, folkstyle and Greco-Roman champion during his career, Metzger was a three-time junior national freestyle champion and two-time junior national Greco-Roman champion before launching his collegiate career at Oklahoma. In 2012, at the age of 52 after a 20-year absence from the world stage, he made a strong run at earning a spot the U.S Olympic Team but fell short in his quest.

5. **Kenny Monday (14 years: 1981-1992; 1995-1996; 14 top-three placements)**
NCAA: 1982 (2nd), 1983 (2nd), **1984 (1st)**
Olympics: 1988 (1st), 1992 (2nd), 1996 (6th)
World Games: 1989 (1st), 1991 (2nd)
World Cup: 1988 (2nd)
Pan American Games: 1991 (1st)
U.S. Freestyle Championships: 1985 (1st), 1988 (1st), 1991 (1st), 1995 (3rd), **1996 (1st)**
Goodwill Games: 1990 (2nd)

Only the second U.S. wrestler to compete in three Olympiads, Monday was a four time U.S. Freestyle champion, an NCAA champion (1984), an Olympic gold medalist (1988) and silver medalist (1992), a World champion (1989) and a Pan Am Games champion (1991). He also won the rugged Tbilisi tournament and was named Outstanding Wrestler, and earned silver medals in the World Games, World Cup and Goodwill Games. A four-time undefeated (140-0-1) high school state champion at Tulsa Washington (1977-80), Monday won a U.S. Junior National championship in 1977. At the 1992 Olympic Games, Monday shut out four straight opponents and only gave up a single point in the gold-medal match, losing 1-0. Following a two-year retirement, he came back in 1995, and in 1996 he won a U.S. Freestyle title and made the Olympic team. In the Atlanta games, Monday placed sixth.

Kenny Monday (Courtesy Oklahoma State University)

The list of the 26 most prolific NCAA wrestlers, based on career wins, contains 17 men who wrestled in the 1980s including the winningest collegiate wrestler of all time, **John Fisher** of Michigan. Fisher racked up 183 wins, eight more than fellow Wolverine **Otto Olson** (175).

Most Prolific NCAA Wrestlers, Career Wins

Rank	Wins	Wrestler	Weight	School	Years
1.	183	John Fisher	134	Michigan	1984-1989
2.	175	Otto Olson	174	Michigan	1996-2002
3.	174	Wade Hughes	126	George Washington	1982-85
4.	169	Howard Harris	190-HWT	Oregon State	1977-80
5.	168	Larry Bielenberg	HWT	Oregon State	1974-77
6.	167	Pat Santoro	142	Pittsburgh	1986-89
7.	166	Joe McFarland	118-126	Michigan	1980-85
8.	164	Jack Cuvo	118	E. Stroudsburg	1986-89
9.	162	Barry Davis	118-126	Iowa	1981-83, 1985
T10.	160	Jeff Catrabone	158-167	Michigan	1995-98

T10.	160	Michael Swift	142-150	California (PA)	1990-93
T12.	159	Cael Sanderson	184	Iowa State	1999-2002
T12.	159	Ed Giese	118	Minnesota	1982-86
14.	158	Tom Brands	126-134	Iowa	1989-92
15.	156	Jim Jordan	134	Wisconsin	1984-86
T16.	155	Jim Baumgardner	177-190	Oregon State	1981-84
T16.	155	Jim Martin	118-126	Penn State	1986-89
T16.	155	Cole Konrad	HWT	Minnesota	2003-2007
19.	154	John Smith	126-134	Oklahoma State	1984-85, 87-88
T20.	153	Wade Schalles	150-158	Clarion	1970-73
T20.	153	Ben Askren	174	Missouri	2004-2007
21.	151	Ed Potokar	177	Ohio State	1980-83
T22.	150	Dan Chaid	177-190	Oklahoma	1982-86
T22.	150	Matt Demaray	150	Wisconsin	1989-92
T22.	150	Kerry McCoy	190-HWT	Penn State	1993-95, 97
T22	150	Rob Koll	150-158	North Carolina	1985-88

Of note, Michigan placed four wrestlers in the top 10 including Fisher and Olson. The Wolverines' **Joe McFarland** is sixth on the list and **Jeff Catrabone** is tied for ninth. Oregon State had two wrestlers in the top five: **Howard Harris** at No. 4 and **Larry Bielenberg** at No. 5 and Jim **Baumgardner** was tied at No. 14. Wrestlers from the 1980s occupied seven of the top nine spots.

John Fisher, 134 pounds, Michigan (1984-1989)

The winningest wrestler in NCAA history with a 183-21 record, Fisher had the misfortune of wrestling in the same weight class as two of the greatest wrestlers of all time:

John Fisher, Michigan, the winningest wrestler in NCAA history. (Courtesy University of Michigan)

Wisconsin's **Jim Jordan** and Oklahoma State's **John Smith**. In the 1985 NCAA Championships, the eighth-seeded Fisher won his first two matches but ran into top-seeded Jordan in the quarterfinals and fell, 6-1. In the consolations, he won three straight matches before falling in the third-place match to fourth-seeded **Alan Grammer** of SIU-Edwardsville. He finished with a 45-10 record.

After taking a medical redshirt in 1986 after a 9-1 start, Fisher came back with a vengeance in 1987. He again won his first two matches in the NCAA event as the No. 3 seed, but was upset by sixth-seeded **Paul Clark** of Clarion, 4-2. Fisher won three consolation matches before dropping an 11-2 major decision to **Jeff Gibbons** of Iowa State and settling for fourth. He posted a 39-5 mark for the season.

His junior year (1987-88), Fisher placed third in the NCAA's and compiled an impressive 45-3 record overall. With a No. 2 seed, Fisher blew past his first two opponents only to suffer a 14-4 loss to Iowa's seventh-seeded **Joe Melchiore** in the quarterfinals. Once again, Fisher had to battle through the consolations and defeated Edinboro's **Dan Willaman**, 13-7, for third place.

At 41-0 his senior season, Fisher earned the top seed at 134 over Melchiore. After easy wins of 8-0, 16-1 and 16-3, he met Oklahoma's fourth-seeded **T.J. Sewell** in the semifinals. In his closest attempt to reach the finals, he was beaten in overtime, 6-6, 8-1, by Sewell. He faced Melchiore in the third-place bout and was pinned by the Hawkeye. He finished his final season at his best-ever 45-2, the third season he had registered 45 wins, and left with a national record 183 career wins.

Although he never wrestled **John Smith** in the NCAA's (always in opposite brackets), he met the defending Olympic champion and four-time defending World champion in the 1992 Olympic Trials at 136.5 pounds. Smith had not lost a match to an American wrestler in four years and had beaten Fisher 15-0 and 9-0 the last two times they met. In one of the biggest upsets in history, Fisher defeated a rusty Smith 4-2 in the opening bout of their three-match finals. Smith rallied to narrowly win the next two matches, 3-1 and 6-5 to earn the Olympic berth.

CHAPTER 22

Andre Metzger, Technically the Best

If it were possible to earn a doctorate in wrestling, **Andre Metzger** would be Dr. Andre Metzger, PhD. His knowledge of the world's most difficult sport is beyond encyclopedic. After all, he has wrestled and won more matches than anyone in history: more than 2,000 bouts and 1,870 victories, with an estimated winning percentage of .935.

"Beginning in the late 1970s, I wrestled 350 matches a year for five years, then slowed down to about 160 per year after that," said Metzger. "Toward the end of my career I was wrestling 80-90 matches a year."

He added several matches onto the total with a comeback attempt to make the 2012 U.S. Olympic Team and in 2014 trying to make the U.S. World Team. "I may come back in 2016 to try to make the Olympic Team at 74 kilos (163 pounds)," he said. Is he serious? Those who know him, know he is dead serious about wrestling. They also know him as the fiercest competitor they ever met.

"A comeback at age 56 for Metzger? I wouldn't bet against it," said **Gene Mills**, two-time NCAA champion at Syracuse, four-time all-American and winner of every international freestyle event in 1981. "Andre was so intense. He couldn't even play a video game without chewing his tongue off trying to win. He was intense in practice, in his matches and in playing video games. He hated to lose at anything. We'd make fun of him, but we all loved him. He's a great friend. For him to come back in 2012 and 2014 and do what he did was just amazing. He's definitely got a passion for wrestling."

Metzger's passion began in ninth grade with a pin in 27 seconds over his first opponent. He was hooked for life. "Early in my career, I lost a match really bad. My Dad said 'if you had hit your move, you would have won.' I said 'Dad, he beat me 31-1.' But the next time I wrestled that kid, I hit my move and won, 7-6. I was tenacious and I got that from my Dad. He put blindfolds on me and made me wrestle to learn not to look at where I was going to attack."

Following a stellar high school career that included a state championship, Metzger wrestled in the 1979 World Championships in San Diego. All he did was take the bronze medal to become the youngest American to medal in the World Championships in history at the age of 19. (Author's Note: In 2015, **Kyle Snyder**, Ohio State redshirt sophomore, was a few months younger than Metzger when he won a gold medal in the World Championships held in Las Vegas, NV). As the top wrestling recruit in the country in 1979, Metzger narrowed his choices to Iowa, Iowa State, Oklahoma and Oklahoma State – the Big Four.

"He was recruited by everyone," said **Stan Abel**, University of Oklahoma coach. "I was waiting at the Lansing airport for my assistant coach **Jim Humphrey** to arrive from Colorado where he was recruiting. He was running late, so I called Andre to tell him. When Hump arrived, I told him that all the other coaches were there: **Tom Chesbro** of OSU, **Dan Gable** of Iowa and **Harold Nichols** of Iowa State and their assistants. He said "Oh, my God. What are we going to do?" I said, 'we're going to sign Andre. Who would you rather close the deal than us? They've already had their chance to say everything they wanted to.'

"I flew up to Michigan because Andre had said he was signing with Iowa," said Gable. "He was the top recruit in the country. When I arrived, there were a lot of cars in front of his house. I thought 'great, he has family, friends and the media.' I walked in the door and the Iowa State and OSU head coaches and assistant coaches were there. I was by myself. I asked Andre 'what are these guys doing here? I thought you were signing with Iowa.' He said he had narrowed his choice down to these schools."

"I had decided I was going to Iowa," said Metzger. "That was before Stan Abel made his pitch."

Abel said Andre had 32 questions written out for the coaches to answer. "You know, what's the wrestling room like? How many workout partners will he have? What are the academics like? What degrees does the university offer? Things like that," said Abel. "I said, hey I can save all of us here a lot of time. I think all these coaches would admit that you will be a national champion at any school. I will tell you why you are going to the University of Oklahoma: you like me and Hump better than these other coaches. You could have heard a pin drop. Then Chesbro says "I don't know about that!"

So Andre and his father took a short walk. When they came back, Andre said "I'm honored that you're here. Having the top four coaches in the U.S. in the same room at the same time doesn't happen very often. You all are great universities, but I've made my choice. I'm going to Oklahoma."

Chesbro said "Which Oklahoma?" Andre answered "The University of Oklahoma."
Gable said "I knew it."

"I really walked into an Oklahoma tornado," recalls Gable. "I wasn't the best speaker back then and I didn't get Andre. It was an eye-opening experience. I learned a lot from that."

Abel took the scholarship papers out of his coat pocket. "Very good choice my good man. Mr. Metzger I'll need your signature and Andre's, too," Abel said.

Abel then held up the papers. "This is the legal limit of a full scholarship: room, board, books, tuition and fees. If anybody offers you more, Andre, they are dishonest. We want to be the best influence on your life we can."

Gable turned to the others. "Well, I think we're finished here."

Oklahoma's four-time all-American **Roger Frizzell** was instrumental in Metzger's recruitment, but not without a speed bump that almost sent Frizzell to rival Oklahoma State.

Frizzell and Metzger had wrestled against each other in several high school and AAU freestyle events (Metzger winning all) and were teammates on the USA All-Star Team that beat the Pennsylvania All-Stars in the prestigious Dapper Dan Classic, both winning their matches by superior decision. "We talked then about how cool it would be to be on the same team together in college," said Frizzell. "It was the beginning of the two of us wrestling back-to-back on the same team."

"I invited Andre to wrestle in the Oklahoma Open as a high school senior," said Abel. "**Bill Luttrell** at Midwest City High School, Roger's wrestling coach, was upset that I had invited Andre and he didn't think Roger would go to OU because of that."

"In the Oklahoma Open, where we met in the finals my senior year, I felt like I had a good chance against Metzger because we would finally be wrestling collegiate style," said Frizzell. "I led the entire match, but, unfortunately, he pulled off an escape with only seconds left on the clock to put us into overtime, where he won. **Jim Humphrey**, the assistant coach at OU, coached Andre in his corner. For a few weeks afterward, I was so upset about it that I started considering OSU in a very real way."

While wrestling at a high school dual, OSU's **Tom Chesbro** ushered Frizzell into a small room away from the gym floor and put the full-court press on him to come to OSU. "I was impressed with Coach Chesbro. He said a lot of good things that I liked. I was seriously considering going to Stillwater. When he told his father, Charles, of his encounter with Chesbro, his father was incensed. "He talked to you without me there? He's not supposed to do that!" said Charles. Frizzell indicated he was seriously considering OSU.

"You can sign with OSU if you want, but I want you to wait four days when you'll have a clearer mind," said his father. "Then, you're going to tell OSU no thanks and sign with OU!"

The night before signing day, Coach Abel and **Bob Stevenson** (Norman geologist and OU supporter) went to Frizzell's house.

"Roger told me that OSU had made another push at recruiting him, but he said he wanted to be a Sooner. He was an OU fan and his dad was an OU fan," said Abel. "I said 'well, we are all on the same page. I want you as a wrestler and for your leadership skills. You will help OU wrestling in more ways than on the mat.'"

Abel then asked Roger something most coaches wouldn't ask. "We are hot and heavy after **Andre Metzger**. I know you wrestled each other in the Oklahoma Open. But one of you can wrestle at 142 and the other at 150 and be teammates and help each other become national champions. Would you mind calling Metzger and let him know you are coming to OU? Roger said 'I'd love to have Andre as a teammate.' He went to his phone and called him. Roger said 'I just told Coach Abel I would love to have you as a teammate. We'd be great workout partners.'"

"**Roger Frizzell** called me and said he was going to OU and he hoped I would go to school there," remembers Metzger. "He never beat me. He was close a few times. We wrestled in the Junior Olympics. I was interviewed the night before the Junior Olympics and the article came out the next day. I said that Roger wasn't tough enough to beat me. He was a mild-mannered guy who actually could beat the hell out of you, but the article made him mad. When we went out of bounds and the ref wasn't looking, he threw an elbow up between my legs and I doubled over and went into a cold sweat from the pain. So much for mild-mannered Roger."

Metzger says Frizzell was very much a worthy opponent and a great teammate.

"My freestyle was better than his, but he was better with collegiate style," said Metzger. "Able was pushing us to learn more wrestling on the mat and Roger was unbelievable on top. He had 'thunder thighs' and would catch arms with his legs. He just bundled people up. He had some innovative moves. His spiral ride was one of the best. He came close to making international teams, but he didn't wrestle as much freestyle as some of us did."

"Andre had a unique style of wrestling that I had never seen before with an unusual technique mix that I just didn't know how to counter," said Frizzell. "In fact, I still consider Andre to be one the very best freestyle wrestlers of all-time. He literally changed the sport and made it exciting to watch, much like Randy Lewis from Iowa."

At Oklahoma (1979-82), Metzger was a four-time all-American and two-time NCAA champ at 142 pounds. At the 1979 NCAA Championships, Metzger roared into the semifinals with three lopsided wins (WBF 7:11, 16-3 and 17-4) before falling to Iowa's **Scott Trizzino**, 10-6, in the semifinals. In the consolations he was defeated 5-1 by Oklahoma State's **Lee Roy Smith**, whom had beaten Metzger 9-7 in the Big 8 Tournament finals, and finished fifth.

In 1980, Metzger again fell to Smith in the Big 8 finals (10-2), but took a number two seed into the NCAA event. He again blew past his first three opponents (17-5, 17-8 and WBF 5:20) before knocking off third-seeded **Bill Cripps** of Arizona State 11-7 in the semifinals to set up a rematch with Smith. Metzger stayed close to the stellar Cowboy senior but was edged 10-7 and had to settle for second.

That same year, Metzger made a serious bid for a spot on the U.S. Olympic Team. At the Final Olympic Team Trials in Madison, WI in May, he was on his way to earning a ticket into the final Olympic camp at Brockport, NY in June. Leading in a late-round match against 1977 NCAA champion **Steve Barrett** of Oklahoma State, Metzger suffered an ankle fracture to end any Olympic hopes that year.

Andre Metzger (right) battles with Big 8 rival Dave Brown of Iowa State. (Courtesy National Wrestling Hall of Fame)

Seeded second in the 1981 NCAA Championships after edging Iowa State's **Dave Brown** in the Big 8 finals (2-2, 1-1 criteria), Metzger scored a fall in 3:29 and reeled off 8-2 and 9-4 wins to reach the semifinals. He pinned Michigan State's **Shawn White** in 1:29 to move into the finals, where he edged Iowa's very tough **Lennie Zalesky**, 10-6, to claim his first NCAA crown.

In his senior season, Metzger took his third straight number two seed into the 1982 NCAA Championships after a stunning 15-11 loss to Nebraska's **Johnnie Selmon** in the Big 8 finals.

"Selmon could throw you into the nickel seats," said Abel. "I told Andre 'do not hook up with this guy.' He said 'why?' I said he's a throwing machine. Metzger said 'I'm one of the best throwers in the country.' I said but that's all he can do. Stay out of the over-and-under. Hit him with your inside trips. He looked at me like 'you don't respect my throws.' I said, why wrestle to that guy's strength?"

Metzger tripped Selmon for a takedown and an early lead. But when they were back on their feet, Metzger hooked up and Selmon threw him for five. "Then he throws him two more times for five and beats Metzger, 15-11," said Abel.

In the NCAA's, Selmon won his first three matches by scores of 18-5, 21-8 and 23-5, using his patented throw. Abel took Metzger aside before his semifinal match with Selmon.

Metzger sits out in an attempt to escape Wisconsin's Mark Schmitz. (Courtesy National Wrestling Hall of Fame)

"This guy has a helluva throw. Wrestle him any way you want," said Abel. "But if I was wrestling, I'd stay out of that area. You're smarter than I am, so wrestle however you want. Every time Selmon tried to hook up, Andre pummeled out."

Mac Bentley, sportswriter for *The Daily Oklahoman*, wrote about the Metzger-Selmon match on March 13, 1982:

*Metzger revenged his loss to Nebraska's Johnnie Selmon with a 3-1 victory at 142 and Dave Schultz walloped **Brad Bitterman** of New Mexico, 15-3, in the Sooners' other two victories. Selmon, who defeated Metzger 15-11 in the Big Eight finals, wasn't ready to quit at the end of the match, which had little of the scoring but just as much action as the earlier meeting.*

"The refs were letting him hang onto me," Selmon said later. "I tried to change up my shots, but he was holding on. The refs should have called him for stalling. He was digging into my sides on my shots, digging in with his nails. It's really frustrating and I lost my temper when they didn't call anything."

Selmon kept going when the whistle blew, and Metzger put an end to it with a head jerk that put Selmon on the mat. Selmon came up ready to fight, but was held off by the referee.

*He was still eager to have words with Metzger when they met as the Sooner went to sign the scorecard, and was even more eager when Metzger made a comment and flashed a taunting smile his way. It took Nebraska heavyweight **Gary Albright** to hold him back that time.*

The Metzger Persona

In the '80s, Assistant Coach **Jim Humphrey** (four-time World Team member and World runner-up in 1977) helped the Oklahoma wrestlers immensely with their freestyle technique.

"He is a good friend and I have so much respect for Hump and for (head coach) **Stan Abel**," said Metzger. "Stan was a stablizing force. We had the greatest team ever assembled that never won the nationals. **Roger Frizzell** was the best wrestler to never win a national title. He would have won but he had **Nate Carr** and **Kenny Monday** at his weight. We were so good with the front headlock that the fans would start to count down ten … nine … eight while the guys were being choked out."

"We wrestled Missouri one year and they had an article in the school paper with the title '**Andre Metzger**: Man without a Friend.' I really had to stay focused and not let that bother me," said Metzger. "I had great friends on the team. When **Richard Evans** won his match that night, he climbed up on a table and shouted 'Missouri: A team without a point!' It felt good that the team fought for me.

Metzger was more than willing to share his techniques with his OU teammates. "I helped Frizzell and **Dave** and **Mark Schultz** with technique," said Metzger. "Dave said to me 'I can't believe you're helping everyone.' I told Dave we were teammates. I knew I might wrestle him sometime, but I wanted our team to be the best it could be.

"Dave and Mark both had problems with Abel. One year, we were wrestling OSU and Dave was angry with Stan and wrestled **Mike Sheets** really close instead of trying to score. He came off the mat and said 'I hope OSU beats us.' I told him right there that he couldn't do that to the team. He played a lot of games like that. But, we all did. We'd see who could get the most takedowns in a period or who could choke a guy out. We got too complacent sometimes."

In his senior season, Metzger wanted to wrestle at 150 so he could take on **Nate Carr** of Iowa State and **Kenny Monday** of Oklahoma State. "But Coach Abel gave me an ultimatum: 'you're going down to 142 or you're off the team. Don't fight it.'"

Metzger's work ethic was Gable-esque. "I worked a lot harder than anyone. I ran 14 miles a day while they were running the three or four miles we did in practice. I worked out three times a day. My conditioning was so good, I could hit the afterburners so many times during my matches. In the wrestling room, I took on a different guy every 15 minutes. They put five guys on me. One-on-one, no one could stay with me because of my conditioning."

The Oklahoma vs. Oklahoma State Bedlam Series matches were electric and legendary, whether in Gallagher Hall in Stillwater or Lloyd Noble Center on the OU campus. Home-team announcers whipped the already rabid fans into a frenzy with lengthy and loud introductions. The crowd noise reached dangerously high decibel levels.

"OSU was always a battle," said Metzger. "I've never been beaten in Gallagher Hall. In the 1984 Olympic Regional Trials I won there. And I beat **Lee Roy Smith** there. He said it was the only time he lost in their house."

Metzger's quest for an Olympic gold once again got sidetracked in 1984 when he got shellfish poisoning and couldn't compete in the final trails at Iowa City.

"I had a low grade fever, was sweating profusely and vomiting and had diarrhea for six months," recalls Metzger. "They didn't diagnose it properly and I almost died. I still have effects from that to this day."

Nine Hands Principle

Metzger gives credit to Coach Abel for teaching him about not dissipating the body. "People don't respect their body enough. All of us had to realize that with wrestling, it isn't about making a major leap, it's about progress an inch at a time. I brought a lot of Judo and Greco-Roman moves into the wrestling room. Throws from Judo. Inside trips from Greco. But I had to drill like crazy and work on footwork. I used my feet like hands. I would catch things with my feet, use my knees and elbows. I still teach that. I invented the Metzger Move in high school. I started with a high crotch, but was hitting it wrong. I started to modify it and came up with my Nine Hands Principle."

Metzger then counts one through nine as he touches his head, both feet, both knees, both elbows, and claps his hands. "Nine hands. Then I cut the body in half and cover. You have to do it properly. Wrestling is a chess game at four levels: the head, the upper body and arms, the body, and the legs. You think with your body and you move with your mind. That is my belief.

"Those nine 'hands' have to be in position constantly without having to think about where they are," he continued. "That's why it's so vital to drill. Repetition is your basis of understanding where all your 'hands' are. The nine 'hands' can really, really make a difference in a wrestler's improvement when they understand. You can have a lot of heart, but not understand your positioning and you can get whipped. But if you understand where the nine 'hands' are, you will get better and better. In my Mertz Series, I use all nine hands in so many different ways."

While wrestling styles obviously differed between collegiate and freestyle, styles also differed between schools in the 1980s. Iowa was the original ground and pound. They just pounded their opponents and kept coming. Iowa State and Oklahoma State focused on a well-rounded approach with emphasis on riding. Oklahoma was different.

"At OU, we would segregate the body with technique. We would rip you apart in any area. Head, upper body, legs. We learned to attack intelligently," said Metzger. "I took anatomy. I studied the body and its pressure points, the joints. I studied film constantly. When I was younger, my Dad and I would break down film, 8 millimeter and 16 millimeter. We would figure out how to beat an opponent. I loved going into a match where I knew my opponent, but they didn't know me.

"I was studying film one day when Dave and Mark Schultz walked in and asked what I was doing. I said I was watching film. They asked me what movie I was watching. After that, they studied film, too. When I went to coach at Foxcatcher, the first thing I requested was film of the most recent World Championships and I studied them."

Top Wrestlers

When he looks back at his long career, several wrestlers stand out as his toughest opponents: two-time national champion **Dan Hicks** of Oregon State; Iowa's incomparable **Randy Lewis**; four-time all-American, national champion and Olympic silver medalist **Andy Rein**; Oklahoma State's national champion **Lee Roy Smith**, who beat Metzger in the 1980 NCAA finals; Iowa's three-time all-American **Lennie Zalesky**, who met Metzger in the NCAA finals twice; and **Lee Kemp**, three-time NCAA champ, three-time World champion and 1980 U.S. Olympic Team member.

"I wasn't scared of anyone. I wrestled **Dan Gable** a couple of times. The first time, he faked a headlock and took me down. But the next time, I took him down several times," said Metzger. "Coach **Stan Abel** wanted to wrestle me when I was at OU and said 'go ahead, give me what you've got.' Unfortunately, I hurt him. I didn't mean to. I hurt his neck with a front headlock and inside trip. It jammed his head down to his chest. I felt so bad. He was out cold for a long time."

Metzger's worthiest foe was Russian **Arsen Fadzaev**, two-time Olympic gold medalist and six-time World champion.

"I never beat him. He's the only wrestler to beat me that I didn't avenge the defeat," said Metzger.

Metzger was runner-up to Fadzaev in the 1986 Goodwill Games, World Championships and World Cup. He was third to Fadzaev in the 1987 World Cup and was set to meet his nemesis in the 1987 World Championships in Clermont-Ferrand, France.

"The coaches wanted me to do a media interview the day of my match with Fadzaev," he said. "The Russians wanted to interview me. I didn't want to do it, but the coaches insisted. So a translator and I were picked up in a taxi at 8:30 in the morning. We were driving around and the driver acted like he was lost and the interpreter kept saying she did not know why the driver was confused on where to go. I didn't get back until 5:45 p.m., just 15 minutes before the weigh-in. At the weigh-in, the Russian coach tried to put his toe on the scale so I wouldn't make weight. When the match finally started, I just didn't have any energy, I was so hyped up about what they were trying to do to me to make me lose focus. Whenever we wrestled the Russians, they would rent the room above us in the hotel and all night long we'd hear the sound of a ball on the floor above."

Metzger taps the table in a very specific pattern he remembers to this day. Bump … bump. Bump, bump, bump. "All night long," he said.

"I always believed there was nobody who could beat me. I hated to lose. It was part of my nature," he said. "I had a positive attitude. I had to be confident. I knew I was always prepared. When you prepare and plan, you expect something good to happen."

Good things have happened to Metzger, the winningest wrestler of all time. But there have been bad things, too: broken noses, wrists and ankles, severe knee injuries, back injuries, too many dislocated fingers to count. And the insanity of the Foxcatcher situation that haunts him to this day.

"Every time I tried to tell someone in authority about what was going on at Foxcatcher, and there were a lot of people, they just looked the other way because of the money," said

Metzger. "When they prostituted themselves like that, they didn't feel the pain right away. It came later when they had to deal with the morality.

"Wrestling taught me to have good character. Stand tall no matter what happens. The wrestling life is so structured. You have to adapt under pressure. That happens in life. You have to put emotions behind you and focus on the moment. Stay in the moment. You have people in front of you who motivate you to get better. You have people behind you who are trying to pass you. You can't depend on other people on the mat; you are out there by yourself, all alone. No one can take credit for what you do. I'm excited where the sport has the potential to go. Life isn't easy. Neither is wrestling."

Not even for the winningest amateur wrestler of all time.

CHAPTER 23

The Coaches

The 1980s not only produced the best wrestlers in history, many of those wrestlers went on to become head coaches of high school, college and international teams. By my count (and there could be others. I apologize for anyone I inadvertently left out), 47 wrestlers from the 1980s became head NCAA coaches. Incredibly, 24 were still coaching in 2015.

1980s Wrestlers Who Became Head Coaches (47); 24 still head coaches (as of 2015)
BOLD = member of All-Decade Team (15)
Clar Anderson, Duke (1997-2012)
John Azevedo, Cal Poly (2003-2011)
Bruce Baumgartner, Edinboro (1991-97)
Jim Beichner, Buffalo (1995-2013)
Terry Brands, University of Tennessee-Chattanooga (2002-2005)
Tom Brands, Iowa (2007-present); Virginia Tech (2005-2006)
Mark Cody, Oklahoma (2011-present); American University (2002-2011)
Barry Davis, Wisconsin (1993-present)
Mike DeAnna, Edinboro (1984-90)
Kevin Dresser, Virginia Tech (2006-present)
Rob Eiter, Pennsylvania (2008-2013)
Tom Erikson, Lyon College (2015-present)
Tim Flynn, Edinboro (1997-present)
Jim Gibbons, Iowa State (1985-1992)
Duane Goldman, Indiana (1992-present)
Dave Grant, Northern Illinois (1996-2011)
Joel Greenlee, Ohio (1997-2015)
Jim Heffernan, Illinois (2009-present)
Russ Hellickson, Ohio State (1986-2006); Wisconsin (1982-1985)
Wade Hughes, Howard University (2000-2002)
Kevin Jackson, Iowa State (2009-present)
Zeke Jones, Arizona State (2014-present); University of Pennsylvania (2005-2008)
Rob Koll, Cornell (1995-present)

Glen Lanham, Duke (2012-present)

Steve Martin, Old Dominion (2003-present)

Mark Manning, Nebraska (2000-present); University of Northern Iowa (1997-2000)

Joe McFarland, Michigan (1999-present)

C.D. Mock, North Carolina (2002-2015)

Mike Moyer, George Mason (1985-1995)

Brad Penrith, University of Northern Iowa (2000-2010)

Greg Randall, Boise State (2003-present)

Andy Rein, Wisconsin (1986-1993)

Roger Reina, University of Pennsylvania (1986-2005)

Jesse Reyes, Purdue (1992-2007)

Wes Roper, Missouri (1987-1998)

Joe Russell, George Mason (2011-present)

Tom Ryan, Ohio State (2006-present); Hofstra (1995-2006)

Gil Sanchez, Clemson (1992-1995)

Pat Santoro, Lehigh (2008-present); Maryland (2003-2008)

Mark Schultz, Brigham Young University (1994-2000)

Brian Smith, Missouri (1998-present)

John Smith, Oklahoma State (1991-present)

Lee Roy Smith, Arizona State (1993-2001)

Pat Tocci, Kutztown University (1996-2000)

Jay Weiss, Harvard (1995-present)

Jim Zalesky, Oregon State (2006-present); Iowa (1997-2006)

Lennie Zalesky, California Baptist (2011-present); UC-Davis (2000-2009)

Coaches with Multiple Top 5 Finishes in the 1980s (National Championships in bold)

Dan Gable, Iowa, 9: **1980-86 (1st)**, 1987 (2nd), 1988 (2nd)

Stan Abel, Oklahoma, 8: 1980 (4th), 1981 (2nd), 1982 (3rd), 1983 (4th), 1984 (5th), 1985 (2nd), 1986 (2nd), 1989 (4th)

Tom Chesbro, Oklahoma State, 5: 1980 (2nd), 1981 (4th), 1982 (4th), 1983 (2nd), 1984 (2nd)

Joe Seay, Oklahoma State, 5: 1985 (4th), 1986 (3rd), 1987 (4th), 1988 (4th), **1989 (1st)**

Jim Gibbons, Iowa State, 5: 1985 (3rd), 1986 (4th), **1987 (1st)**, 1988 (3rd), 1989 (3rd)

Dr. Harold Nichols, Iowa State, 4: 1980 (3rd), 1981 (3rd), 1982 (2nd), 1983 (3rd)

Rich Lorenzo, Penn State, 4: 1984 (3rd), 1986 (5th), 1987 (3rd), 1988 (5th)

Bobby Douglas, Arizona State, 3: 1980 (5th), **1988 (1st)**, 1989 (2nd)

Dale Bahr, Michigan, 2: 1985 (5th), 1989 (5th)

Thad Turner, Lehigh, 2: 1981 (5th), 1983 (5th)

COACH PROFILES

John Azevedo, Cal Poly-San Luis Obispo (2003-2011)

John Azevedo served as head coach for eight years at Cal Poly-San Luis Obispo, replacing **Lennis Cowell**. During his tenure, his teams posted a 54-63 dual record. He coached three NCAA runners-up – **Chad Mendes** in 2008, **Chase Pami** in 2010 and **Boris Novachkov** in 2011 – and 10 NCAA all-Americans. Mendes was undefeated and the top seed at 141 in the 2008 NCAA Championships. In the finals, he was decisioned 5-2 by Ohio State's sixth-seeded **J Jaggers**. In 2010, the seventh-seeded Pami reached the finals against Harvard's top-seeded **J.P. O'Connor** and dropped a tough 6-4 decision. Novachkov, the No. 3 seed at 141 and 31-1 on the season, was edged 3-2 by top-seeded **Kellen Russell** of Michigan.

Azevedo served as an assistant coach at Cal Poly for two years prior to becoming head coach. Previously, he held assistant coaching positions at the University of Wisconsin from 1988-1989, University of Notre Dame from 1984-1986, and Cal State-Bakersfield from 1981-1984.

He was head coach at Calvary Chapel High School in Santa Ana, CA, for 12 years, winning seven California State Championships and 10 CIF Championships while posting a 183-18 record in dual meets. He was named National High School Coach of the Year in 1993.

Azevedo was a high school all-American and won two NCAA Division I championships and two NCAA Division II championships while at Cal State-Bakersfield. He was a three-time Division I all-American. In 1980, he went 53-0 with 23 pins and went on to win the U.S. Olympic Trials at 125.5 pounds. He didn't get to fulfill his dream of Olympic gold when the U.S. boycotted the Moscow Games. He was an alternate on the 1984 U.S. Olympic Team, a two-time U.S. Freestyle champion (1977, 1981) and placed fourth in the 1982 World Championships.

He was inducted into the California Wrestling Hall of Fame in 2000.

Clar Anderson, Duke (1997-2012)

In his 15 seasons, Anderson compiled a career record of 101-125-2. He helped lead 14 Blue Devils to the NCAA Championships, including two-time all-American and 2009 NCAA heavyweight runner-up **Konrad Dudziak**. He was named the Atlantic Coast Conference (ACC) Coach of the Year in 2004 after guiding Duke to a third-place finish at the ACC Championships with four All-ACC selections and four NCAA qualifiers.

Anderson's 2008 team registered a 12-9 overall dual record, the most wins by a team in his career. His wrestlers ranked among the nation's top programs in grade point average, including the highest in 2007 and 2008. Ten Duke wrestlers earned NWCA All-Academic honors under his watch. He served as an assistant coach at Oklahoma State for one year, then at North Carolina State from 1991-94.

A 1985 graduate of Oklahoma State, Anderson was a two-time all-American. He won the 134-pound title at the 1983 NCAAs and was fifth in 1984. He had a 73-17-4 record at OSU after transferring from Auburn where he earned all-American honors in 1981 with a sixth-place finish in a weight division (134) that included All-Decade Team members **Jim**

Gibbons, Iowa State (1ˢᵗ), **Darryl Burley**, Lehigh (2ⁿᵈ), **Ricky Dellagatta**, Kentucky (3ʳᵈ) and **Randy Lewis**, Iowa, (7ᵗʰ).

Bruce Baumgartner, Edinboro (1991-1997)

The legendary wrestler joined the coaching staff of **Mike DeAnna** at Edinboro University in 1984 when it was a Division II school. In 1986, the university earned Division I status and became a force at the NCAA tournament with several top-ten finishes. Baumgartner succeeded DeAnna as the head coach and from 1991through 1997 he led Edinboro to a 70-36 record, producing 11 all-Americans. In his final season, 1996-97, the Fighting Scots finished 14-0 in duals, the best in school history, and earned a sixth place finish at the NCAA Division I National Championships. Baumgartner became Interim Director of Athletics at Edinboro in 1997, with the interim tag removed the following year.

As a three-time all-American at Indiana State, Baumgartner won a national title at heavyweight in 1983, and placed second in 1982 and 1981. His international wrestling career is the greatest in history among U.S. wrestlers: four Olympic medals (gold in 1984 and 1992, silver in 1988, and bronze in 1996). He won a total of nine World Games medals (gold in 1986, 1993 and 1995; silver in 1989, 1990 and 1994; and bronze in 1983, 1985, 1987, and 1996). He was inducted into the National Wrestling Hall of Fame in 2002.

Jim Beichner, University of Buffalo (1995-2013)

In his first season as head coach (1995-96), **Jim Beichner** had an immediate impact on the Buffalo wrestling program. He took a team that was winless the previous season and carved out a stunning 10-4 dual campaign and a third-place finish in the East Coast Association (ECA) tournament. That success resulted in coaching honors in New York State Division I and the ECA Conference, as well as being named Rookie Coach of the Year by the *Amateur Wrestling News*.

Starting with a tiny budget, virtually no facilities and just three scholarships, Beichner built Buffalo into an Eastern wrestling power. Today, the program has an ample budget, is fully staffed with three full-time coaches and one volunteer and is a certified USA Olympic Wrestling Training Center.

Beichner compiled a 151-120-4 record at Buffalo, with 47 of his wrestlers competing in the NCAA Championships. He was named Coach of the Year in the Mid-American Conference in 2011.

As a wrestler at Clarion University, Beichner was a two-time all-American at 190 pounds, placing fifth in 1984 and sixth in 1985. He posted an impressive 125-22 record, tied for third on the school's all-time list. He put together three undefeated dual campaigns and had a career-best 40-4 record in 1985. He was selected twice to the prestigious East-West All-Star Classic and captained Clarion to its third undefeated season in 38 years of competition.

Beichner was a four-time Pennsylvania State Athletic Conference champion (1983-1986) and a two-time Eastern Wrestling League champion (1984-1985).

He has been inducted into four halls of fame: Cassadaga Valley Hall of Fame (1982);

Eastern Wrestling Hall of Fame (1993); Clarion University Sports Hall of Fame (2000); and Chautauqua Sports Hall of Fame (2004).

Terry Brands, University of Tennessee-Chattanooga (2002-2005)

Terry Brands served as head coach at the University of Tennessee-Chattanooga for three seasons (2002-05) and led the Mocs to the 2005 Southern Conference title, while crowning three conference champions and placing two all-Americans at the NCAA Championships: **Michael Keefe** (5th at 141) and **Jon Sioredas** (5th at 165). For his efforts that season, Brands was named Southern Conference Coach of the Year. Following a tough initial campaign in 2002-03 with a 6-17 dual record and two NCAA qualifiers, Brands compiled a very respectable 25-16 dual mark in his next two seasons and sent five qualifiers to the NCAA both years.

Prior to his stint at UT-Chattanooga, Brands was an assistant coach at Iowa (1992-2000), Nebraska (2000-01) and Montana State-Northern (2001-02). Brands rejoined the Hawkeye staff in 2008 after a three-year stint (2005-08) as USA Wrestling's National Freestyle Resident Coach in Colorado Springs, CO. He was promoted to associate head coach at Iowa in 2011.

He has helped the Hawkeyes win seven NCAA and Big Ten titles, while crowning 19 NCAA and 26 Big Ten champions. Iowa's dual record of 115-12-1 during his tenure includes three undefeated seasons (14-0 in 1995, 17-0 in 1996 and 18-0 in 2000).

During the last seven seasons (through 2014-2015), Brands has helped Iowa to two NCAA and three Big Ten team titles, crowning six NCAA champions, 40 all-Americans, nine Big Ten champions and 46 academic All-Big Ten honorees. Iowa owns a 118-10-1 dual record since Brands returned to the staff in 2008.

He has led the Hawkeye Wrestling Club since returning to campus, and in 2014 he was named USA Wrestling's **Terry McCann** Freestyle Coach of the Year.

Brands was one of the nation's greatest freestyle wrestlers, winning World gold medals in 1993 and 1995 at 125.5 pounds (57 kg) when both U.S. teams won World Team Titles in freestyle. In 1993, he won his world title with brother Tom, who was the World champion at 136.5 pounds (62 kg). Terry and Tom were named 1993 USA Wrestling Athlete of the Year, 1993 **John Smith** Freestyle Wrestler of the Year and 1993 *Amateur Wrestling News* Man of the Year. The Brands brothers became the first U.S. brothers to win a World title during the same year.

Brands placed second at in the 1996 U.S. Nationals and the 1996 Olympic Team Trials, falling just short of making the U.S. Olympic Team. He qualified for the 1997 and 1999 U.S. World Teams, but did not compete due to injury. In 2000, he made a comeback and won the U.S. Olympic Team Trials at 127.75 pounds (58 kg). He earned a bronze medal at the 2000 Olympic Games in Sydney, Australia.

A two-time World Cup champion (1994, 1995), Brands won a gold medal at the 1995 Pan American Games; captured three U.S. Nationals titles and was runner-up three times. He was inducted into the National Wrestling Hall of Fame as a Distinguished Member in 2006.

Brands was a two-time NCAA champion, three-time all-American and three-time Big

Ten champion for the Hawkeyes (1989-92) at 126 pounds. He ended his career at Iowa with a 137-7 record.

He earned a Bachelor of Science in Human Development from the University of Iowa in 1992. He and his wife, Michelle, have a son, Nelson, and a daughter, Sydney.

Tom Brands, Iowa (2006-present); Virginia Tech (2005-2006)

Tom Brands became head coach of the Iowa Hawkeyes in 2006 after serving as an assistant coach from 1993 to 2004. He was named National Wrestling Coaches Association Assistant Coach of the Year in 2000. He also served as head coach at Virginia Tech for two years, with his 2005 team setting a school record for most dual victories in a season (16). That team won the Atlantic Coast Conference title and had five individual conference champions.

Brands led the Hawkeyes to national titles in 2008, 2009 and 2010. In his first season, Iowa placed eighth, but then strung together three straight team championships. Over the past five seasons, the Hawkeyes finished third, third, fourth, fourth and second (2015). His overall record as Iowa's head man is 157-15-1 with three national crowns and a conference record of 64-6.

As a competitor, Brands was the dominant 134-pounder from 1990-1992 winning three straight NCAA titles and compiling a 158-7-2 record with 46 falls for Iowa under **Dan Gable**. In 1993, he won gold in the World Games, captured a gold medal in the 1996 Olympics at Atlanta and was a four-time U.S. Freestyle champion. Brands was inducted into the National Wrestling Hall of Fame as a Distinguished Member in 2001.

Mark Cody, Oklahoma (2011-present); American University (2002-2011)

In four seasons at Oklahoma, Cody has compiled a 37-31 dual record and his squads have placed in the top 20 at the NCAA Championships all four seasons. He has coached two national champions at OU – **Kendrick Maple** in 2013 and **Cody Brewer** in 2015 – and four wrestlers have earned eight all-American placements.

In his first year (2011-2012), Cody led the Sooners to a 13th-place finish at the NCAAs with Maple (141) and Nick Lester (147) earning all-American status. OU moved up a notch to 12th at the NCAA Championships in 2013 on the shoulders of Maple, who became Cody's first national champion at OU by defeating **Mitchell Port** of Edinboro, 4-3, at 141 pounds. The Sooners posted their best NCAA tourney finish under Cody in 2014, placing 10th behind all-American performances by **Andrew Howe** (second at 174), Maple (8th at 149) and Brewer (8th at 133). In 2015, the Sooners slipped to 18th at the national tournament, but Brewer turned a ridiculous No. 13 seed into gold by winning the title at 133 pounds.

Not only have Cody's Sooners found success on the mat, they have also excelled in the classroom as he's coached a total of 11 National Wrestling Coaches Association Division I All-Academic team selections, including three in 2011-12 and two in 2012-13. In 2014, OU placed a nation-best six wrestlers on the squad and tied for 11th place on the All-Academic Team standings with a combined 3.16 GPA.

Prior to OU, Cody coached nine years at American University, leading the Eagles to a program-best fifth-place finish at the 2011 NCAA Championships. The team produced three all-Americans after qualifying six for the tournament, while also posting a school record 3.48 GPA. He coached 14 all-Americans and 16 NCAA qualifiers and 21 academic all-Americans. Previous coaching experience included assistant stints at Oklahoma State, Nebraska, Bloomsburg University and Missouri.

As a student-athlete, Cody was a three-time all-American. He spent two years at the State University of New York at Delhi before transferring to Missouri in 1983. In 1985, Cody placed sixth at the NCAA Championships and was named Mizzou's Most Outstanding Wrestler. Cody still ranks in Missouri's single season top-10 for falls (17) and winning percentage (.875). He graduated from Bellevue University with a Bachelor of Science degree in business. As a member of the New York Athletic Club, he was a 198-pound finalist at the 1988 U.S. Olympic Trials.

A native of Binghamton, N.Y., Cody and his wife, Holly, have four sons: George, Charlie, Henry and Norman.

Barry Davis, Wisconsin (1993-present)

Barry Davis has been the head coach at Wisconsin since first wearing the interim tag for a season (1993-94). In 22 years, Davis has an overall dual record of 216-154-11. In 2010, Davis was named the National Coach of the Year by the National Wrestling Coaches Association as the Badgers registered their best finish in school history (fourth) in the NCAA's. Sophomore **Andrew Howe** won his first NCAA Division I title at 165 with a 37-0 record. Davis was an assistant coach at Iowa from 1988-92, helping guide the Hawkeyes to four top-six finishes, including NCAA championships in 1991 and 1992.

Davis was the winningest wrestler at the winningest program in Division I, Iowa. He graduated in 1985 with a career record of 162-9-1 (.945). He still holds school records for wins in a season (46 in 1982) and career wins (162) and is fourth in career-winning percentage. After placing seventh at 118 as a freshman, he won national titles at 118 (1982) and 126 (1983 and 1985). Iowa won NCAA team titles all four years that Davis competed. He was named Outstanding Wrestler of the 1985 NCAA tourney. On the international level, Davis won a silver medal in the 1984 Olympics in Los Angeles and was a member of the 1988 U.S. Olympic Wrestling Team but did not place. In addition, he won a silver medal in the 1987 World Championships.

Barry Davis, University of Wisconsin. (Courtesy University of Wisconsin)

He was inducted into the National Wrestling Hall of Fame in 2007 as a Distinguished Member.

Mike DeAnna, Edinboro (1984-1990)

Mike DeAnna became the head wrestling coach at Edinboro University in 1984, following longtime head coach **Fred Caro** (21 seasons). DeAnna guided his teams to five top-ten NCAA finishes in six years, earning the 1986 NCAA Division II National Coach of the

Year Award. He compiled a career record of 54-34-1 (.612) while helping the Fighting Scots transition to Division I competition in the 1986-87 season.

One of the best wrestlers ever developed in the Greater Cleveland area, DeAnna was a three-time Ohio high school champion at Bay Village with a 104-5-1 mark. He was undefeated in his final three seasons going 83-0 during his three-title run. He earned first-team high school all-American honors and captured two U.S. Wrestling Association National Freestyle titles. At the University of Iowa, he was a four-time all-American, twice reaching the NCAA finals, and a four-time Big Ten Champion. After graduation he won National AAU Freestyle titles in 1983 and 1984 and was named second alternate to the 1984 U.S. Olympic freestyle wrestling team.

Kevin Dresser, Virginia Tech (2006-present)

Kevin Dresser was a two-time high school wrestling state champion and four-time state tournament placer, forging a 112-11-1 record. At the University of Iowa, he was a two-time Big Ten champion, two-time NCAA all-American and a national champion at 142 pounds in 1986. That year, he was the winner of the **Mike Howard** Award as the most valuable wrestler for the Hawkeyes.

He was an assistant coach at Iowa under **Dan Gable** before becoming head coach at Grundy (VA) High School. His teams won Virginia state championships eight consecutive years. Dresser then moved to Christiansburg (VA) High School and registered five consecutive state titles during his tenure, along with three runner-up finishes in 10 seasons.

When fellow Hawkeye **Tom Brands** departed Virginia Tech in 2006, Dresser became head coach for the Hokies. Through the 2014-2015 season, Dresser owns a dual meet record of 126-48. He has coached 10 wrestlers to 14 all-American placements and led Tech to two ACC tournament titles (2013 and 2014), as well as an official dual meet title in 2015. He was named ACC Coach of the Year in 2013, 2014 and 2015 and Virginia's coach of the year five times (2011-2015) by the Virginia Sports Information Directors (VaSID).

Virginia Tech's best finish in the NCAA tournament (eighth) came in 2014 when they had three all-Americans and the school's first national finalist in **Devin Carter** at 141 pounds. In 2015, the Hokies won the ACC's dual meet title and placed 10th at the NCAAs with four all-Americans as the team scored its most points ever at the event. Dresser's team beat eventual national champion Ohio State in a dual and the team finished third at the **Cliff Keen** Las Vegas Invitational.

In 2009, Dresser was inducted into the Iowa High School Athletic Association Wrestling Hall of Fame. In 2013, Dresser was honored with the Lifetime Service Award given in recognition of years of dedication to the development of leadership and citizenship in the youth through wrestling by the Virginia Chapter of the National Wrestling Hall of Fame. He was inducted into the Iowa Wrestling Hall of Fame in 2014 and the Roanoke Valley Wrestling Hall of Fame in 2015.

Rob Eiter, Pennsylvania (2008-2014)

Rob Eiter was head coach at the University of Pennsylvania from 2008 to 2014 after serving as an assistant for the Quakers from 2006-08. He coached four NCAA all-Americans: **Scott Griffin** (2010), **Zack Kemmerer** (2011), **Micah Burak** (2012) and **Lorenzo Thomas** (2014). As a team, Penn was honored by the NWCA as an All-Academic Squad and was one of 17 Penn programs honored in the NCAA's annual Academic Progress Report (APR).

The Quakers had their best NCAA performance under Eiter at the 2011 tournament (31st) with four wrestlers advancing to the Round of 12, the most since 2000 when Penn finished ninth overall as a team. At the EIWA Championships, Eiter guided his teams to finishes of second (2010), third (2009), fourth (2012) and fifth (2011). Kemmerer won a school-record 39 matches to become the first unanimous first-team All-Ivy selection in Eiter's tenure. Other first-team All-Ivy wrestlers under Eiter include **Rick Rappo** (2008 and 2009) and **Cesar Grajales** (2009). Heavyweight **Kyle Cowan** was named Ivy League Rookie of the Year in 2011, just the fifth Penn wrestler to earn that honor. In 2009, Eiter led the Penn program to a third-place finish at the EIWA Championships and six Quakers advanced to the NCAA Championships in St. Louis.

Eiter served as an assistant at Northwestern University from 2002-06 and was an assistant at Clarion (PA) University from 1993-1997). He was head coach of the U.S. Women's Team that took the gold medal in the 1999 Women's World Championships, the only time the women have accomplished that feat. Eiter followed that up by coaching the U.S. women's squad to a first-place finish at the 2001 Women's Pan-American Games. In 2007 and 2008 he served as head coach of the U.S. Junior Women's World Championships teams that placed fifth and third.

Prior to coaching, Eiter represented the U.S. in nine elite international competitions. In 1992 he was an alternate on the U.S. Olympic Team and in 1996 he placed eighth in the Atlanta Olympic Games. He also competed in the 1993 and 1995 World Championships and was a five-time U.S. Open national champion and won two silver medals at the World Cup.

A 1991 graduate of Arizona State, Eiter resides in New Jersey with his wife, Courtenay; their daughter, Stella, and their son, Troy.

Tom Erikson, Lyon College (2015-present)

The newest member of the fraternity of head coaches who wrestled in the 1980s, Tom Erikson was named head men's and women's wrestling coach at Lyon College in Batesville, AR, in July 2015. A former assistant coach at Purdue for 13 years, Erikson has more than 25 years coaching experience at all levels. Most recently, Erikson was head coach of USA Wrestling national team which participated in the Medved Cup in Minsk, Belarus. He also coached Team USA against Team India in an exhibition dual in Oklahoma City, OK in 2014. In addition, he served as an assistant coach at Hamilton Heights High School in Arcadia, IN and served as team leader of Team Indiana.

Erikson was a two-time NCAA all-American heavyweight for Oklahoma State University, placing fourth in 1986 and third in 1987, and was a three-time U.S. Olympic

Team alternate (1988, 1992 and 1996). He was a two-time NJCAA national champion (1984, 1985) and a member of the All-Big 8 Academic Team (1986).

He is a member of the Bloom (IL) High School Athletics Hall of Fame (1986), the Illinois Wrestling and Officials Association Hall of Fame (1996), The Midlands Hall of Fame (2004) and the Indiana Wrestling and Officials Association Hall of Fame (2010).

He is a graduate of Bloom High School and earned an Associate Arts degree from Triton College in Illinois. He continued his education at Oklahoma State University and later graduated from Western Governor's University with a Bachelor's in Marketing and Management.

Erickson and his wife, Randi, have a son, Bowdi, and a daughter, Jadlynn.

Tim Flynn, Edinboro (1997-present)

With a 198-73-5 dual record in 18 seasons, Tim Flynn is the winningest coach in Edinboro history. During his reign, the Fighting Scots have won 14 of 18 Eastern Wrestling League Championships and the Pennsylvania State Athletic Conference Tournament title 15 times in his 18 campaigns.

In 2015, Flynn's wrestlers registered the school's finest NCAA performance in history with a third-place finish and four all-Americans including two second-placers and two third-placers. The team's next-best performance was the previous season when the Fighting Scots placed fifth with three all-Americans. Edinboro under Flynn has had five top-10 finishes and 13 top-20 placements.

In 2014, Flynn was named the NWCAN NCAA Division I Coach of the Year. He shared InterMat Coach of the Year honors with Minnesota's J Robinson, and was selected WIN's **Dan Gable** Coach of the Year. During his 18- year career Flynn has produced 37 all-Americans, 134 national qualifiers and three national champions.

The 2005-06 Fighting Scots finished with a perfect 12-0 record, the only Division I team in the country to go undefeated that season. Flynn's 2006-2007 squad finished with a 17-1 dual mark, the most wins in school history.

Joining the program as an assistant coach prior to the start of the 1992-93 season, Flynn assisted Head Coach **Bruce Baumgartner** to a 56-21 record during his five-year period as an aide, including a perfect 14-0 dual match record and a school-record sixth-place finish at the 1996 NCAA Championships.

As a competitor at Penn State, Flynn captained the 1986-87 team while earning all-American honors at 134 pounds. He went 30-10-1 as a senior, winning the EWL title and finishing seventh in the NCAA Tournament. He compiled a 105-32-2 record, still ranking among the all-time career leaders in victories for the Nittany Lions. He also won the EWL title as a junior in 1986 while competing at 126 pounds, finishing with a 30-7-1 mark. He qualified for Nationals as a sophomore as well.

Flynn graduated from Penn State in 1987 with a Bachelor's in Business Management. He later earned his Master's in Business Administration with a concentration in Finance in 1990.

Jim Gibbons, Iowa State (1985-1992)

In 1985, Jim Gibbons became the head coach at Iowa State at age 26 and became the second-youngest coach to win a national title behind Oklahoma State's Myron Roderick (23) when the Cyclones ended Iowa's nine-year reign in 1987. For that accomplishment, he was named National Coach of the Year. In 1991, he was named Big Eight Coach of the Year. He coached seven individual NCAA champions and had 33 all-Americans while compiling a 96-32-1 career coaching mark.

Jim (left) and Joe Gibbons. (Courtesy Iowa State University)

Gibbons wrestled at ISU for **Dr. Harold Nichols** and earned all-America status three times. In 1981, he won a national title at 134 pounds in a weight class that included two-time national champion and four-time all-American **Randy Lewis**; future two-time national champion and four-time all-American **Darryl Burley**; three-time all-American **Ricky Dellagatta**; and future national champion **Clar Anderson**. Following his collegiate career, Gibbons served as an assistant coach at his alma mater for two years before taking over the head coaching duties.

He retired from coaching in 1992 and currently serves as market president at First American Bank in Ames, IA. He is a frequent color commentator on wrestling broadcasts. He and his wife, Anne, have three daughters, Genna, Grace and Samantha.

Duane Goldman, Indiana (1992-present)

Duane Goldman has served as head coach at Indiana for 24 seasons with his wrestlers appearing in 24 NCAA Tournaments, the most in school history. His 275 career dual match victories are also a school record. In the 2015 NCAA's, **Taylor Walsh** placed second at 165 pounds to become the 28th all-American under Goldman.

Under the guidance of Goldman, **Angel Escobedo** won a 125-pound national championship (2008) and became the first four-time all-American in school history, while **Joe Dubuque** won back-to-back NCAA crowns in 2005 and 2006, also at 125.

Goldman served as an assistant under former Indiana head coach and current Michigan head coach **Joe McFarland** before being elevated to the top spot in 1992. Prior to arriving in Bloomington, he spent a year as an assistant at Army.

As a collegiate wrestler at Iowa, Goldman was an NCAA champion (1986) and four-time all-American (three second-place finishes), compiling a 132-10 record under **Dan Gable**.

He won a gold medal at the Pan-American Championships in 1987, was a member of the 1987 World Cup Team and won two Canadian Cup Championships. He was an alternate on the U.S. Olympic team in 1988.

Goldman earned his Bachelor's in General Studies at the University of Iowa in 1986. He went on to earn his Master's from Iowa in administration in 1997. During the summer of 2000, Goldman accompanied former assistant coach **Charles Burton** to the 2000 Sydney

Olympics, where he served as an assistant coach and training partner. In 2008, he was inducted into the **Glen Brand** Wrestling Hall of Fame.

He and his wife, Patricia, have two daughters, Aphten and Avery, and one son, Garret.

Dave Grant, Northern Illinois (1996-2011)

Dave Grant registered a career record of 127-110-6 during his 15 years at the helm at Northern Illinois, posting five straight 10-win seasons from 2002 through 2006. Under his guidance, **Jeremy Goeden** (1997, 1998), **Scott Owen** (2002, 2003) and **Ben Heizer** (2003, 2004) each repeated as all-Americans during their careers to account for more than half of NIU's 11 wrestling all-Americans. In 2004, Heizer had the school's first NCAA runner-up finish since 1973. The 2003 NCAA tournament marked the first time in school history two wrestlers were awarded all-American honors in the same year. That year, the Huskies had the most dual victories (15) under Grant. He led his wrestlers to 20 individual Mid-American Conference titles and qualified 40 wrestlers for the NCAA Championships during his career.

The Huskies had two 14-win seasons in 2002 and 2005. In 2004, they finished second in the Mid-American Conference and had a school-record nine wrestlers place at the MAC Summit, including Heizer and **Sam Hiatt**, who brought home conference crowns for the second consecutive year. Heizer, Hiatt and **Josh Wooton** all represented the Huskies at the 2004 NCAA Championships and guided NIU to a 23rd-place national finish.

NIU's 29 wins during the 2002 and 2003 seasons is the top two-year win total in school history, while its 38 wins from 2001-04 tied for tops in program history. In 2003, the Huskies finished 22nd at the NCAA meet and climbed as high as 15th during the regular season. In addition to sharing the MAC regular season championship with Central Michigan, NIU boasted dual match wins over the 13th-ranked Chippewas, No. 5 Ohio State and No. 8 Missouri.

In 2001-02, the Huskies earned the third-best record in school history with a 14-4 mark, and finished second in the MAC. Grant was recognized as the MAC Coach of the Year.

As the top assistant for the University of Minnesota for 10 seasons, Grant helped guide the Golden Gophers to a regular spot in the nation's top 20 during his tenure (1986-96) at the school, with four finishes in the top 10 between 1989 and 1993. In Grant's 10 seasons, Minnesota produced 14 wrestlers who earned a total of 23 all-America honors, along with five NCAA finalists and one national champion.

As a collegian, Grant transferred to the University of Northern Iowa from the University of Kentucky after the Wildcats dropped their wrestling program. He gained all-America status for the Panthers in 1984 with a solid 32-11-1 record and an eighth-place showing at the NCAA Championships at 158 pounds. He finished with a career record of 86-37-4 (.693).

Grant received his Bachelor of Arts in physical education and coaching from the University of Northern Iowa in 1985 and gained his Master's in kinesiology from Minnesota in 1997. He is married to the former Kris Langsdorf.

Joel Greenlee, Ohio (1997-2015)

Hired as an interim coach for the 1997-98 season due to an illness of then-head coach **Harry Houska**, Joel Greenlee served as head coach of the Ohio Bobcats for 18 seasons. Greenlee's accomplishments during his first season at Ohio earned him the NWCA National Assistant-Coach-of-the-Year award in 1998. His 1997-98 team finished ninth at the NCAA Tournament, the Bobcats' best finish since 1973, and won the regular-season MAC title with a 5-0 record. He coached **Dwight Gardner** (158) to the school's first individual national title since 1978. In 2005, Ohio's **Jake Percival** became the MAC's first-ever four-time all-American. Prior to coming to Ohio, Greenlee was an assistant coach at the University of Northern Iowa from 1989-97.

Greenlee was a two-time all-American at Northern Iowa, placing fourth in 1988 and second in 1989 when he lost a razor-thin 1-0 decision to three-time national champion **Carlton Haselrig**. That year, he won Midlands Tournament and Midwest Championships titles and was named the Outstanding Wrestler at both events. He has the highest winning percentage in UNI history with an .878 (127-16-4) career mark. He also holds Panther records for dual victories (58) and dual victories in a season (20 in 1986-87).

Greenlee finished second at the U.S. Olympic Team Trials in 1992 and was an alternate on the U.S. Olympic Team. He won the Cerra Pelado Tournament in Cuba in 1993 and the Cuban All-Star Tournament in 1992.

He and his wife, Roxann, have a son, Walker, and a daughter, Madison.

Jim Heffernan, Illinois (2009-present)

After serving as an assistant coach under **Mark Johnson** for 19 years (17 at Illinois, two at Oregon State), Jim Heffernan became head coach at Illinois in 2009. He was named the National Wrestling Coaches Association Assistant Coach of the Year in 1995 and 2001 after the Illini's fifth-place national finish and second-place finish in the Big Ten. Under Heffernan, Illinois' best finish in the NCAA Championships was fifth in 2001.

During Heffernan's tenure, Illinois has finished in the top-10 at the NCAA championships on 11 occasions and in the top 15 in 16 of the last 19 seasons. He has coached nine individual national champions in the last 17 seasons. In 2015, Illinois qualified all 10 wrestlers (fourth time in school history) and **Isaiah Martinez** rolled to a 39-0 record and a national championship at 157. In 2014, 125-pounder **Jesse Delgado** became Illinois' first back-to-back champion and probably would have made it three in a row in 2015 but was limited to just 15 matches during the season because of injury and was forced to default in the national tourney due to injury.

While at Illinois as an assistant and head coach, Heffernan has sent 133 wrestlers to the NCAA championships. During the past 16 seasons, the Illini have produced 47 all-Americans and eight national champions.

Heffernan began his coaching career as a graduate assistant at the University of Iowa, then had stints as an assistant at Lehigh University and Oregon State before joining Johnson at Illinois in 1992. He also coached the Cadet Wrestling Team at the world championships in Istanbul, Turkey, in 1992, and the USA World Espoir Team in 1989.

A 1987 graduate of the University of Iowa, Heffernan was a four-time all-American and Big Ten champion, while being a member of three Hawkeye NCAA and four Big Ten championship teams. Heffernan won an NCAA title in 1986 at 150 pounds and captained the Hawkeyes as a senior in 1987 when he was named Iowa's Male Athlete of the Year. During his career, Iowa won 70 of 74 duals.

Heffernan and his wife, Rebecca, live in Champaign with their son, Sean, and daughter, Alex.

Kevin Jackson, Iowa State (2009-present)

Kevin Jackson is in his sixth season as Iowa State's head wrestling coach. In 2014-15, the Cyclones had their best regular season performance since 2010. They finished with an 11-2 dual record (.846) and ended the season ranked eighth. ISU was second to Oklahoma State in the Big 12 Championships, qualifying seven men for the NCAA Championships. **Kyven Gadson** won a national title at 197 for ISU.

In his first year at the helm, Jackson coached two NCAA individual champions en route to a third-place finish at the 2010 NCAA Championships. He was honored as *Amateur Wrestling News* magazine's 2010 Rookie Coach of the Year for his 13-2 dual record and 4-0 mark in the Big 12.

Prior to Iowa State, Jackson served eight years (2001-08) as the National Freestyle Coach for USA Wrestling. He was the first full-time freestyle wrestling coach for the organization and took two United States' teams to the Olympics. Two of his athletes – **Cael Sanderson** (2004) and **Henry Cejudo** (2008) – won gold medals. His 2001 freestyle team won the World Cup, the 2003 team placed second and the 2006 squad finished third at that meet. Jackson was a freestyle resident coach at the Olympic Training Center, head coach for the U.S. Army team at Fort Carson (1998-2001) and head coach of the Sunkist youth development program. During that tenure, he personally trained 2000 Olympic champion **Brandon Slay**.

He was a four-time all-American (LSU and Iowa State) and captained the 1987 national championship team, the Cyclones' last. Internationally, Jackson established himself as one of the world's best, capturing gold medals at the 1992 Olympic Games in Barcelona, Spain and at the World Championships in 1991 and 1995. He is one of just five wrestlers in U.S. history with three career world-level titles. He also won two Pan American Games titles (1993 and 1995) and three U.S. Open titles, placing second five times. In 1998, Jackson became the first American to win the Takhti Cup tournament in Tehran, Iran.

Jackson's success earned him a number of major awards, including the 1995 **John Smith** Award as National Freestyle Wrestler of the Year, 1992 *Amateur Wrestling News* Man of the Year and 1991 USA Wrestling and USOC Wrestler of the Year.

He is a member of the FILA International Wrestling Hall of Fame, the National Wrestling Hall of Fame (Distinguished Member in 2003), Greater Lansing Area Sports Hall of Fame (1993) and the Iowa State University Athletics Hall of Fame (2007).

He earned a Bachelor of Sports Science from the U.S. Sports Academy/University of Americas in 2005. Jackson and his wife, Robin, have five children: Cole, Bailee, Trinity, Brynn and Kira.

Zeke Jones, Arizona State (2014-present); Penn (2005-2008)

Zeke Jones is the seventh wrestling coach in Arizona State history. In his first season, the Sun Devils qualified six wrestlers for the NCAA Championships with **Blake Stauffer** claiming a fourth-place finish and all-American status at 184.

A member of ASU's 1988 NCAA Wrestling Championship team, Jones was a three-time all-American and Pac-10 Champion for the Sun Devils. A national runner-up at 118, Jones sits at No. 4 in ASU's career record book in both overall victories (134) and dual victories (59). He also holds the school record for dual match victories in a season with 22 during the 1989-90 campaign.

An Olympic silver medalist for the United States in 1992, Jones was the 1991 World Champion at 52kg, a four-time World-Cup Champion, and coached United States' Olympians in the 1996, 2000, 2004, and 2012 Olympic Games. As U.S. Olympic Team head coach, Jones team members won two gold medals and one bronze at the London Games in 2012. At the 2004 Athens Games, Jones served as freestyle coach and saw his charges win a gold and two silvers.

In the four World Championships during Jones' tenure, Team USA placed third in the 2011 World Championships, fifth in 2013, and seventh in 2009. He also led the team to five individual World Champion medals. Under Jones, Team USA placed third in 2012 and 2013, and sixth in 2010 in the Freestyle World Cup. In addition, Team USA won eight Junior World medals, five University World medals and four Cadet World medals with Jones at the helm.

Prior to his international coaching, Jones was head coach at the University of Pennsylvania where he compiled a 33-17-1 record. Following the 2006 campaign, *Amateur Wrestling News* named Jones the Rookie Head Coach of the Year. He also was an assistant coach at West Virginia, Arizona State and Bloomsburg University. Jones coached teams that have finished in the NCAA Final Four twice, in the top-10 four times and won six conference team championships. Individually his wrestlers have won six NCAA titles and 38 conference crowns, with 30 all-American honors and 80 NCAA qualifiers.

Jones is a Distinguished Member of the National Wrestling Hall of Fame (2005) and a member of the Arizona State University Hall of Fame and the Michigan Wrestling Hall of Fame.

Rob Koll, Cornell (1995-present)

Rob Koll is the **David R. Dunlop** '59 Head Coach of Wrestling at Cornell. His teams have won 16 Ivy League titles, crowned 12 national champions and achieved 56 all-American designations and 51 individual EIWA championships. The Big Red has had at least one individual NCAA champion in seven of the last eight years. Koll is the school's career leader in wins with a 261-82-5 (.757) career record, including

Coach Rob Koll (Courtesy Cornell University)

89-15-1 (.852) over the last seven years. His teams have finished second in the NCAA event twice (2010 and 2011).

Over the past 11 years, Cornell has produced 45 all-Americans, ten national champions, eight top five team finishes at the NCAAs, nine straight EIWA titles and 13 consecutive Ivy crowns. Koll has sent at least one wrestler to the NCAA championships in each of his 21 seasons, including sending a school-record nine wrestlers to the national meet in 2005, 2009, 2011, 2012 and 2015.

In 2015, **Gabriel Dean** won a national title at 184 pounds to start a new streak of national champions at Cornell after the team did not mount the winner's podium in 2014. In 2013, **Kyle Dake** became the first wrestler to win national titles at four different weight classes and the first to win four titles without a redshirt season. He was The **Dan Hodge** Award winner as collegiate wrestler of the year and the inaugural *Sports Illustrated* Male College Athlete of the Year. Dake was unbeaten at 165 pounds.

A three-time EIWA Coach of the Year Award recipient (2007, 2010, 2011), Koll was honored as Intermat's NCAA Coach of the Year and **Dan Gable** Coach of the Year in 2010 and was named the NWCA Division I Coach of the Year in 2005. Koll came to Cornell as an assistant coach under **Jack Spates** prior to the 1989-90 season.

Koll won a national championship at 158 in 1988 and was the winningest wrestler in school and Atlantic Coast Conference history at 150-20-1. He was North Carolina's first four-time all-American and second wrestler in Tar Heel history to win a national title. Koll was the 1988 recipient of the Patterson Medal, given to the most outstanding senior athlete at North Carolina.

He won gold medals at the 1990 and 1993 World Cup events, won the 1992 World Cup Grand Prix and was an alternate on the 1992 U.S. Olympic team. In addition, he was a 1989 Pan-Am Games champion. He won national freestyle championships in 1990 and 1991 and was the runner-up at the 1989 Olympic Festival in Oklahoma City.

His father, the late **Bill Koll**, was a three-time NCAA champion at Iowa State Teachers' College (Northern Iowa) and was twice named the tournament's Outstanding Wrestler. Bill Koll was inducted into the National Wrestling Hall of Fame in 1977.

Koll and his wife, Rachel, live in Lansing and have two sons, William and Daniel.

Glen Lanham, Duke (2012-present)

The 12th head coach in Duke wrestling history, Glen Lanham is building the Blue Devil program one step at a time. From two NCAA qualifiers but no wins at the national event in his first season, Lanham had his first all-American in 2014 (and second in program history) when **Conner Hartmann** went 6-2 and placed fifth at 197 to help Duke to a tie for 29th. The following season, Lanham took five wrestlers to the NCAA Championships and finished 28th – the highest in school history – thanks to Hartmann's sixth-place all-American finish after losing 4-1 to eventual national champion **Kyven Gadson** of Iowa State in the semifinals. **Immanuel Kerr-Brown** (157) added to Duke's point total by winning three matches in the consolations before being eliminated.

Lanham served as an assistant coach at Duke for two seasons before taking over the helm and was an assistant at Oklahoma State (which won two NCAA titles during his time there), North Carolina and Purdue. He had an extremely successful run as head wrestling coach at perennial power Midwest City (OK) High School.

As a collegian, he garnered all-American honors at both OSU (5th at 158 in 1987) and the University of Tennessee (8th at 158 in 1985). He earned his Bachelor of Arts in Human Service with an emphasis in juvenile counseling in August of 1988.

Lanham resides in Pittsboro, N.C., with his wife Melanie.

Mark Manning, Nebraska (2000-present); University of Northern Iowa (1997-2000)

In his 15 years at Nebraska, Mark Manning has coached 39 all-Americans and led the Huskers to five top-eight finishes at the NCAA Championships. He is the winningest coach in school history with a 201-74-3 record. He won back-to-back Big 12 Coach-of-the-Year awards in 2008 and 2009 after guiding Nebraska to a runner-up conference finish in 2008 and share of the conference crown in 2009. NU placed fourth at the NCAA Championships both seasons with nine Huskers earning all-America honors, and **Jordan Burroughs** capturing the 157-pound national title with a perfect 35-0 record in 2009.

Manning was named the 2011 FILA Freestyle Coach of the Year after helping Burroughs capture the gold medal at the World Championships in Istanbul, Turkey. Burroughs also won a gold medal at the 2012 London Olympics, where Manning served as a volunteer coach for the U.S. Freestyle Team. Burroughs went on to win a second world title in 2013, and added a bronze medal in 2014.

In addition to their success on the mat, Husker wrestlers under Manning have earned 79 academic all-conference selections, including 38 academic All-Big Ten awards during Nebraska's first four seasons in the conference. Three Huskers were named to the 2014 NWCA All-Academic Team. In 2012, Nebraska turned in the nation's best team grade-point average (3.46) for the first time in school history.

The 2003-04 Huskers posted one of the best wrestling seasons ever at NU with a 19-3 overall record, tying the second-highest win total in NU history. The Huskers posted two team titles during the season, winning the prestigious Las Vegas Invitational and winning the Virginia Duals with a 25-13 defeat of Lehigh in the finals. Manning coached his first NCAA national champion at Nebraska, as **Jason Powell** claimed the title at 125 pounds with a 17-2 technical fall in the finals to lead NU to a fifth-place finish.

The 2007-08 the Huskers won a share of the Big 12 championship for the first time in school history. Seven NU wrestlers qualified for the NCAA Championships, where the Huskers finished fourth, the second-best finish in school history (3rd in 1993).

History was made in 2011, when Manning helped Burroughs become the first two-time national champion in school history by winning the 165-pound title at the NCAA Championships. Burroughs was awarded the school's first-ever Hodge Trophy, given annually to the nation's top wrestler.

Prior to Nebraska, Manning coached three seasons at Northern Iowa (1997-2000) and compiled a 23-24-2 dual record while the Panthers improved in each of his seasons, finishing 11th in the NCAA Championships in his final season – the best in seven years. He also was an assistant coach at Oklahoma and North Carolina. He coached two U.S. Olympic teams as an assistant in 1996 and 2000 and was the head coach at U.S. Olympic Festivals in 1991, 1993 and 1995. He coached the U.S. freestyle team at the 2001 FILA World Championships and was an assistant on the U.S. delegation to the FILA World Championships eight times. In 2009, Manning was a coach for the U.S. Freestyle World Team at the World Wrestling Championships in Herning, Denmark.

He wrestled collegiately at Nebraska for one year, before transferring to the University of Nebraska-Omaha. After redshirting a season, Manning went on to become a two-time NCAA Division II national champion and three-time all-American under Coach Mike Denney. Manning posted a 121-23 record for the Mavericks, while capturing titles at 150 pounds in 1983 and 1985. He was inducted into the NCAA Division II Hall of Fame for his accomplishments as a wrestler and coach in 1999. He was a member of the U.S. freestyle team from 1986 to 1989. He won a silver medal at the 1989 Pan American Games.

The Vermillion, SD, native received his bachelor's degree in physical education from Nebraska-Omaha in 1985, with a specialization in exercise science. He earned his Master's in sports administration from North Carolina in 1989.

Manning and his wife, Carrie, were married in August of 2006. Mark has four sons: Matthew, Connor, Ryan and Will.

Steve Martin, Old Dominion (2003-present)

In his 11th season as head coach in 2014-15, Steve Martin led seven wrestlers into the NCAA Championships, tying a school record set in 2012. **Chris Mecate** and **Alexander Richardson** each earned all-American honors, marking the first time since 1991 that two ODU wrestlers achieved that feat in the same season. The Monarchs finished 22nd in the NCAAs and also placed second at the Mid-American Conference Championship. **Tristan Warner** was the recipient of the NCAA's Elite 89 academic recognition award for the second consecutive season, becoming just the second Division I wrestler to earn the award in back-to-back seasons.

ODU sent 51 overall wrestlers to the NCAA Championships in the past 11 seasons under Coach Martin. He has led Old Dominion to double-digit dual victories in nine of his 11 seasons with the program.

The 2008-09 season was perhaps one of the greatest in ODU wrestling history. The team was ranked 16th in the country in the final dual meet rankings and went a perfect 5-0 in league duals to claim the regular season CAA title. They posted victories over nationally-ranked Hofstra and Virginia Tech and had a Top 20 finish in the NCAA Tournament with the school's second-ever national finalist. Martin was named the Virginia Sports Information Directors Association (VaSID) Coach of the Year.

Martin's father, the legendary **Billy Martin**, is considered the father of Virginia wrestling. He won 22 state wrestling team titles in 23 years at Great Bridge High School. Steve nearly matched his father's success, leading Great Bridge to 13 state championships in 14 years with 40 state champions, 98 state place-winners, 35 all-Americans and six high school national champions.

Martin was awarded the National Wrestling Coaches Association state and regional coach of the year in 1995 and 2000. The Norfolk Sports Club named him the **Bob Bates** Award winner as the Outstanding Metropolitan Coach of the Year.

Following an all-American (1989) career at Iowa, Martin graduated in 1991 and got his Master's degree from George Washington University in 1996. Steve and his wife Lori live in Chesapeake, VA. They have four children: Madison, Macy, McKenna and Max.

Joe McFarland, Michigan (1999-present)

Joe McFarland has led Michigan to three Big Ten dual-meet championships (2004, 2005 and 2006) and a streak of eight consecutive top-10 finishes at the NCAA Championships (2001-2008), including a school-best NCAA runner-up performance in 2005. He ranks third on Michigan's career wins list with 182 and has mentored 21 different student-athletes to five NCAA individual titles, 49 all-America citations and 16 Big Ten individual crowns. Among McFarland's most decorated pupils are two-time NCAA champions and four-time Big Ten champions **Kellen Russell** (2008, 2009, 2011, 2012) and **Ryan Bertin** (2002-2005).

He became the ninth wrestling coach in school history after seven seasons as an assistant coach under **Dale Bahr**. He was named the National Wrestling Coaches Association's Assistant Coach of the Year in 1994.

Formerly the head wrestling coach at Indiana University (1990-92), McFarland produced one of the most impressive first-year improvements in Big Ten Conference history when he guided the Hoosiers to a perfect 14-0 dual

Joe McFarland, Michigan (Courtesy University of Michigan)

meet record, the program's first undefeated season since 1946. IU placed eighth at the NCAA Championships that season and claimed runner-up honors at the Big Ten Championships. Indiana also was the only unbeaten team in NCAA Division I in 1989-90 and reached the No. 5 national ranking in the final dual-meet listing by *Amateur Wrestling News*. He coached three all-Americans and three Big Ten champions and was named the 1990 Big Ten Conference Coach of the Year, the only rookie coach to be so honored. He also was named *Amateur Wrestling News'* recipient of the 1990 "Rookie Coach of the Year" award.

As a Wolverine wrestler (1981-82, 1984-85) he was 166-24-4 (third best in school annals), while his 48 wins (1983-84) are a single-season record. He served as team captain as a junior and senior while earning all-American honors four times including two runner-up finishes at 126 pounds (1984 and 1985). He won a Big Ten title in 1984, and reached the conference finals all four seasons. McFarland also won the prestigious Midlands Tournament in 1982 and 1983.

Internationally, he was the silver medalist at the 1986 World Championship, a bronze medalist at the1987 Tbilisi Tournament, and 1988 World Cup Championship gold medalist. He also was named the Outstanding Wrestler of the 1988 USA-USSR dual meet in Orlando, FL.

A graduate of North Olmstead (OH) High School, McFarland was a two-time Ohio state champion. He earned his Bachelor's from the University of Michigan in 1985. McFarland resides in Whitmore Lake with his wife, Linda.

C.D. Mock, North Carolina (2002-2015)

North Carolina's first-ever NCAA wrestling champion, C.D. Mock coached the Tar Heels for 12 seasons. The 2005 and 2006 Atlantic Coast Conference Coach of the Year, Mock was named head coach in 2002, and compiled a 108-105-3 record.

Mock guided the Tar Heels to a 22nd-place finish at the 2013 NCAA Championships and a 25th-place finish in 2014. The performances were highlighted by **Evan Henderson**, who earned all-American honors by placing sixth in 2013 and fourth in 2014 at 141, the best finish for a Tar Heel in 18 years.

Early in his tenure, Mock's teams won back-to-back ACC titles in 2005-2006. In 2005, Mock guided two-time All-America **Evan Sola** to a sixth-place finish at 133 pounds and a 24th-place team finish – UNC's best since 1997.

Prior to the 2003-04 season, Mock worked as an assistant coach for three years and was involved in all aspects of North Carolina wrestling. He was an integral part of the 2003 Atlantic Coast Conference championship squad.

In 1982, Mock became North Carolina's first NCAA champion and helped the Tar Heels to a fifth-place finish at the NCAA Championships. He finished that season a perfect 35-0 en route to the national title at 134 pounds and also received the prestigious Patterson Medal, which is presented to the UNC senior student-athlete that best demonstrates athletic excellence.

Mock won three ACC titles and was a two-time all-America. He posted a career record of 108-9, good for a .923 winning percentage, which ranks third all-time in school history. He also had a career record of 64-4 in ACC competition.

Mock lives in Chapel Hill with his wife, Mickie, a UNC graduate and former member of the gymnastics team, daughter Chelsea and son Corey.

Mike Moyer, George Mason (1985-1995)

In 1985, Mike Moyer began his ten-year coaching career at George Mason University in Fairfax, VA. Moyer advanced 27 wrestlers to the NCAA Division I Wrestling Championships, four earning all-American Honors, including GMU's first in 1991, **Scott Kirsch**; two-time all-American and three-time NCAA qualifier, **John Curtis**; and **Matt Finacchio**. In 1995, Moyer's final team posted an 11-0 record, the third undefeated wrestling season in school history, and again captured the Colonial Athletic Association championship. Moyer was named CAA Coach of the Year for the second time and Virginia Coach of the Year for the fourth time. He ended his career as the winningest wrestling coach in school history with a 126-29-2 record.

He served as a graduate assistant wrestling coach at James Madison University and took his first head coaching position at Chowan Junior College in Murfreesboro, NC.

Moyer began his wrestling career at Wilson High School in West Lawn, PA, competing in three PIAA State Wrestling Tournaments. He notched an 89-14-2 record under Coach **William Moyer**, his father. At West Chester State College (PA), Moyer wrestled in three NCAA Division I Championships at 158 where such legends as **Dave Schultz**, **Rick Stewart** and **Jim Zalesky** dominated. In 1981, Moyer defeated the 10th seed in the first round, but was edged by the future two-time national champion Zalesky of Iowa, 7-3, in the second round.

He was Executive Director of the GMU Patriot Club from 1995 to 1999 and served as Chairman of the NCAA Wrestling Committee from 1997 to 1999. He became Executive Director of the National Wrestling Coaches Association in 1999 and serves on the National Wrestling Hall of Fame and USA Wrestling Boards.

Moyer was honored with the Lifetime Service to Wrestling Award, through the Virginia Chapter of the National Wrestling Hall of Fame in 2010.

Brad Penrith, University of Northern Iowa (2000-2010)

Brad Penrith ended his tenure at Northern Iowa with a 90-75-4 record. He coached 69 NCAA Division I national qualifiers in 10 seasons. He served as an assistant to **Mark Manning** for three years before being named UNI's ninth head wrestling coach in 2000. He also was an assistant coach at Nebraska for five seasons, along with stops at Boise State and Arizona State.

During his own competitive career, he was a three-time Big 10 champ and a three-time all-American at Iowa, winning a national title at 126 pounds in 1986 when the Hawkeyes won their national record ninth consecutive team championship. Penrith had NCAA runner-up finishes in 1987 and 1988 and was a silver medalist at the World Games and a gold medalist at the Pan American Games in 1991. In addition, he was an alternate on the 1992 U.S. Olympic Team and won three U.S Open titles. He was a four-time state medal winner in high school and claimed a New York state championship as a sophomore.

He is married to the former Laura Wood of Waukee, Iowa.

Greg Randall, Boise State (2002-present)

Greg Randall has led Boise State to four Pac-12 Championships, five runner-up finishes, and eight top-25 finishes at the NCAA Championships in his 13 years as head coach. Prior to taking over as just the third head coach in 41 years, Randall also served as an assistant coach for the Broncos from 1992-93 through 2001-02. He was named head coach following the retirement of longtime head coach **Mike Young**. The Broncos are 118-63-1 in dual competition under Randall with 11 wrestlers earning 15 all-America honors. BSU wrestlers have claimed 31 individual Pac-12 Championships under Randall's guidance.

Boise State set two school records at the 2011 NCAA Championships by placing ninth and qualifying a wrestler at every weight class. Other top finishes include 11th (2010), 12th (2003, 2009), 19th (2013), 24th (2006, 2008) and 25th (2014).

In 2008, Boise State registered the third-highest score in Pac-12 Tournament history

(152.5) and qualified nine wrestlers for the national tournament. That performance earned Randall his first Pac-12 Coach of the Year award. A year later, Randall repeated as Pac-12 Coach of the Year, winning the conference championship with six individual champions. The Broncos won Pac-12 Championships in 2004, 2008, 2009 and 2011, finished runner-up in 2003, 2005, 2010, 2012 and 2013, and finished third in 2006 and 2014.

In 2006 Randall guided his first NCAA individual champion as a head coach with **Ben Cherrington** capturing the national title at 157.

Randall also served as an assistant coach at BSU from 1992 through 2002. He was named head coach in 2002 and was named "Rookie Coach of the Year" by *Amateur Wrestling News* in his first campaign.

Randall was a three-time all-American at Iowa under **Dan Gable**, helping the Hawkeyes to four of the school's nine straight national titles (1978-86). He had two runner-up finishes (1984 and 1986) and a fifth (1985) at 134 pounds. He was a Big 10 champion in 1985 and participated in the East-West All-Star Wrestling Classic three straight years (1985-87). Following his 1987 season Randall received Iowa's **Mike J. McGivern** Award, presented each year to the team's most courageous wrestler.

He was a gold medalist in the 1989 Pan American Games, a runner-up at the U.S. Open Nationals and placed second at the 1989 U.S. Olympic Festival.

A four-time state high school champion, Randall was inducted into the **Glen Brand** Wrestling Hall of Fame in 2002, and into the state of Iowa High School Hall of Fame in 1995. He was a two-time junior national champion.

Randall, and his wife Chris, have three children: Rylee, Shea and Brittlyn.

Andy Rein, Wisconsin (1986-1993)

Rein became the 14th head coach of his alma mater in 1986, leading the Badgers to an overall record of 81-41-3 during his tenure. Rein was recognized for his coaching abilities in both 1987 (Rookie Coach of the Year by *Amateur Wrestling News*) and 1992 as the Big Ten Coach of the Year after leading the badgers to Big Ten runner-up finishes. His 1987 team also registered 15 dual wins and produced two all-Americans in **Jeff Jordan**, fourth at 150, and **Paul McShane**, fourth at 158, and placed 11th in the NCAA. Two more 11th-place finishes followed in 1988 and 1989, with Rein notching his first national champion when **Dave Lee** took the 167-pound crown. In 1991, **Matt Demaray** won an NCAA title at 150 and repeated that feat in 1992. His title and all-American seventh-place finishes by **Matt Hanutke** (118) and **Dan Flood** (126) lifted the Badgers to their highest finish (seventh) since 1980 when Rein won the 150-pound NCAA title and led Wisconsin to a seventh-place finish.

Wisconsin registered seven top-25 placements (and six top 15's) under Rein, who produced three national championships between two wrestlers and 12 all-American honorees.

While a wrestler at Wisconsin, Rein won two Big Ten titles and was a three-time all-American. He went undefeated (40-0) in his run to the NCAA crown in 1980. Rein became just the second Wisconsin wrestler to win an Olympic medal when he earned the silver at the 1984 Olympics in Los Angeles at 149.5 pounds. Other international success included gold medals at the 1983 Tbilisi Tournament and the 1979 Pan American Games, and silver medals at the 1982 World Cup and 1985 Super Champions Tournament in Japan.

Roger Reina, University of Pennsylvania (1986-2005)

Hired in 1986 as the youngest head coach in Division I at the time, Roger Reina became the winningest wrestling coach in Penn history with a record of 205-106-6 – more than double the next most wins at Penn. Three of his teams placed in the top 12 at the NCAA's, with a high of ninth – the school's third-best finish. Reina coached 17 NCAA all-Americans and seven of Penn's eight multiple medalists. He coached two-time NCAA finalist **Brandon Slay** (a 2000 Olympic champion) and 2000 NCAA champ, **Brett Matter**.

His teams set an Ivy League mark with seven straight titles. He coached the Quakers' first-ever EIWA team title and four straight from 1996-1999, a league first in 42 years. After no individual titles from 1945-95, his 1997 team tied Lehigh's league mark (7), among 31 won from 1996-2005.

He was elected Ivy Coaches Chairman, President of the EIWA and President of the NWCA. He was a four-time National Coach of the Year nominee and a three-time EIWA Coach of the Year. Roger is Director of Major Gifts for Penn's Health System, raised two children and attends every home meet.

Reina's 1996-97 team scored an all-time EIWA record 183 points and set the record for largest margin of victory (79.5 points). The Quakers also crowned a school- and EIWA-record eight finalists and six EIWA champions. In 2000, Penn sent seven wrestlers to the NCAA Championships and returned with a National Champion (Matter at 157), three semi-finalists and three NCAA all-Americans.

Reina was a member of the **Dave Schultz** Wrestling Club coaching staff, where he has guided multiple open-level all-Americans, National Champions, World Team and Olympic Trials place winners. His greatest achievement was coaching 1998 Penn graduate **Brandon Slay** to a berth on the 2000 Olympic Team. Slay went on to capture the gold medal in Sydney, Australia. He also served as coach for both the National Championship Pennsylvania Cadet and Junior teams in Freestyle and Greco-Roman.

He received the 1997 Pennsylvania Amateur Wrestling Federation's "Contributor of the Year" Award. Reina also served as tournament director for the 1992 Olympic Freestyle Trials held at the University of Pennsylvania.

Jesse Reyes, Purdue (1992-2007)

Jesse Reyes posted a 179-120-3 dual meet record during his 15 seasons at Purdue and coached 16 all-Americans and four Big Ten champions. Under Reyes, Purdue's best NCAA finish was 14th in 2003 with two all-Americans: **Chris Fleeger** (125) and **Ryan Lange** (174) and eight qualifiers. Top-seeded Fleeger placed second, losing a narrow 3-2 decision, and fourth-seeded Lange placed 8th, while both claimed Big Ten individual titles. Reyes' 2004 squad had a memorable dual campaign with an 18-6 mark that set a school record for most dual victories during a single campaign. At the Big Ten Championships, the Boilermakers placed sixth, the best finish by a Purdue squad at the tournament during the Reyes era. In

2001, Reyes posted his 100th career coaching victory in his ninth season at Purdue to surpass **Claude Reeck** as the school's all-time wrestling victory leader.

He served as an assistant coach at Michigan State for three seasons before his hiring as Purdue's head coach in 1992. He was an assistant coach at Arizona State and Oklahoma State and a graduate assistant at Cal State-Bakersfield. Arizona State and Oklahoma State posted three top-five finishes during Reyes' association with their programs. He also helped coach Team USA to a third-place finish at the 1998 Junior World Freestyle Championships.

As a wrestler, Reyes went 151-22-1 at Cal State-Bakersfield. As team captain, he led the Roadrunners to three consecutive Division II national titles and a second-place finish in his freshman year. He won an NCAA Division I national championship at 142 in 1984, as well as Division II titles in 1983 and 1984. He earned the Most Valuable Wrestler award at the 1983 Division II National Championships.

Reyes graduated from Cal State-Bakersfield with a Bachelor in Business Administration in 1984. He furthered his education by taking classes in physical education and athletics administration while at Michigan State. Reyes and his wife, Yolanda, reside in Lafayette with daughters Brisa and Maya.

Wes Roper, Missouri (1987-1998)

Wes Roper served as the University of Missouri's wrestling coach for 12 seasons (1986-98), coaching nine wrestlers to 11 all-American designations and building an overall record of 73-94-4. Under Roper, who took the head job just four years after his graduation from MU, the Tigers registered seven top 25 team placements at the NCAA Championships including bests of 16th (1992), 18th (1994) and 19th (1988 and 1993). The Tigers had their best dual performance under Roper in 1992 at 8-6. In 1993, **Shaon Fry** placed second at 167 pounds in the NCAA Championships, the highest MU placement since Roper's fourth-place finish in 1982. Fry also placed third the following year.

On the mat, Roper stands second all-time in Mizzou history with 131 wins. He ranks first all-time in major decisions in a season (12 in 1981-82) and fifth all-time in victories in a season (40 in 1980-81). In 1982, he capped his career by placing fourth at 150 pounds at the NCAA Championships in an extremely tough weight that featured **Nate Carr** of Iowa State, **Kenny Monday** of Oklahoma State and **Roger Frizzell** of Oklahoma. Roper led Mizzou in wins three straight seasons, winning 34 matches in 1980, 40 in 1981 and 35 in 1982. He was named the school's most outstanding wrestler in 1980 and 1982 and set a school record for most points in a career that stood for 25 years.

Roper is a financial consultant with A.G. Edwards and lives in Kirksville, MO with his wife, Becky, and sons Derek and Austin. He was inducted into the Missouri Hall of Fame in 2006.

Joe Russell, George Mason (2011-present)

In his four years as head coach at George Mason, Joe Russell's charges have posted a 26-57 dual record. Over that period, four wrestlers have qualified for the NCAA Championships with heavyweight **Jacob Kettler** earning trips to two NCAA events (2013 and 2015). **Gregory**

Flournoy (157) joined Kettler in the 2015 tournament and registered the only match win by a Patriot wrestler under Russell. Other qualifiers were **Vincent Rodriguez** (125) and **Mendbagana Tovuujav** (197) in 2012.

Russell was an assistant coach on three NCAA championship teams (2001, 2002, 2007) at Minnesota under legendary **J Robinson**, coaching 11 individual national champions, six Big Ten title teams, 31 individual conference champions and 84 all-American honorees.

He was presented the Medal of Courage from the National Wrestling Hall of Fame in 2007. The Medal of Courage is presented annually to a wrestler or former wrestler who has overcome what appeared to be insurmountable challenges. In 1985, a motorcycle accident left Russell partially paralyzed on the left side of his body. He spent three weeks in a drug-induced coma and the process of recovery was long and grueling, but he recovered fully.

In 1998, he served as the coach of Team USA in a dual versus Germany and was selected as the coach for the USA Wrestling Tour de Monde team in Hungary. In 1999, he coached Team USA in a dual meet against Cuba and coached the U.S. 17-and-under team at the Cadet World Championships in Denmark. For his efforts, Russell was voted the 1999 USA Wrestling Person of the Year for the University and FILA Junior Age Divisions.

In addition, he coached the U.S. Junior Team at the 2000 Pan American Championships in Peru; the USA All-Stars in the First Annual Utah Greco-Roman Challenge in Utah; and the USA team at the Junior Pan American Championships in Toronto.

Russell wrestled at Minnesota from 1988-92. In his senior season, he served as team captain, was named to the Academic All-Big Ten team and was the winner of the team's **Dean Fraser** Most Courageous Wrestler award. He also competed for Athletes in Action on a summer tour to Australia and New Zealand.

He earned his Bachelor of Arts in 1992 and completed his juris doctorate in 1995. He is a licensed attorney and completed his master in sports management in 2006.

He and his wife, Sadie, have a son, Taft.

Tom Ryan, Ohio State (2006-present); Hofstra (1995-2006)

In 2015, Tom Ryan led Ohio State to the program's first-ever national championship, ending Penn State's four-year reign as **Logan Steiber** and **Nathan Tomasello** captured national titles. The Buckeyes also won the Big Ten title for the first time in 64 years. For his accomplishments, Ryan was named the 2015 Big Ten, NWCA and InterMat Coach of the Year.

Ryan has coached four different student-athletes to eight national championships: Steiber (4 titles), and two-time champions **J Jaggers**, **Mike Pucillo** and Tomasello. Under Ryan, the Buckeyes have finished in the Top 10 in seven of the last eight seasons, including runner-up finishes in 2008 and 2009.

A three-time National Coach of the Year, Ryan and his staff have coached 14 NCAA finalists, 23 all-Americans, nine Big Ten champions and 48 Academic All-Big-Ten honorees.

In 2008, national champs Jaggers and Pucillo led the Buckeyes to

Tom Ryan, head coach of 2015 NCAA champion Ohio State University. (Courtesy Ohio State University)

a second-place NCAA finish, which was repeated in 2009 in one of the closest finishes in NCAA history. Ohio State narrowly lost to Iowa by 4.5 points, their best finish in history at that time.

Prior to Ohio State, Ryan was head coach at Hofstra from 1995-2006. He earned Eastern Collegiate Wrestling Association and Colonial Athletic Association Coach of the Year honors seven times. He also was named New York State Coach of the Year twice. Leading Hofstra to six consecutive conference titles, his teams had the nation's longest unbeaten conference streak at 46-0-1. He has a lifetime career record of 222-126-1 (113-42 at Ohio State). He also was an assistant coach at Indiana from 1992-94.

As a wrestler, Ryan was an EIWA champ as a sophomore at Syracuse in 1989, then transferred to Iowa to wrestle for **Dan Gable**. In 1990 as a junior, he lost a narrow 8-7 decision to future four-time champion **Pat Smith** of OSU in the NCAA finals and placed third his senior year, both at 158.

Ryan earned his bachelor's degree in education from Iowa in 1993. He and his wife, Lynette, have four children, Jordan, Jake, Teague and Mackenzie.

Gil Sanchez, Clemson (1992-1995)

Gil Sanchez had a brief three-year career at Clemson, but took the program to new heights upon arrival. In his rookie season (1992-1993), the Tigers finished 13th in the NCAA Championship, third in the ACC Tournament and posted a 13-9-1 record. Sanchez was only the fourth rookie coach in any sport in Clemson history to lead a team to a top 20 finish. For his efforts, he was runner-up for Rookie Coach of the Year honors. Leading that team was NCAA 118-pound national champion **Sammie Henson**, only the second champ in Clemson wrestling history.

In 1994, Henson repeated as the 118-pound NCAA kingpin and seventh-seeded **Tim Morrissey** placed third to earn all-America honors as the Tigers placed a school-best seventh in the tournament. Earlier, Clemson had placed second in the ACC Tournament with three individual champions – tying school records for both. Clemson's 1995 team ran into difficulties on and off the mat, forcing Sanchez to resign with the Tigers holding a 4-13 dual mark. Sanchez ended with a 31-28-1 career record.

Sanchez was an NCAA runner-up for Nebraska at 134 pounds in 1987, falling to **John Smith** in the finals. He also was an All-Big 8 Academic selection and posted the winningest season in NU history with a 46-3 record. All three losses were to Smith, whom he beat in a dual in November – the last collegian to do so. His 29 falls in 1987 took his career total to 50 and he finished with a 96-25-3 career mark.

He earned his B.S. in education from Nebraska in 1988.

Pat Santoro, Lehigh (2008-present); Maryland (2003-2008)

Pat Santoro is the **Lawrence White** Head Coach of Wrestling at Lehigh. In his first season as head coach (2008-2009), he led Lehigh to a school-record 23 dual wins (starting 15-0), a runner-up finish in the EIWA and was named EIWA Coach of the Year. He garnered a second EIWA Coach of the Year honor in 2012 and has led 11 wrestlers to 12 EIWA individual titles, eight wrestlers to 15 all-American designations and has coached one national champion, **Zack Rey** (2011). He registered his milestone 100th dual win in the last match of 2015 and has a career record of 100-34-1 while leading Lehigh to six consecutive top 25 finishes in the NCAA tournament.

In 2015, Santoro's Mountain Hawks had three all-American placements, including a runner-up finish by **Nathaniel Brown** at 184. That made it four of the past five seasons that Lehigh had three all-American placers at the NCAA event. In 2014, he again had three all-Americans including **Darian Cruz**, the first true freshman all-American for Lehigh in 34 years.

Santoro's top squads were in 2011 and 2012 when Lehigh placed eighth in the NCAA Championships. In 2012, Rey and **Brandon Hatchett** placed second and two additional all-American placements pushed the Mountain Hawks into the top 10. In 2011, it was Rey's national title and three-time all-American **Robert Hamlin's** second-place finish that led Lehigh.

At Maryland, Santoro guided the Terrapins to their first ACC championship in 35 years in 2008 and was named ACC Wrestling Coach of the Year. In 2007, his squad registered a school record-tying 17 dual wins. He had a 48-41-1 dual record in five seasons. He was named NWCA National Assistant Coach of the Year in 2003 for his work at Lehigh just before becoming the Terps' head coach. He also served as an assistant at Duquesne and Penn State.

Santoro was a two-time national champion (1988, 1989) at the University of Pittsburgh and the school's only four-time all-American. He was a three-time Eastern Wrestling League champion and the recipient of Pittsburgh's Golden Panther Award in 1989, recognizing the outstanding athlete of the year. Internationally, he was a four-time member of the U.S. National Team and served as an alternate for the 1996 Olympic Team and the 1999 World Team. He placed fourth at the 2000 U.S. Olympic Trials, third at the 1992 Olympic Trials and was runner-up in the 1992 U.S. Open Freestyle Championships.

He earned his Bachelor's in psychology from Pittsburgh in 1992. He and his wife Julie have a daughter, Leah, and a son, Mack.

Mark Schultz, Brigham Young University (1994-2000)

Mark Schultz was hired as head coach at Brigham Young University in 1994 to turn the program around. With no NCAA qualifiers in his first two seasons, Schultz helped produced two qualifiers in 1996 and averaged four qualifiers per year over the next four years. BYU's best season under Schultz was in 2000 when five wrestlers made it into the NCAA Championships and all five scored points for the Cougars led by **Rangi Smart** at 165. Smart won his first bout and registered two consolation wins to narrowly miss the top eight. BYU's lone all-American during Schultz's reign was **Aaron Holker** who was seventh at 133 pounds in 1999. BYU dropped its wrestling program following the 2000 season.

A superstar at Oklahoma, Schultz won three NCAA titles over three stellar Iowa wrestlers: 1981 at 167 pounds over **Mike DeAnna**; 1982 over **Ed Banach** (177); and 1983 over

Duane Goldman (177). His closer-than-it-looks 16-8 win over Banach in 1982 is rated by many as the best finals match in history. Not only did it earn Schultz his second of three titles, it stopped Banach's attempt to become the first wrestler to win four championships. Internationally, Schultz was an Olympic gold medalist in 1984 and World Champion in 1985 and 1987. In addition, he won a World Cup title in 1982 and was a four-time U.S. Open Freestyle champion (1984-87).

He and his late brother, **Dave Schultz**, were the most successful brothers in U.S. amateur wrestling. He was inducted into the National Wrestling Hall of Fame in 1995.

Brian Smith, Missouri (1998-present); Syracuse (1997-1998)

Brian Smith is the winningest wrestling coach in University of Missouri history with a career record of 223-90-3 and his winning percentage of .711 is tops for the program. He has taken the Tiger program to national prominence and its highest NCAA finishes in history: third in 2007 and fourth in 2015. His teams have posted 13 consecutive seasons with a dual record at or above .500. Smith has coached 20 all-Americans to 33 top-eight performances and five Tigers to six national titles. **Ben Askren** was the first Mizzou wrestler to win an NCAA championship and the only Tiger to win back-to-back national titles (2006 and 2007). Other national champs under Smith are **Mark Ellis** (2009), **Max Askren** (2010), true freshman **J'den Cox** (2014) and **Drake Houdashelt** (2015).

In 2012, Smith's wrestlers won the school's first-ever conference championship, crowning four titlists and sending 10 wrestlers to the NCAA event (also a school first and the only school to qualify all 10 wrestlers that year). For his efforts, Smith was honored as Big 12 Coach of the Year.

In 2013, Missouri left the Big 12 and became a wrestling member of the Mid-American Conference (MAC). The Tigers won the conference championship, ending an 11-year reign by Central Michigan, set a conference scoring record (136 points) and sent all 10 wrestlers to the NCAA's. He was named Mid-American Conference Coach of the Year.

At least one Mizzou wrestler has reached the NCAA tournament in each of Smith's 17 seasons and his squads have finished among the top-20 programs at the NCAA Championships in 13 of the last 14 years. The Tigers had a school-record five all-Americans in both 2009 and 2015.

In 2007, Smith was named **Dan Gable** Coach of the Year by W.I.N. Magazine. He also was head coach at Syracuse in 1997-1998.

Smith was a two-time NCAA qualifier, reaching the quarterfinals in 1990. He was a three-time All-Big Ten wrestler and a four-time letterman at Michigan State from 1986-1990 and is among the top-25 on Michigan State's all-time wins list with 84 career victories. He also is tied for 19th on MSU's single-season list with 32 victories in 1990.

John Smith, Oklahoma State (1991-present)

You only need one word to describe John Smith: Legend. Smith has coached at OSU for 25 seasons, longer than any other Cowboy mentor except the legendary **Edward Gallagher** (also 25 seasons). His career record through the 2015-16 season of 384-59-6 (.861) makes him the winningest coach in school history.

His teams have won 18 conference championships (including 2016) and five NCAA wrestling team titles (1994 and 2003 through 2006). In 2006, Smith won his fourth consecutive NCAA team title and surpassed his coach, **Tom Chesbro**, as the all-time winningest coach in school history. The Cowboys crowned two national champions in **Johny Hendricks** (165) and **Jake Rosholt** (197). It was Rosholt's third national championship and fourth all-American performance. In 2005, the Cowboys compiled a 21-0 dual meet record and capped the season with one of the most dominant showings in the history of the NCAA Championships with five

John Smith has led Oklahoma State to five NCAA titles. (Courtesy Oklahoma State University)

NCAA champions: **Zack Esposito** (149), Hendricks (165), **Chris Pendleton** (repeating as champion at 174), Rosholt (197) and **Steve Mocco** (heavyweight). The 2004 season saw Pendleton win his first NCAA crown and the Cowboys capture Smith's second championship. In 2003, the Pokes went 17-0, won the Big 12 title with six champions and took down the NCAA crown with two winners in **Johnny Thompson** (133) and Rosholt (184) and five additional all-Americans.

Smith has won 14 conference coach of the year awards (Big 8 and Big 12) and two NWCA National Coach of the Year honors (1994 and 2003) while coaching 29 NCAA individual champions (most among active coaches) and 111 all-Americans (second among active coaches).

As a competitor, Smith was a three-time all-American and two-time NCAA champion at OSU (1987 and 1988) with a 154-7-2 record. He holds school records for career victories (154), single-season victories (47), career bonus-point wins (113), single-season bonus-point wins (39), and single season bonus-point win percentage (.907).

From 1987 to 1992 he won *six consecutive world titles* including Olympic gold medals in 1988 and 1992 and World Games gold medals in 1987, 1989, 1990 and 1991. His 1987 win marked the first time in history that a collegiate wrestler won a world title while still in school. His international record was an astonishing 100-5. Smith was the first American to be chosen Master of Technique and Wrestler of the Year by the International Wrestling Federation (FILA); the first wrestler to receive the **James E. Sullivan** Award as America's outstanding athlete; and the first wrestler ever nominated for the World Trophy, which he received in 1992. Other recognition includes: Man of the Year by *Amateur Wrestling News* in 1988; Athlete of the Year by USA Wrestling in 1989; Sportsman of the Year (U.S. Olympic Committee) in 1990; and 100 Greatest Olympians of All Time in 1996. In 2004, Smith received the Titan Award (U.S. Olympic Committee) and in 2005 was named, along with his younger brother **Pat Smith**, as one of 15 wrestlers on the NCAA's 75th Anniversary Team. Smith was inducted into the National Wrestling Hall of Fame and the Oklahoma Sports Hall of Fame in 1997 and enshrined in the FILA International Wrestling Hall of Fame in 2003.

He and his wife, Toni, have three sons – Joseph, Samuel and Levi – and two daughters, Isabell and Cecilia.

Lee Roy Smith, Arizona State (1993-2001)

In his nine-year career at Arizona State, Smith led the Sun Devils to nine NCAA appearances, five top-10 national finishes and four Pac-10 titles. His highest NCAA finish was fourth in both 1993 and 1995. He coached 27 all-Americans at ASU, including two national champions: **Ray Miller**, 1993 (167) and **Markus Mollica**, 1993 (158) and 1995 (167). Smith ended his ASU coaching career with an overall dual record of 91-58-1 (.607).

Smith was named Pac-10 Coach of the Year in 1993 and 1998, and was selected Co-Coach of the Year in 1997. He was named Rookie Coach of the Year by *Amateur Wrestling News* in 1992-93.

Smith took the ASU post after serving as USA Wrestling's freestyle coach for the United States national team from 1989 through the 1992 Olympics. At the Barcelona games, Smith guided the USA to three gold (including the second Olympic gold for his brother, **John Smith**), two silver and one bronze medal, placing men in the top seven in all 10 weight classes. In 1997, Smith coached the USA Wrestling team at the World Championships in Siberia.

In the three years prior to the Olympics, he coached six individuals to world freestyle wrestling titles (including brother John) and helped guide the U.S. National Team to three runner-up finishes at the World Championships.

From 1987-89, Smith was a member of the Swiss Wrestling Federation national coaching staff. In that capacity, he conducted training camps for Swiss National Team members prior to international competition, helping the Swiss team to its best-ever showing at the Freestyle World Championships in Clermont-Ferrand, France, in 1987.

Smith began his coaching career first as a graduate assistant coach and then as an assistant coach for his alma mater, Oklahoma State University, from 1982-87. He helped guide the Cowboys to five top-four NCAA finishes and three Big Eight Conference titles.

Competitively, Smith was a two-time Oklahoma high school state champion at Del City and a two-time Junior National champion. Smith also was a three-time all-American at Oklahoma State and earned four Big Eight individual titles. He won an NCAA title at 142 pounds in 1980 and helped the Cowboys to second-place finishes at the NCAAs in 1977 and 1980.

Smith was the National Open Freestyle champion from 1980-82 and the World silver medalist in 1983. At the U.S. Olympic Trials in 1984, Smith and rival **Randy Lewis** battled through controversial matches and rematches, protests, suits and counter-suits before Lewis was awarded the spot on the team and won a gold medal in Los Angeles.

He currently serves as executive director of the National Wrestling Hall of Fame in Stillwater, OK. He and his wife, Lisa, have two daughters, LeAnne and Shannon.

Pat Tocci, Kutztown University (1996-2000)

In 1996, Pat Tocci became head wrestling coach at Kutztown University (PA) where he built a nationally recognized NCAA Division II program. In his four-year career, Kutztown advanced nine wrestlers to the NCAA Division II Championships, two who became all-Americans. Five of his student-athletes received academic all-American honors.

Tocci attended Brown University (1989-1993) where he competed in the 118-pound weight class. After graduation, he served as an assistant wrestling coach under **Jay Weiss** at Harvard.

Originally from Bethlehem (PA), he placed third in the 1989 PIAA State Tournament competing for Liberty High School. He was a 1988 Espoir national champion, a Greco-Roman national champion, a Freestyle Junior National all-American and a Senior Level Greco-Roman all-American. He was an assistant coach at Bethlehem (PA) Catholic High School for two years.

He currently serves as senior director for the National Wrestling Coaches Association.

Jay Weiss, Harvard (1995-present)

Jay Weiss is The **David G. Bunning** '88 Head Coach for Harvard Wrestling. The two-time EIWA Coach of the Year has mentored two national champions, 17 EIWA champions and 19 all-American's during his 21 seasons. Prior to Weiss, Harvard had just seven all-American's in almost 80 years of wrestling. Winning titles under Weiss were **Jesse Jantzen** (2004) and **J.P. O'Connor** (2010). Jantzen was the first Harvard wrestler to win an NCAA title since 1938 with his victory at 149.

Weiss' 2001 EIWA championship squad boasted two individual champions and six NCAA qualifiers, the largest contingent to ever represent Harvard at the event. Weiss was honored as EIWA Coach of the Year for the second time in his career after earning Harvard's first such distinction in 1998. In addition to the six wrestlers who made the NCAAs in 2001, Harvard has placed four in the meet seven times under Weiss. The Crimson finished 20th as a team at the NCAA meet in 1999, 22nd in 2002, 2004 and 2007, 23rd in 2010, 28th in 2000 and 29th in 1998.

In 2015, Harvard had three men earn All-Ivy League honors, including **David Ng** who made an appearance at the NCAA Championships at heavyweight. The 2014 season saw two Crimson wrestlers reach the NCAA Championships: EIWA champion **Todd Preston** who reached the quarterfinals at 141 before falling and **James Fox** (197), who made his third consecutive trip to nationals.

Weiss received the **Bob Bubb** Coaching Excellence Award in 2009 for the accomplishments he and his team made in the classroom and in competition. The award is presented annually to one coach across each division of collegiate wrestling, and is intended to recognize an outstanding coach who epitomizes the qualities and characteristics of a role model and mentor for developing young student-athletes. Weiss was one of two recipients of the United States Marine Corps Excellence in Leadership Award in 2007. He also was named the Wrestling USA 2008 Massachusetts Person of the Year.

A 1990 Franklin & Marshall graduate and four-year starter on the wrestling team, he was an EIWA runner-up and an NCAA qualifier as a senior. He graduated with the school record for most wins in a season with 29, and ranked second in all-time career wins.

His wife, Jennifer, is the head coach of the Harvard women's volleyball team. They have two sons, Colby and Keegan.

Jim Zalesky, Oregon State (2006-present); Iowa (1997-2006)

Jim Zalesky's Oregon State teams have won six conference championships and finished either first or second eight times. He has mentored nine all-Americans and 22 conference champions. His teams captured four consecutive Pac-12 titles (2012-2015) and five of six with a title in 2010, and his 111 victories are third-most in school history.

In 2014, OSU became just the third team in Division I history with 1,000 dual wins when it defeated Southern Oregon in its season-opener. That was Zalesky's 100th dual win. His career record at Oregon State is 111-41-2 and 238-75-2 overall in 18 years as a head coach, split evenly between OSU and Iowa. At Iowa, his teams won three consecutive national championships (1998-2000).

The Beavers finished 12-1 overall in 2015, were 6-0 at home, won the conference championship, had five wrestlers capture individual conference titles, seven NCAA qualifiers, and five student/athletes on the Pac-12 All-Academic team.

Zalesky was named Pac-12 wrestling coach of the year in 2012 after winning the conference championship, sending eight wrestlers into the NCAA Tournament and placing tenth. Three Beavers earned all-American honors. In 2010 he earned his first conference coach of the year award following a Pac-10 title and an 18-3 dual record that included a 17 match win streak.

At Iowa, he compiled a 127-34 dual meet record, serving as head coach from the 1997-98 season through the 2005-06 season. His Hawkeye teams captured three Big Ten team titles and won 10 NCAA individual titles and 45 all-America honors. He was named the Big Ten Coach of the Year in 2000 and 2004 and the National Wrestling Coaches Association Coach of the Year in 1998 and 1999. His coaching career also includes three years as an assistant coach at Minnesota and seven seasons as an assistant under legendary Iowa coach **Dan Gable**. He was named the National Wrestling Coaches Association Assistant Coach of the Year in 1992 and 1997.

As a collegian, he was a four-time all-American and three-time NCAA champion at 158 pounds, ending his Iowa career with an 89-match winning streak. He was named Outstanding Wrestler at the 1984 NCAA Championships and *Amateur Wrestling News* named him the Wrestler of the Decade for the 1980s.

Zalesky was inducted into the National Wrestling Hall of Fame in 2004 as a Distinguished Member, the University of Iowa Letterman's Club Hall of Fame, the Iowa High School Athletic Association Wrestling Hall of Fame in 2002, and the Iowa Wrestling Hall of Fame in 1994.

He is a 1984 graduate of Iowa. He and his wife, Teri, have four children: Nicolette, Jaclyn, Zackery and Lucas.

Lennie Zalesky, California Baptist University (2011-present); UC-Davis (2001-2010)

Lennie Zalesky was hired as California Baptist University's second wrestling coach in 2011 and helped transition the program to full NCAA Division II and Rocky Mountain Athletic Conference (RMAC) membership. In four seasons, Zalesky led CBU to a 39-24-1 overall dual record. He has coached 19 all-Americans and four individual national champions at CBU. The Lancers won a program-best 13 duals in the 2014-15 season.

The Lancers had an impressive debut in NCAA Division II in 2013-14, posting an 11-4-1 dual mark (3-1 in the RMAC) and defeated two Division I opponents. CBU placed second in its first-ever Division II Super Region IV and Rocky Mountain Athletic Conference Championships, with half of its lineup advancing to the NCAA Div. II Championships. Three Lancers won regional/conference titles, with three wrestlers going on to earn NCAA all-American status. CBU took 12th place overall nationally in its inaugural campaign in the NCAA.

In the 2012-13 season, Zalesky led the Lancers to a first place finish at the NCWA National Championship, grabbing the second title in program history. CBU had two individual champions – **Bradford Gerl** at 141 and **Zach Merrill** (at repeat champ at heavyweight) – and nine all-Americans. It was CBU's third tournament victory of the season.

In his first season, Zalesky led the Lancers to a runner-up finish at the 2012 NCWA National Championship, with six Lancers earning all-American honors and two winning individual titles – **Jimmy Martinez** at 125 and Merrill at heavyweight.

Zalesky was head coach at NCAA Division I UC Davis before the program was dropped prior to the 2010-11 season. In those nine seasons, he coached numerous Pac-10 placers, five conference champions and had 30 athletes qualify for the NCAA Championships. Perhaps his best season came in 2007 when he was named Pac-10 Coach of the Year and also coached the Aggies' first-ever NCAA Division I National Champion in any sport (**Derek Moore**, 141 pounds), which helped UC Davis finish 22nd at the NCAA National Championships, its best showing ever. Moore finished 24-0 and was named Outstanding Wrestler.

His first coaching job came at his alma mater where he served under **Dan Gable** from 1986-90. He then spent eight seasons as the head wrestling coach at Palmer High School in Palmer, Alaska. In 2010, he was inducted into the Alaska Wrestling Hall of Fame. He also spent two seasons as an assistant coach at the University of Indiana and then was the dean of students and wrestling coach at Culver Military Academy in Culver, IN, for two years prior to taking the UC Davis job in the summer of 2011.

Zalesky was a three-time all-American wrestler at Iowa, helping the Hawkeyes to four straight national championships, and he notched a record of 73-2-1 in his last two seasons. He was twice the national runner-up at 142 pounds and won three Big Ten titles. Internationally, he won silver medals in the 1983 Pan American Games, the 1984 World Cup, 1984 Tbilisi Tournament in Russia and the 1983 Canadian Cup.

He graduated from Iowa in 1983 with a degree in finance and later earned another Bachelor's in Education and Russian Language in 1990, also from Iowa. He earned a Master's from Indiana in Slavic linguistics and literature in 2000. He was recognized five times in the 1990s for outstanding achievement by the American Council of Teachers of Russian.

Zalesky and his wife, Maria, have two children.

CHAPTER 24

Schultz vs. Stewart: The Upset That Wasn't

When the wrestling world talks about the biggest upsets in collegiate wrestling, **Larry Owings'** (Washington) 1970 finals victory over unbeaten **Dan Gable** (Iowa State) at Northwestern University is always the first match mentioned. It is so well known and documented, that people simply refer to it as Gable-Owings. Also talked about are **Darrion Caldwell's** (North Carolina State) 11-6 win over top-seeded and defending national champion **Brent Metcalf** (Iowa) at 149 pounds in 2009; **Mark Perry's** (Iowa) upset of defending champion **Johny Hendricks** (Oklahoma State) at 165 pounds in 2007; and **Damion Hahn's** (Minnesota) 5-4 upset of top-seeded **Jon Trenge** (Lehigh) at 197 in 2003.

But two of the most talked about upsets in collegiate wrestling history took place in the Golden Era of Amateur Wrestling and both were at the 1981 NCAA Championships in Princeton, NJ. In the finals at 134 pounds, sixth-seeded **Jim Gibbons** of Iowa State knocked off top-seeded **Darryl Burley** (Lehigh), 16-8, and three matches later **Rick Stewart** (Oklahoma State) pinned the heavily-favored **Dave Schultz** (Oklahoma) at 4:56 to win his second straight NCAA title at 158.

Wrestlers and wrestling fans remember that Stewart, trailing in the match, hit a fireman's carry and pinned the Oklahoma and international superstar at the end of the second period. **Stan Abel**, Oklahoma's head coach at that time, remembers the match like it was yesterday.

"David could be moody and tough to coach," said Abel. "He was ahead of Ricky 3-1. David was walking into him and Ricky was trying to hit the fireman's carry. The first two or three carry attempts went off the mat. I was yelling at David 'Do not walk into him. Make him come to you.' The only chance Ricky had, and don't get me wrong, he was a helluva athlete and the defending champion, but his only chance was if David kept coming into him. I grabbed David. 'David, listen to me. Do not walk into that man!' David kind of waved at me dismissively as if to say 'I can handle this.' Ten seconds later, David walked in, Ricky hit an outside carry and got a leg through. When Dave reached back, Ricky hit the half, reared back and pinned him. David got up and never said a word."

Abel says he and Schultz never talked about that match until a year later.

"I was eating in the athletic dining hall and David came in and asked if he could sit with me. We sat there eating chili. David was a pretty quiet guy and wasn't saying anything. Then, out of the clear blue, he says 'I should have listened to you.' I looked up and smiled. 'You damn sure should have.'"

Schultz's Oklahoma teammate **Andre Metzger** remembers the match vividly. "When Stewart hit the near arm-far leg, he dumped Dave on his butt. Dave went to his side, and I can still see this in slow motion in my mind, Dave reached back to whizzer and I was like screaming in my head 'don't whizzer!' He needed to bail right there, but Ricky hit the half and it was over."

"I was there for the 158-pound NCAA finals in 1981 when Ricky Stewart hit the fireman's carry on Schultz," said **Joe Gibbons**, Iowa State. "Dave tried to whizzer out, but his head was down and Ricky went double trouble and locked it up. People were shocked since Dave had beaten him two or three times that year, but Stewart was the defending national champion and a great wrestler in his own right."

Sportswriter **J. Carl Guymon**, who has covered college wrestling for 45 years and attended every NCAA Tournament during that time, remembers the match well.

"Ricky had one of the best firemen's carries I've ever seen," said Guymon. "Two other guys had great ones: **Ron Ray** of OSU and former OSU coach **Myron Roderick**. Myron could take anyone down with his firemen's, even when he was coaching. Dave Schultz was a great wrestler and everyone assumed Dave would win the match. But Ricky caught Dave and all of a sudden, he had him on his back. I was thinking 'four-point move' and then bam! Schultz was pinned. It stunned everyone."

Ricky Stewart working to finish his world-class fireman's carry. (Courtesy Oklahoma State University)

And everyone knows the outcome. Not everyone knows the story behind the story.

"Dave and I were the same age and were at Oklahoma State at the same time," said Stewart. "After I redshirted my first year, I grew over the summer and was comfortable at 158. Dave also wanted to wrestle at 158. He told me I should wrestle at 150 and he would wrestle at 158 all season, then we would switch for the Big 8 Tournament. I didn't agree to that and he didn't want to pull to 150, so he ended up transferring to UCLA. I don't think the team chemistry at OSU was a good fit for Dave. He was a freestyler. We focused on Oklahoma State style."

Schultz then transferred to Oklahoma when UCLA dropped its program. In his first year at OU (1980-81season), Schultz rolled to a perfect 29-0 record. The media started calling him "The Chairman of the Board." During his march to the NCAA tournament, he easily defeated Stewart in the first OU-OSU Bedlam match and romped past OSU's future superstar **Mike Sheets** 20-4 in the second Bedlam bout. In the Big 8 championship tourney,

Schultz again beat Stewart (4-2) to take the conference crown at 158. Of significance was the fact that Stewart attempted three fireman's carries in the bout, only to have Schultz roll out of them at the edge of the mat.

Standing on the medal podium in OSU's Gallagher Hall, Schultz placed his hand on Stewart's shoulder, leaned down and said "Hey, Rick, second place isn't so bad is it?"

"I know he was trying to get inside my head, but that didn't sit well with me. That hurt my pride. I knew I had to make some changes," said Stewart. "In practice for the next two weeks, I changed my carry to a near arm-far leg, an outside fireman's, so he wouldn't be able to roll. I worked on that really hard."

At the NCAA Championship, Schultz opened with an 11-5 decision over **Rick O'Shea** of Oregon. He registered an easy 18-6 win over Lehigh's **Jim Reilly** in the second round and then dominated unseeded **Jim Farina** of Iowa State, 14-1. Farina had placed third in the Big 8 tournament behind Schultz and Stewart. In the semifinals, Schultz survived a 6-5 decision over Cal State-Bakersfield's **Perry Shea** to reach the finals.

On the other side of the bracket, Stewart was doing his best to make a rematch with Schultz a reality. An opening round 22-4 drubbing of Oregon State's PAC-10 champion **John Ohly** was followed by an 11-5 win over #11 **Tom Janicik** of Northwestern and a quarter-finals romp past seventh-seeded **Jan Michaels** of North Carolina, 25-8. In the semifinals, Stewart handled Iowa's future three-time national champion and National Wrestling Hall of Fame Distinguished Member **Jim Zalesky**, 8-4, to set up the much anticipated finals match against Schultz.

The two grapplers were tentative in the early going. Stewart was hit with two stalling points and Schultz with one, while Dave picked up an escape point early in the second period. Schultz was leading Stewart 3-1 near the end of the second period when he went for a takedown.

"I countered with the near arm-far leg and he went straight down, fell like a ton of bricks," said Stewart. "The half was staring me in the face. I put it in for the pin."

The crowd's reaction was one of shock as Stewart jumped up, triumphant.

"Ricky ran across the mat and jumped into my arms and was crying, coach, coach," said Abel.

Sounds unusual for a wrestler to celebrate with the opposing coach, doesn't it Stan?

"No, Ricky and I were good friends," said Abel. "He was just so excited to have beaten Dave. I was happy for Ricky, but not happy for Dave or our team."

"I was in the stands for the 158-pound finals match between Dave Schultz and Ricky Stewart," said **Mike Moyer**, West Chester's 158-pounder who had lost to Zalesky, 7-3, in the second round. "It was like Ali-Frazier. The crowd was really into it. When Stewart hit Schultz with the fireman's carry and pinned him, the crowd went nuts. Everyone was like 'Did you see that? Did that just happen?' The one word that came out of everyone's mouths was 'Wow!'

As Stewart stood on the gold medal riser between runner-up Schultz and third-place finisher **Perry Shea**, he put his hand on Schultz's shoulder, leaned down and said "I guess second place isn't too bad, is it?"

It was one of the biggest upsets in NCAA finals history that really wasn't an upset. It was a textbook example of adaptation and motivation. Stewart adapted his patented firemen's carry and derived great motivation from his Big 8 Tournament loss and Schultz's earlier mind games. Payback can be rough. However, the loss to Stewart motivated Schultz to return to OU for his senior season and a shot at a national championship.

"I saw Dave back at the motel where OU and Mizzou wrestlers were on the same floor," said **Wes Roper**, Missouri's 158-pounder. "Dave told me he hated collegiate wrestling and wanted to focus on freestyle. But now after losing, he had to come back. He detested riding time, but won the NCAA title the next year by riding out **Mike Sheets** in the finals in O.T.!"

Wrestling up a weight at 167 in 1982, Schultz avenged a 4-3 loss to Sheets in the Big 8 finals two weeks earlier by taking a paper-thin 4-4, 1-1 criteria decision and securing his only national championship. Stewart was upset by **Perry Shea** in the semifinals at 157 and missed registering his third straight NCAA title. He placed third with a 3-2 decision over OU's **Isreal Sheppard**.

After an undefeated career at Duncan High School and three state championships, Stewart became a four-time all-American at OSU with two national championships under his belt.

"Ricky Stewart was a great collegiate wrestler with superior strength and an unstoppable fireman's carry," said **Roger Frizzell**, Oklahoma's outstanding four-time all-American at 150. "But because he didn't wrestle freestyle, he doesn't get nearly the credit he deserves in the wrestling community."

CHAPTER 25

Remembering Dave Schultz

An international superstar throughout his career, Schultz wrestled for Oklahoma State as a freshman before transferring to UCLA then to the University of Oklahoma. He dazzled the wrestling world even before he got out of Palo Alto (CA) High School by winning a college tournament over the defending NCAA Champion. Schultz was a two-time Sooner NCAA finalist, winning the title in 1982 over Cowboy great Mike Sheets in overtime by criteria. He was 61-4 at OU. As a freshman at Oklahoma State in 1978, Schultz placed third at 150.

Dave Schultz (Courtesy Nancy Schultz)

Dave Schultz won 10 Senior National titles (eight in Freestyle and two in Greco-Roman) over a 19-year span, at three weight divisions: 149.9 lbs., 163 lbs. and 180.5 lbs. In international competition, Schultz won a 1983 World Championship and a 1984 Olympic gold medal, four World Cup and two Pan American Games titles. He is the only American to twice win the prestigious tournament in Tbilisi and was a seven-time World and Olympic medalist.

Dave and his brother, **Mark Schultz**, along with **Lou** and **Ed Banach**, were the first American brothers to each win gold medals in the same Olympics (1984), and likewise the only American brothers to win both World and Olympic championships.

Schultz was an assistant coach at the University of Oklahoma, Stanford University and the University of Wisconsin. On January 26, 1996, while serving as coach of Team Foxcatcher, he was murdered in cold blood by the mentally-ill John du Pont.

Wrestling Resume for David L. Schultz

Among the accomplishments in Dave Schultz' long wrestling career:

- 1977 California state champion for Palo Alto High School
- Outstanding wrestler 1977 California high school state championships
- 1977 Senior National title in Greco-Roman at the AAU Nationals (while still in high school)

- 1977 Pan American Games Greco-Roman champion
- 1982 NCAA champion for the University of Oklahoma at 167
- Three-time NCAA all-American (placing 3rd at 150 for Oklahoma State in 1978; 2nd at 167 for Oklahoma in 1981 and 1st in 1982)
- 1983 Senior Freestyle World champion at 163
- 1984 Olympic gold medal in freestyle at 74 kg/163 lbs.
- 1987 Pan American Games freestyle champion
- 1986 Goodwill Games gold medalist
- 1994 Goodwill Games silver medalist
- Three-time World silver medalist (1985, 1987, 1993)
- Two-time World bronze medalist (1982, 1986)
- Five-time World Cup champion (1980, 1982, 1985, 1994, 1995)
- Three-time World Cup silver medalist (1978, 1981, 1983)
- Two-time Tbilisi Tournament champion (1984, 1991)
- Three-time Deglane Challenge champion (1983, 1990, 1991)
- Ten-time Senior Nationals champ in both freestyle and Greco-Roman
- Outstanding wrestler at US Nationals 1984, 1987 and 1993
- Assistant wrestling coach for University of Oklahoma, Stanford University, and University of Wisconsin
- Wrestling coach for Team Foxcatcher
- National Wrestling Hall of Fame, 1997 (posthumously)

Remembrances

Jim Scherr, Nebraska (1982-1984)

This was in the press statement by USA Wrestling issued the day after Dave's murder on January 26, 1996 by executive director Jim Scherr:

"USA Wrestling is deeply shocked and saddened to hear of the death of Dave Schultz, one of the great athletes and individuals ever involved in the sport of wrestling.

"We have truly lost a giant, an ambassador of goodwill around the world. Few people have made such an impact on the sport as Dave. His legacy will encompass much more than the numerous medals and honors which he won on the mat.

"The record books will forever tell the story of Dave's excellence as a wrestler. A 1984 Olympic gold medal, a 1983 World title, plus a Goodwill Games title, a Pan American Games title, four World Cup titles and ten national titles. He was truly one of the best ever to lace up a pair of wrestling shoes.

"But what records won't tell you is the kind of person Dave was and impact he made on all of us in wrestling. There literally wasn't a wrestler Dave wasn't willing to help. He had a profound impact on virtually all of the elite athletes in the U.S. the last fifteen years, as a competitor, coach and friend. He will be irreplaceable among the wrestling community. He touched the lives of thousands of people, all who were enriched by his spirit.

"He shared his love and enthusiasm for wrestling with everybody that he met. Through his unique personality, he made friends wherever he traveled and was loved by wrestling fans here in the United States and all over the world."

Roger Frizzell, Oklahoma (1980-83)

Dave Schultz was one of the best wrestlers of the past century in my view. He was an outstanding wrestler in college style, but even better in freestyle. Few people knew that he also was an outstanding wrestler in Greco-Roman.

He was my teammate and daily workout partner at OU for three years. He was the finest wrestling technician I had ever met and he was one of the best counter wrestlers in our sport's history. He studied moves and adapted them to fit his own unique style. Dave was one of the hardest workers you would ever find and he spent hours in the mat room outside of practice perfecting his technique by drilling ever part of the move again and again.

Dave and I also traveled together to freestyle tournaments around the world including the Junior World Games in Mongolia. Once again, we spent hours together training. Over time, I began to pick up some of his style and techniques. When I wrestled overseas, people thought I was Dave's and Mark's brother, which was the greatest of compliments.

I also learned in very personal way that Dave was a fierce competitor. I went up a weight class to 163 pounds for the Senior National Freestyle Championships and wrestled Dave in the semifinals. Dave beat me 2-1 in one of the toughest matches I ever wrestled in any tournament. It was nearly impossible to find a way to score on him and he went on to win the tournament.

Dave was a close friend and a true ambassador of the sport. He helped shape the sport of wrestling in the U.S. and around the world in the process.

Andy Rein, Wisconsin (1977-1980)

I had the privilege of having Dave as both a teammate and as an assistant coach at the University of Wisconsin. Dave had a tremendous love for his family and the sport of wrestling – spending quality time as a husband/father and coach/athlete. This is what Dave wanted to do and he did them well.

Dave had a unique combination of that California "free spirit" and a tremendous focus and dedication to the competitive sport of wrestling. Outside of his family life, wrestling was most important to Dave. While on the mat, Dave was always in a learning (or beating) mode – innovative and thoughtful, always wanting to get better. He was known to always have his wrestling shoes with him just in case there was an opportunity to step on the mat.

We competed together on teams to Tbilisi (Soviet Georgia) and the 1984 Olympics. I remember Dave coming up to me after I won the Tbilisi tournament in 1983. Dave said "Rein, that was awesome. You wrestled just like them (Russians). You didn't do anything!" Dave went on to win two Tbilisi titles and had the respect and friendship of many Russian and foreign athletes and coaches. He was a true ambassador.

In 1986, Dave came to the University of Wisconsin where we coached together for three years. I am not sure Dave knew what he was getting into with the change of seasons in the Midwest. During the winter months of wrestling season, Dave would wear his Russian

Ushanka hat and American goggles riding his mountain bike through the snow to the wrestling office and practice. The wrestlers on the team loved him and the other UW coaches were in constant wonder – who is this guy?

Lennie Zalesky, Iowa (1979-1982)

I trained with Dave quite a bit during 1983-84. I was the weight class beneath him. I was on several teams he was on at the same time like the Tbilisi Tournament, duals of 1984 and the Henri Deglane Challenge in France. He also trained at Iowa for several weeks.

One of the things I remember most about Dave is how he would handle the end of each practice. If I or anyone else were to give him troubles in a certain technical area during practice, he would ask what we were doing and then drill/wrestle hard for 15-20 minutes in that area to erase the problem from his wrestling.

I found him to be the most difficult guy to wrestle or workout with. Everything hurt and he felt like he weighed 30 pounds more because of the pressure he could put on you, mainly with his boney hips. I was excited to work out with him the first time he asked, but never too enthused after that.

Barry Davis, Iowa (1981-83, 1985)

I think Dave Schultz was one of the greatest technicians the U.S. has ever seen. I think because of his death, it hurt our sport and set us back. He not only was a great wrestler, but also supported everyone else to be the best they could be on and off the mat.

Jim Heffernan, Iowa (1983, 1985-87)

I worked out with Dave on several occasions, but never did compete against him. He had graduated from Oklahoma the year prior to when I started school. Following our workouts, Dave was very good about taking the time to help me and give constructive criticism on how he thought I could improve, and what I could do differently. From that point on, even as an opposing coach, he always made a point to say something positive to me.

Steve Martin, Iowa (1985-1991)

Dave was an awesome guy. He helped me out when I was at low points in college even though he was at Wisconsin and I was at Iowa. He really cared and had a way of making you think about the problem and made you want to please him.

Wes Roper, Missouri (1977-1982)

I wrestled Dave my junior year (1981) when I moved up a weight to 158 from 150. He dominated the 158-pound weight that year, but in the NCAA finals Ricky Stewart of OSU pinned Dave after hitting a great fireman's carry. Dave had dominated Ricky in earlier matches that year. I saw Dave back at the motel where OU and MU wrestlers were on the same floor. Dave told me he hated collegiate wrestling and wanted to focus on freestyle. But now after losing, he had to come back. He detested riding time, but won the NCAA title the next year by riding out Mike Sheets in the finals in O.T.!

Joe Gibbons, Iowa State (1982-1986)

I was at Foxcatcher and I spent a lot of time with Dave Schultz. He was the toughest guy I ever worked out with. I hated those workouts. He was so deceiving. He wrestled so relaxed, then he would explode on you. He just needed an inch. He would hit you with a gut wrench or an ankle twist and you thought 'If I don't turn, bones are going to break.' He put you into situations where muscles would get torn if you didn't turn. Schultz could hurt you.

I was there for the 158-pound NCAA finals in 1981 when Ricky Stewart hit the fireman's carry on Schultz. People were shocked since Dave had beaten him twice that year, but Stewart was the defending national champion and a great wrestler.

INDEX

Funk, Mike 34, 42, 44, 58, 64

Futrell, Bernard 103

G

Gable, Dan vii, 5, 8, 11, 46, 47, 49, 50, 52, 53, 55, 62, 83, 86, 90, 91, 92, 116, 121, 127, 141, 147, 150, 154, 156, 158, 159, 164, 170, 174, 176, 180, 181, 183

Gadson, Kyven 162, 164

Gallagher, Edward 177

Gardner, Dwight 161

Gardner, Rulon 114

Gerl, Bradford 181

Ghaffari, Matt 109, 110, 115, 119

Gibbons, Jeff 34, 39, 82, 90, 139

Gibbons, Jim vii, 3, 15, 17, 34, 51, 53, 60, 69, 78, 80, 90, 91, 149, 150, 151, 159, 183

Gibbons, Joe vii, 18, 29, 31, 32, 54, 58, 64, 78, 80, 82, 90, 91, 159, 184, 191

Gibbons, Tim 90

Gibson, Greg 105, 115, 119

Giese, Ed 21, 31, 138

Ginther, John 44

Giura, John 17, 114

Gleasman, Jason 110

Glenn, Dan 11, 72

Glenn, Derek 11, 15, 17, 49

Goeden, Jeremy 160

Goldman, Duane 24, 27, 28, 30, 31, 33, 48, 50, 58, 61, 65, 79, 86, 96, 149, 159, 176

Gonzales, Joe viii, 5, 6, 10, 11, 46, 50, 72, 78, 104, 112, 115, 118, 121, 124, 126, 127, 128, 129, 131, 132

Gonzalez, Peter 38

Gorriarian, Manuel 11

Gotcher, Larry 39, 43

Govig, Bert 105

Grajales, Cesar 157

Grammer, Alan 29, 31, 138

Grant, Dave 149, 160

Greenlee, Joel 37, 44, 149, 161

Gressley, Jim 38, 40

Griffin, Jack 42

Griffin, Scott 157

Guerrero, Eric 114

Gust, Brian 104

Gutches, Les 110, 114

Guymon, J. Carl 64, 184

H

Hajkenari, Abbas 89

Hall, Dean 37, 41

Hall, Dennis 109, 110, 114, 115

Hallman, Bob 25

Hamilton, Steve 42, 58, 65

Hamlin, Robert 175

Hanlon, John 7

Hanrahan, John 16

Hanutke, Matt 170

Harris, Howard 5, 6, 7, 10, 13, 21, 57, 60, 66, 74, 79, 137, 138

Hart, Dave 65

Hartmann, Conner 164

Hartupee, John 14, 72, 122

Haselrig, Conrad 79

Haselrig, Ken 36

Hatchett, Brandon 175

Hatta, Tadaaki 129, 131, 132

Heard, Charlie 22, 25, 87

Heffernan, Jim vii, 23, 29, 31, 32, 34, 36, 49, 58, 66, 68, 78, 86, 149, 161, 190

Heffernan, John 36, 44, 67, 82

Heizer, Ben 160

Heller, Charlie 16, 52, 59

Hellickson, Russ 104, 115, 116, 119, 120, 149

Henderson, Dan 109, 110

Henderson, Evan 168

Hendricks, Johny 177, 183

Henson, Josiah 117

Henson, Sammie 114, 174

Heropoulos, John 30, 33

Heugabel, Reiner 105, 131, 133

Hiatt, Sam 160

Hicks, Dan 147

Higgins, Darrin 36

Hodge, Dan 3, 4, 11, 116, 164

Holcomb, Mike 27

Holker, Aaron 175

Holzer, Werner 117

Hooks, Rod 2

Horner, Gary 44

Houck, Mike 115, 119

ABOUT THE AUTHOR

Reginald E. Rowe

REGINALD E. ROWE covered his first high school wrestling match in 1974 as sports editor of The Duncan (OK) Banner daily newspaper and has been a fan of amateur wrestling ever since. He has won multiple awards for sports writing, column writing, editorial writing and public relations programs. He and his wife, Sally, live in Pineville, MO.

Printed in the United States
By Bookmasters